Wellbeing Ranking

'In an era where people's voice are increasingly difficult to prioritize above those of experts, and local specificities often lose out to average effects, this thoughtful book will hopefully reignite interest in engaged inquiry. It offers us on-the-ground experiences about finding out what it means to be better off or worse off – the heart of what drives international development. The editor has found a wonderfully reflective style that makes the ideas eminently useful for self-critical professionals. This is how inquiry best evolves.'

Irene Guijt is a Research Associate, RAPID Programme,
Overseas Development Institute.

'Wellbeing ranking is the centre piece method of participatory poverty research. This excellent volume provides a much-needed reminder of its continuing value to the broader applied research community.'

Jeremy Holland, Associate Consultant, Social Development Team,
Oxford Policy Management

'Using wealth ranking under the guidance of Barbara Grandin in Kenya in the mid-80s was a very exciting and hugely inspirational experience. Its use in a base-line and planning survey for Intermediate Technology Development Group, now Practical Action, in one of their early animal health care projects demonstrated the way that this simple technique is able to reveal impressive detail about lives, livelihoods, and especially livestock management. The information we gathered was instrumental in designing approaches which could really meet people's needs and resources. It was also formative in my understanding about the need for a thorough consideration of communities and the context for development work. It is remarkable that this was all revealed through a simple card-sorting exercise, and one that the participants themselves also seemed to enjoy doing. I am delighted that Barbara's groundbreaking work is receiving the recognition it deserves in this book.'

John Young, Head of the Research and Policy in
Development Programme (RAPID)

Wellbeing Ranking

Developments in applied community-level poverty research

Edited by John Rowley

PRACTICAL ACTION
Publishing

Practical Action Publishing Ltd
The Schumacher Centre
Bourton on Dunsmore, Rugby,
Warwickshire CV23 9QZ, UK
www.practicalactionpublishing.org

ISBN 978-1-85339-845-2 Hardback
ISBN 978-1-85339-846-9 Paperback
ISBN 978-1-78044-845-9 Library Ebook
ISBN 978-1-78044-846-6 Ebook

A catalogue record for this book is available from the British Library.

<http://dx.doi.org/10.3362/9781780448459>.

Rowley, John (ed.) (2014) *Wellbeing Ranking: Developments in applied community-level poverty research*, Rugby, UK: Practical Action Publishing.

Since 1974, Practical Action Publishing has published and disseminated books and information in support of international development work throughout the world. Practical Action Publishing is a trading name of Practical Action Publishing Ltd (Company Reg. No. 1159018), the wholly owned publishing company of Practical Action. Practical Action Publishing trades only in support of its parent charity objectives and any profits are covenanted back to Practical Action (Charity Reg. No. 247257, Group VAT Registration No. 880 9924 76).

Cover design by Mercer Design
Indexed by Liz Fawcett
Typeset by Allzone Digital Services Limited
Printed by Hobbs the Printers Ltd

Contents

http://dx.doi.org/10.3362/9781780448459.000

About the editor

John Rowley is an international development professional with over 30 years' experience working for national and international NGOs, government agencies, bilateral and multilateral donors and commercial companies in the UK, Africa and elsewhere.

CHAPTER 1

Introduction: wealth ranking and wellbeing ranking

John Rowley

This chapter explains the origins of this book, its contents and intended readership. It provides an explanation of wellbeing and wealth ranking, and the key steps in carrying out a ranking at community level. The description of the contents should help readers to find sections that are most relevant to their interests, and although the book can be read from start to finish, the chapters can also be read separately and in a different order. This chapter challenges recent trends in international development and suggests that there is an increasing need for better understanding of changes that are occurring at community level. This is why methods such as wellbeing ranking are important and why a book promoting them is appropriate.

Keywords: wellbeing, well-being, ranking, poverty, wealth, development, health, happiness, local

How this book came about

The long process by which this book (Rowley, 2014e) came to be written started when Barbara Grandin's original 1988 manual on wealth ranking was out of print and it was difficult to find a copy. I wanted a copy because I use wealth ranking methods in my work as a freelance consultant working for international development agencies, and find it hugely valuable. It seems unlikely that there is any way quicker and simpler than wealth ranking to find out about and understand wealth and other differences within a community. Understanding these differences and how they change seems so important to people working in the international development aid sector that it seemed wrong that the key text about the method should be so difficult to obtain.

The publisher provided me with a scan of the text, but when they said they were planning to reprint Barbara Grandin's original manual, I suggested that it should be updated. They agreed and asked for an outline of a new publication. Then, as I interviewed people who had other specialist knowledge about wealth and wellbeing assessments, the book turned into an edited compilation. This is clearly a much better book than the one I originally had in mind, and has led to more work and worry about writing and editing than I could have imagined.

http://dx.doi.org/10.3362/9781780448459.001

A note on context

Understanding differences in wellbeing is obviously important to people working in international aid agencies, and throughout the 1990s there was a lot of interest in what wealth ranking could do. It was a key part of the World Bank 'Voices of the Poor' project in 1999–2000; this is probably the greatest use of the method to have been sponsored by a large multilateral agency. During the first decade of the 21st century, the number of publications on wealth or wellbeing ranking has appeared to decline and there have been very few published since 2010. This may be indicative of a gradual loss of interest in participatory methods, or perhaps participatory approaches, within the development aid sector.

At the same time, there has been a significant increase in interest around ideas of wellbeing, and a range of models have been developed to look at the many dimensions that make up ill or wellbeing. The aid sector tends to look at its work as aiming to reduce poverty, but there is a broad acceptance that poverty takes many forms and is more than just an absence of material wealth. The recent broader interest in wellbeing assessments has produced a number of models that can be applied to a wide range of situations where there is no explicit poverty focus. Wellbeing offers positive ways of looking at work in the aid sector as a means of increasing wellbeing, rather than the more common approach, which is as a means of reducing poverty. Wealth ranking should not be seen as poverty ranking.

Wealth or wellbeing

The original wealth-ranking tool (described in Box 1.1 'What is wealth and wellbeing ranking?', see p. 3) initially focuses on ideas of economic wealth: the most common understanding of material wealth and the usual use of the words 'rich' and 'poor'. People who have tried to do wealth ranking know that, during the exercise, a wide range of other differences between people emerge; criteria for ranking people or households tend therefore to include issues of social, spiritual and emotional wellbeing alongside questions of health, happiness and attitude. There are examples of these findings in Chapter 4: 'Some practical examples and what users say about wellbeing ranking' (Rowley, 2014c).

Definitions of wellbeing tend to cover some or all of these components, so the phrase is vague and very broad. Attempts to assess wellbeing oblige people to come up with better definitions of the separate components that can be seen to make up an overall consideration of wellbeing.

Quite often, the different components of wealth and wellbeing tend to correlate, or at least appear together, in relation to particular people or groups. For example, those who are well off in one area of wellbeing are also well off in another, and being materially wealthy may lead to higher levels of other forms of wellbeing.

Box 1.1 What is wealth and wellbeing ranking?

Originally, the ranking method was called 'wealth ranking', and the starting point was an enquiry into levels of material wealth. As the process brings up diverse elements of people's livelihoods, including health, respect and social links as well as spiritual, emotional and other issues, it is more accurately seen as a description of wellbeing. This point can be made clearly to a given audience by introducing the method as an enquiry into wellbeing, and finding an appropriate word or phrase to open up a broader discussion.

Wellbeing ranking is a simple interview tool through which people sort members of their community into different wellbeing groups. The names are written on pieces of card or paper, and the participant sorts these into groups to indicate different levels of wellbeing.

Chapter 5 ('Methodological issues in wellbeing ranking', Rowley, 2014) provides detailed discussions of the different methodological steps involved, each of which can be carried out in several ways. There is a more detailed guide on conducting wellbeing ranking in Annex 1.

At the core of the method is the practice of ranking, through which items are compared and placed either in the same category, or a higher or lower category. The process does not require any absolute assessments of wellbeing but only of relative positions. It is comparatively easy to decide that one person or household is better off or less well off than another. It is not necessary to reveal details of specific wealth or other characteristics of any particular person, and this makes the method easy to use and powerful.

The major steps in a conventional ranking exercise are:

1. Make a list of all the households in the community.
2. Write the name of each household on a separate card.
3. Select the participants to do the ranking exercise.
4. Ask the participants to sort the cards into different wellbeing categories. They take the cards one by one, either creating a number of wellbeing categories as they go or placing them in predetermined categories from highest to lowest.
5. Score the results of the sorting for each card.
6. Discuss with the participants the criteria they have used for the sorting.
7. Repeat the process so that you have at least three replicates.
8. Calculate the overall wellbeing score for each household.
9. Create a list of all the households in the community split into different categories of wellbeing.

There are possible variations to many of these steps. For example: the ranking may be of individuals or of households; the ranking may be done by individuals or small groups; the number of categories may be set by the facilitator or determined by the participants; and it is not always necessary to develop a final list split into wellbeing categories.

A wellbeing ranking can serve a range of purposes including:

- facilitating a discussion;
- determining local beliefs;
- selecting beneficiaries for a development intervention;
- describing changes, progress over time, or impact of an intervention;
- forming part of a socio-economic analysis;
- supporting more quantitative methods of enquiry, e.g. household surveys.

In this book, most references to 'wellbeing' recognize that wealth ranking or other assessments of 'wealth' tend to include the wider range of criteria such as health, prestige and happiness, which are in fact better described as aspects of wellbeing. Some of the work described in Chapters 3 ('The history of wellbeing ranking techniques', Rowley, 2014d) and 4 ('Some practical examples and what users say about wellbeing ranking', Rowley, 2014c), however, is termed as 'wealth ranking' because this was the term used in the original reports.

The focus

The book focuses on the work of development aid agencies and many of the examples described are drawn from non-governmental organizations (NGOs). It covers ways in which wellbeing ranking has been used, and describes real experiences of the use of methods to assess wellbeing, from which readers will be able to draw their own lessons. Later chapters cover the development of wellbeing assessments using other methods, such as household surveys and questionnaires.

The book points out the value and interest in developing an understanding of wellbeing through the genuine and rich descriptions provided by local people regarding their situation and conditions. This may not seem contentious, but there are trends among international development agencies that seem to promote simple global statements of what development is, and what should be addressed and changed by development aid work. There is a tension between the one-dimensional measures of approaches such as the Millennium Development Goals, and the complex and specific measures that emerge from assessments of wellbeing. The book looks at ways to address this tension.

Who the book is for

The book will be of most interest to people working in the development aid sector, including social development consultants, community activists, and those who design, assess, monitor and evaluate community-level initiatives. Some of these readers might use the methods described in the course of their work. Others may find it helpful as background information, and in finding and using other methods to assess wellbeing. It may also be relevant to researchers doing relatively small-scale research in the areas of wealth, poverty, inequality and assessment of wellbeing.

This is not an academic text and it will not contribute to the substantial work dedicated to the study of wealth according to its many definitions. However, some students of wealth, poverty and development may find it helpful to see how some of these elements can be assessed in real situations.

What the book contains

The writers in this book are mostly practitioners, despite their association with academic institutions, and are writing about their experiences of working with wealth and wellbeing methods.

I was particularly pleased when I tracked down Barbara Grandin, who agreed to contribute her recollections of the time during which the method was developed and the original manual published. In Chapter 2, 'How wealth ranking was developed' (Grandin, 2014), she provides some background to the development of the method, including the lack of tools available to assess economic questions at a time when a great deal of anthropological research was focused on social issues.

I have also drawn up a short history of the development and use of wealth and wellbeing ranking, and this is presented in Chapter 3: 'The history of wellbeing ranking techniques' (Rowley, 2014d). The chapter looks at the evolution of the thinking around wellbeing, as well as the use of assessment methods. This seems to follow a trajectory whereby participatory tools were initially received with enthusiasm and used by increasing numbers of people, then used more and more poorly and, gradually, abandoned. The overview of the history covers the possibility of using both quantitative and qualitative methods in tandem to reinforce each other. This would appear to be very sensible in theory, but seems to be rarely done in practice.

In Chapter 4, 'Some practical examples and what users say about wellbeing ranking' (Rowley, 2014c), I have collected observations on using the method from authors in the journals *RRA Notes* and *PLA Notes*, where practitioners discuss their work with some frankness. These are the views of the people actually trying to make development projects work, who do not need to publish in addition to doing the routine reporting of their jobs. I found that the tone and content of the articles was almost always self-critical, but useful to people who wanted to try out the tools in their own work.

The history and the records in *PLA Notes* raise a number of methodological issues related to the practicalities of carrying out wellbeing ranking. I have put these together in Chapter 5, 'Methodological issues in wellbeing ranking' (Rowley, 2014b), which will be of interest to those who are keen to know exactly how the methods have been used and tested. Although the way a tool is used is often important, with participatory tools there are also questions around the attitude and approach of the person using the tool.

In keeping with the tone and style of *PLA Notes*, I have adopted a more personal and reflexive approach in Chapters 4 (Rowley 2014c) and 5 (Rowley, 2014b). The content, also in line with *PLA Notes*, is offered for readers to pick through and find items or observations that are helpful to them. The more personal tone is a deliberate contrast to the more objective and academic style of the other contributors.

Anton Simanowitz describes his work with participatory wealth ranking in Chapter 6, 'Using participatory wealth ranking in a South African microfinance organization: the value of scale' (2014). His work has a particular place in the history of the use of wealth ranking, because it includes one of the most convincing cases of extending wealth ranking from the local community level to a wider application across very large numbers of households in a large number of communities. This appears to resolve a major issue that can arise when using participatory methods, which are often seen to provide results that are relevant and useful to the community in which they are developed, but become less relevant outside their original context. This issue is particularly important for assessments of poverty where comparisons between regions and countries are required and transferable results necessary. Simanowitz makes clear some of the conditions and skills required to deliver high-quality results that can be transferred from one location to another.

Claire Heffernan and Frederica Misturelli explore these issues in more detail in Chapter 7, 'Wellbeing ranking, semi-structured interviews and practitioner bias: Personality traits and participatory narratives' (2014). They present evidence on the ways that personality factors and professional backgrounds affect the results of semi-structured interviews. The importance of these issues and the dangers of bad practice are often discussed, but there is little concrete evidence of the impact of personal bias. These authors' findings suggest that interviewers need to be extremely careful in their interviews and in interpreting their work. It may be that being aware of bias and looking for it is easier to achieve than eliminating bias from interview work.

In Chapter 8, 'Wellbeing assessment in practice: lessons from wellbeing and poverty pathways' (Marshall et al., 2014), Sarah White and her colleagues describe how they have taken forward work on the development of models of wellbeing, by developing and testing a multi-dimensional model in rural communities in Zambia and in India. This is real research in real communities, and a model is developed from local understanding of wellbeing. Two crucial areas are covered: first, that the multi-dimensional model can be useful in bringing out areas of ill-being and wellbeing that might not emerge with a narrower focus on poverty; and, second, just how much work and attention to detail is required to test a model and interpret the results. The authors also discuss the issues involved in finding a way of describing wellbeing that is locally relevant and applicable over a wide range of locations and situations.

Roger Williamson in Chapter 9, 'Wealth-ranking to wellbeing: Where next for development?' (2014), look at the changes that have occurred in thinking about wellbeing in the time since Barbara Grandin published the wealth-ranking field manual. They review a range of high-level tools used to assess poverty, including those used at national and international levels such as the Millennium Development Goals. The different tools are assessed alongside the thinking that surrounds them, and key issues in their use are brought together and presented. Williamson observes that problems can emerge from treating wellbeing as a simple concept, or focusing on a single aspect such as happiness; from adding up the components of wellbeing to create some composite score; or from imagining that the assessment of wellbeing takes place in a politically neutral environment.

Chapter 10, 'Conclusions about wellbeing assessments and ideas for the future' (Rowley, 2014a), reviews the issues raised in the other chapters and provides an overview of some of the methods used to assess wellbeing; the strengths and weaknesses of the methods; and the uses that the assessments might serve. It concludes that people in the development aid sector need to conduct careful assessments of wellbeing in the design and evaluation of development initiatives and that there are methods that can help ensure assessments are reliable. The assessments can be useful in managing individual development programmes and also for understanding more generally how and when people benefit from the work of the development aid sector.

There is not, however, a strong focus on wellbeing in high-level development aid processes such as the Millennium Development Goals, and this is not likely to change in the post-2015 agenda. The drive from large donors for evidence of impact expressed in simplistic quantitative measures works against the use of more meaningful evaluations of changes in people's lives that can be produced through wellbeing assessments. This book provides evidence of the value of gaining a more genuine understanding of the situation of local people; of the importance of local views and local differences. The final chapter asks if there is a way to integrate the more genuine understanding provided by wellbeing assessments with the demands of high-level processes for simple statements of impact.

References

Grandin, B. (2014) 'How wealth ranking was developed', in Rowley, J. (ed.) *Wellbeing Ranking: Developments in Applied Community-level Poverty Research*, pp. 9–12, Rugby: Practical Action Publishing, <http://dx.doi.org/10.3362/9781780448459.002>

Heffernan, C. and Misturelli, F. (2014) 'Wellbeing ranking: Semi-structured interviews and practitioner bias: Personality traits and participatory narratives', in Rowley, J. (ed.) *Wellbeing Ranking: Developments in Applied Community-level Poverty Research*, pp. 89–110, Rugby: Practical Action Publishing, <http://dx.doi.org/10.3362/9781780448459.007>

Marshall, N., White, S.C., Gaines, Jr S.O. and Jha, S. (2014), 'Wellbeing assessment in practice: Lessons from wellbeing and poverty pathways', in Rowley, J. (ed.) *Wellbeing Ranking: Developments in Applied Community-level Poverty Research*, pp. 111–126, Rugby: Practical Action Publishing, <http://dx.doi.org/10.3362/9781780448459.008>

Rowley, J. (2014a) 'Conclusions about wellbeing assessments and ideas for the future', in Rowley, J. (ed.) *Wellbeing Ranking: Developments in Applied Community-level Poverty Research*, pp. 153–162, Rugby: Practical Action Publishing, <http://dx.doi.org/10.3362/9781780448459.010>

Rowley, J. (2014b) 'Methodological issues in wellbeing ranking', in Rowley, J. (ed.) *Wellbeing Ranking: Developments in Applied Community-level Poverty Research*, pp. 49–70, Rugby: Practical Action Publishing, <http://dx.doi.org/10.3362/9781780448459.005>

Rowley, J. (2014c) 'Some practical examples and what users say about wellbeing ranking', in Rowley, J. (ed.) *Wellbeing Ranking: Developments in Applied Community-level Poverty Research*, pp. 33–48, Rugby: Practical Action Publishing, <http://dx.doi.org/10.3362/9781780448459.004>

Rowley, J. (2014d) 'The history of wellbeing ranking techniques', in Rowley, J. (ed.) *Wellbeing Ranking: Developments in Applied Community-level Poverty Research*, pp. 13–32, Rugby: Practical Action Publishing, <http://dx.doi.org/10.3362/9781780448459.003>

Rowley, J. (ed.) (2014e) *Wellbeing Ranking: Developments in Applied Community-level Research*, Rugby: Practical Action Publishing

Simanowitz, A. (2014) 'Using participatory wealth ranking in a South African microfinance organization: the value of scale', in Rowley, J. (ed.) *Wellbeing Ranking: Developments in Applied Community-level Poverty Research*, pp. 71–88, Rugby: Practical Action Publishing, <http://dx.doi.org/10.3362/9781780448459.006>

Williamson, R. (2014) 'Wealth ranking to wellbeing: Where next for development?', in Rowley, J. (ed.) *Wellbeing Ranking: Developments in Applied Community-level Poverty Research*, pp. 127–152, Rugby: Practical Action Publishing, <http://dx.doi.org/10.3362/9781780448459.009>

About the author

John Rowley is an international development professional with over 30 years' experience working for national and international NGOs, government agencies, bilateral and multilateral donors and commercial companies in the UK, Africa and elsewhere.

CHAPTER 2
How wealth ranking was developed

Barbara Grandin

In this chapter, Barbara Grandin tells the story of how she developed and tested methods of wealth ranking. She explains how the focus of anthropological research at that time tended to ignore economic considerations, and how a piece of work on assessing levels of respect in a small Italian town helped her to explore levels of wealth and produce a reliable methodology for doing wealth ranking.

Keywords: wellbeing, well-being, ranking, development, anthropology, ownership, prestige

As a student of Anthropology in the early 1970s, I was influenced by theories of cultural ecology, which basically attempts to understand how people made a living and how adaptations to the environment (broadly defined to include wider political and economic systems) affected social organization and culture. I was also very interested in development anthropology and saw a potential role for the anthropologist as 'culture broker': trying to explain to Western technocrats the reasons behind, and the benefits of, peasant activities and associated beliefs, both as discussed by the peasants themselves and as deduced by scientific enquiry.

I was an Africanist and found that the bulk of available ethnographies were produced by British anthropologists from the late 1940s through to the mid-1960s. They provided detailed descriptions of social structure and culture with little or no attention to subsistence and the environment. I remember one telling story: an anthropologist saw a peasant making a small structure of poles and watched and carefully noted exactly how it was constructed, assuming he was watching the construction of a shrine. He was terribly disappointed to find that he had detailed notes on the building of a pig pen.

As I was reading the ethnographies in West Africa, I came across references to pygmy or dwarf cattle in coastal areas. Both anthropologists and animal scientists described these as being sacred, kept only for prestige; not being useful, as they were not milked or used for draft and were slaughtered on ceremonial occasions. It was noted, however, that they were resistant to trypanosomiasis, a disease carried by the tsetse fly, which is endemic in coastal areas. One animal scientist went so far as to assert that the keeping of these cows was an indication of the African peasants' genetic predisposition to own and keep cattle. My thesis topic was born. Why did African peasants keep these cows? What role did they play in the agricultural system?

http://dx.doi.org/10.3362/9781780448459.002

I did my thesis research in south-western Nigeria among Egun speakers. My introduction was typical. The District Officer recommended a community in which Muturu cattle were kept. I was brought to meet the 'chief' and male elders, to whom I described my goal as trying to understand how people made a living and what challenges they had. I was accepted and it was decided that I would take a room in the large concrete block home of an elder. He was a very wealthy man who had a son who lived next door; the son was a school teacher and spoke English fluently.

As I walked through the community, I was struck instantly by apparently large differences in wealth in the community, as evidenced initially by housing, then clothing – easily discernible markers to the neophyte. I was in the field for over two years trying to understand the socio-economic system, with a special focus on the agricultural production system (including access to the means of production), as well as social organization and culture.

Muturu cattle were indeed kept in small numbers, mainly by a few wealthy men. They were neither milked nor used for draft, and were slaughtered primarily for the funerals of 'big men'. I'll never forget my first attempt to do a genealogy of a cow, with emphasis on her acquisition and the fate of her offspring. I began by asking the elder why he kept Muturu cattle. 'I like the way they walk,' was his initial response; my heart began to sink. However, he proceeded to tell me details of the fate of the eight calves that this 11-year old cow had produced: several he still had; others he had loaned out; and others had been sold for the funerals of chiefs and other 'big men'. What I discovered was that the cattle consumed at 'ceremonial' events, especially funerals, were purchased from the owners for substantial sums. The cattle served as a relatively risk-free store of wealth and their manure enabled continuous cropping of fields near the homestead. They were also used to build patron-client relationships, as a wealthy owner would loan out a cow to a friend or relative who would care for it. The recipient got the manure and half of the offspring – and a deep debt to the giver. Owners said they did not milk or use the cattle for draft as the resistance to trypanosomiasis would break down. I did extensive genealogies and never recorded a death from trypanosomiasis, and only rarely from other diseases. They were indeed a fairly risk-free store of wealth.

Towards the end of my stay, I did a formal household composition and agricultural survey, which included a delineation of all fields (with the help of aerial imagery), the land tenure and cropping patterns, livestock holdings as well as labour sources. It showed clear differences in access to the means of production. An extensive survey is fine for an anthropologist with years to spend in the field gathering background information to inform the survey, and with the resources to conduct it and time to analyse it. But how could a development worker, with limited time, come to understand these differences, and how to prevent projects from being commandeered by friends of the chief?

One of my thesis advisors told me of an article by an anthropologist named Sidel Silverman. Researching in Italy, he used a participatory card-sorting technique to rank men into groups in terms of prestige. This was my first exposure to what is now known as a participatory rapid tool and I felt that, if it worked, it could be valuable to development workers. I decided to try a similar technique using wealth instead of prestige, as I felt wealth was more germane to my concerns. While prestige is important in society, it has too many other possible dimensions that could muddy the waters; for example, a well-known healer might have relatively high prestige but be fairly poor. Of course, this kind of observation is now part of the common understanding of wellbeing, but at the time I was unsure if the method would work at all and was trying to simplify the approach. So, I carried out wealth ranking, initially with households as the unit being ranked, as outlined in my manual. I was frankly amazed at how easy it was to do, and how well the subsequent discussion of the piles both fitted with my understanding of wealth differences in the community, and expanded them (for example, providing an insight into food insecurity in the poorest households). In writing my thesis, I was able to compare wealth-ranking results with the results of my conventional survey and the correlations were strong. Number and types of fields, livestock holdings and access to labour were all highly correlated with wealth ranks, as were house type, children in school, and ownership of transportation (e.g. bicycles, motorcycles).

I was not sure if wealth ranking would work in other types of communities, or where there was no anthropologist in residence with time to build a rapport in the community. When I was working with the International Livestock Centre for Africa in pastoral Maasailand (Kenya), I was able to try wealth ranking again. As among the Egun, once informants understood the process it went smoothly. It is really a very natural exercise. People had no difficulty saying who had and who did not have wealth and what constituted it. I was again pleasantly surprised. It brought to light something I had not realized. A couple of households were rated as wealthy, despite appearing to have relatively few animals (as confirmed by our livestock census). The explanation was that they owned many animals under the care of other households. The caretakers did the work and benefited from the milk; the owners spread their risk.

Subsequently, while working with John Young of the then Intermediate Technology Development Group (ITDG, now known as Practical Action), we were able to test wealth ranking in several different communities in Kenya in which we did not have the luxury of spending a lot of time. Again the process went smoothly, and agreement on ranks of individual households was high. In each case we felt that the results were reliable and could be used both to understand the needs of the less well-off households and to try to ensure that development efforts were not hijacked by a male elite. We felt we could help ensure this by making sure that people representative of each of the wealth ranks were met in the course of project development.

We were so happy with the results that ITDG suggested I write a manual about the use of the method. Thus began a new chapter in Participatory Rural Appraisal.

It is always easier to see things with hindsight, and there are a few things I would have done differently were I writing the manual again. First, I wish I had included more about the discussions conducted with each informant about the piles. There is so much that can be discussed and learned in asking questions about the situation of people in each pile. I was afraid of making the manual too complicated, or that in recommending items to be discussed these would be taken as gospel rather than just suggestions that would need to be adapted to each setting. Second, the value of females as informants should have been discussed more thoroughly – particularly in terms of discussions about the piles. Females' rankings did not vary substantially from those of men, but discussions on wealth differences with females bring out fuller information on women's concerns and needs, as well as child nutrition and health, more readily than those with male informants. Finally, I would have stressed the need to meet people from *every* wealth rank in the community. This ensures that the poor and disenfranchised are not ignored without singling them out, but rather keeping the appraisal at the level of the entire community. Although a project may focus on the poorest of the poor, I feel it is important at the outset to ensure that people from all wealth categories feel they are being listened to.

I was very pleased when I heard that the guide was being updated in this book on wellbeing ranking. I am pleased that the methods have been so widely used and modified in different ways to meet individual project needs and constraints.

About the author

Barbara Grandin worked in international development principally in East Africa, where her research led her to develop the wealth-ranking method. She was assisted by John Young, who encouraged her to refine and publish the method. She changed her career direction not long after completing the publication, but was persuaded to share her experiences in writing this chapter.

CHAPTER 3

The history of wellbeing ranking techniques

John Rowley

This chapter looks in a small amount of detail at the early use of wealth ranking techniques by pioneers Silverman, Hill and Grandin. There is a brief look at Grandin's 1988 manual, the 'blue book', but the content is more closely examined in Chapter 4, 'Some practical examples and what users say about wellbeing ranking' (Rowley, 2014). This chapter then covers the reporting of the use of the tools in reviews by Chambers (1997) and then by White and Pettit (2004). It also looks at the large-scale use of wellbeing assessments in the Voices of the Poor project in 2000 and how these assessments were judged (Narayan et al., 2000). It ends with questions raised more broadly on the use of participatory methods and, in particular, on the processes within which the methods are used. The methods work well, it seems, when the principles of participation are respected, and work poorly or fail when these principles are ignored.

Keywords: wellbeing, ranking, prestige, family, household, community, participatory methods

Wealth ranking may be unusual among participatory tools in being associated with a particular practitioner. Most tools and methods seem to be part of a shared pool of ideas and no one is considered to have invented them. On the rare occasions when a method has been copyrighted or trademarked it seems rather odd and not inkeeping with the spirit of participatory work. However, Barbara Grandin's name is associated with wealth ranking in a specific way. This is because of the manual she wrote, published by Practical Action (formerly known as Intermediate Technology Development Group, ITDG) in 1988, which includes detailed instructions for using the method and some interesting accounts of its use in different situations in Kenya. The manual was published with a striking blue cover and is sometimes referred to as the 'blue book'. We will look at Grandin's specific contributions later.

Sydel Silverman (1966)

The earliest use of the method that I can find is Sydel Silverman's (1966) use of the ranking of individuals according to their levels of prestige. The paper inspired Barbara Grandin, who developed the method for use with

http://dx.doi.org/10.3362/9781780448459.003

levels of wealth. Silverman's paper is very well written and has something of the modest self-critical style of many articles in the journal *PLA Notes*. He discusses some of the key elements of using the method that have concerned users ever since.

Silverman is not happy with the use of the word 'ranking' and wishes to call the technique 'stratification'. He is right, in that the method is a stratification created by ranking exercises. Social stratification is a phrase that has specific meanings in anthropology, but is hardly ever used in international development, the sector in which wealth ranking has been used most often. The problem of finding a good name for the method has not been solved. Alice Welbourn suggested the name socio-economic dimension ranking (SEDR) (International Institute for Environment and Development (IIED)/Institute of Development Studies (IDS), 1993). Even at the time, it was recognized that this name was more accurate but it was too cumbersome to be adopted. Anton Simanowitz (see Chapter 6 'Using participatory wealth ranking in a South African microfinance organization: the value of scale', Simanowitz, 2014) uses the phrase 'participatory wealth ranking' and the initials PWR. However, the use of both wealth and wellbeing as a focus of the work has made it impossible to arrive at an agreed title.

Silverman describes his search for the right word to define the task that he was asking participants to carry out. His interest was in prestige, and he soon found the word *rispetto*[1] was the key to the interviews.

He describes how he carefully avoided giving subjects any criteria of judgement of *rispetto*. In the exercise, he only asked them to rank from higher to lower. 'No indication was given of the dimensions of hierarchy that I wanted, for my explicit aim was to permit the informant to establish the terms in which "higher" and "lower" [were] meaningful to him.' (Silverman, 1966) This is an almost perfect definition of a participatory approach.

Silverman addresses the issue of the ranking unit and fixes on the family, an approach which worked well in his surroundings: a village in Italy in 1966. His detailed interviews show that the male head of the family is a key determinant of the ranking. He selects three male informants, who are lifetime residents of the community, from families that had been in the village for generations, and makes no apology for not selecting a representative sample. He needs people who are high-quality informants, capable of the complex sorting task based on their knowledge of the families in the village. He also acknowledges that the method might only work in small communities where it is possible for individual informants to know all the families in the community.

As became standard practice in wealth ranking, Silverman's informants create different numbers of categories of prestige. He specifically asks the informants about the size differences between groups. He then develops an overall categorization of families from the results of the three interviews and, interestingly, comes up with categories and sub-categories, a practice that did not become standard but that clearly has advantages where differences between categories created by the informants vary in nature. Silverman suggests that people are capable of finer distinctions closer to their own position, and this seems likely to be true when people are assessing others on a wide range of conditions.

The nature of the differences between categories is very important for Silverman, who explores the question of how families might move between different categories of prestige. The practice of asking probing questions on how people move between groups is recommended in standard wealth ranking and usually yields interesting insights into perceptions of wealth and wellbeing. Silverman found that there were very important differences in how families could change levels of prestige and that moving from, for example, group 3 to group 2, required quite different changes compared with moving from group 2 to group 1. In some cases, prestige was based on ideas of the origin of the family; gaining the level of respect accorded to the 'old families' of the village might require generations of residence.

As a research anthropologist, Silverman wants to understand the criteria defining categories and the rules by which families are assigned to different categories. He acknowledges that a great many factors come into play and that they are not necessarily clear even to the people who use them: 'There are innumerable discriminable differences between x and y, but only certain ones are relevant.' This is a good definition of 'optimal ignorance'. Nevertheless, he wants to know what the relevant features are.

It is not always the case that people managing a community development project need to know all the factors that differentiate households in terms of their wealth or wellbeing. In some circumstances, perhaps, knowing that there are differences and that a particular group of families are better off than another group may be all that is required.

My last observation on Silverman's paper relates to his remark that the participants were surprised and apparently pleased that they had achieved the task. During the period when wealth ranking was commonly used during the 1990s, this observation was to be made again and again, as facilitators noticed that the participants seemed to enjoy doing and completing the rankings.

Polly Hill (1972)

Polly Hill is mentioned in numerous texts for her wealth-ranking work published in *Rural Hausa – A Village and a Setting* (1972). The book is a remarkable account of economic activities and relationships in a village in northern Nigeria. Reviewed in 1974, as 'an outstanding example of how a close examination of a village contributes to the study of the economic system of a larger society and to ... the problems of rural development' (Ortiz, 1974), the book contains enormously detailed descriptions of different aspects of economic activities and key relationships within and between families.

Polly Hill does not refer to previous uses of wealth ranking and treats the initial exercise with residents in northern Nigeria as something of a game. She discusses the best definition of wellbeing with the initial participants, and they select the ability to withstand the shock of a very late, or very poor, harvest as a useful definition. The rains in 1967 were very late and just before the harvest there was widespread hunger. During the initial ranking she asks the participants to identify which households are hungry and which are not. The participants perform their task so enthusiastically that Hill asks them to continue to classify the units into four economic groups.

Like Silverman, she selects three 'very well informed' men to act as informants who do their ranking exercises 'independently and secretly'.

The unit for ranking in this case is the farming unit, and 174 units are ranked into four different categories by the participants. There are 'only a few' units, which are probably borderline between categories, that need to be adjusted; overall, there is a very strong agreement between the results of the three exercises.

Hill tests the categorization against 12 elements of household make-up (e.g. numbers, ages, and gender of household members) and then against 20 elements of ownership of farm land. The groupings look reliable and she goes on to use them to assess a huge number of other features of wealth and wellbeing. Her initial suspicion that 'this subjective classification reflected genuine economic differentiation' seems to be proved beyond any doubt. Nevertheless, she presents another 20 pages of evidence on differences between the economic groups relating to issues of acquisition and size of land, production of different crops and numbers of animals, moveable property, occupations outside farming, numbers of granaries, ages, numbers of wives, numbers of sons and the amount of land per working man. All the evidence supports the conclusion that the categories identified by the interviewees represent real and meaningful economic differences between the members of the different groups. Hill writes, 'it is time to drop all this pretence and to assert that the analysis will henceforth be based on the definite idea that, in any meaningful economic sense of the word "rich", most of those in Group 1 are "richer" than most of those in Group 2 and so forth' (p.83). The decision to switch from very careful presentation of data to the statement of an overwhelmingly obvious truth comes as a genuine relief.

Hill has little time for household surveys, which she dismisses in several paragraphs before explaining how she started work on wealth ranking. She suggests that it may not be possible to get reliable statistics on income and expenditure in a Hausa village for a wide range of reasons, including: secrecy within and between families; extreme seasonal variations in prices; extreme year-on-year variations in production; flexible breaking-up and coming together of cooking units and farming units; and migration in and out of the village. Hill points out that educated Hausa women would be required as enumerators to interview the secluded women of the village. She is also concerned that a survey would have to be done on a sample of households in the village, while 'one of the great advantages of our approach was that everybody was included'. It is possible that an expert in household surveys could explain how these difficulties might be overcome and how such surveys have been improved since 1972. However, the point is that the decision to use wealth ranking is not taken in a vacuum, but in light of what other methods might be available. Household surveys of income and expenditure are the main alternative used.

Hill makes two other points that I wish to mention here because we come back to them in later chapters in this book. First, she notes that the economic system of the village in northern Nigeria is not 'in some kind of stable balance' but is an 'unstable equilibrium' (p.189). The point she is making is that change is possible and that the wellbeing ranking is only a snapshot of the situation at the time it was done. Second, the poorest of the poor in the village were being cared for by the better-off. These are not symmetrical relationships: the poorest need welfare and find themselves in a patronal relationship. However, the key point is that the relationship exists, and that the wellbeing of their household cannot be assessed without taking this relationship into account.

Barbara Grandin (1988)

Barbara Grandin makes her approach very clear in the manual that first set out the methods of wealth ranking. The manual is described by Chambers (1997) 10 years later as 'seminal for much current practice'. First, Grandin states the importance of understanding inequalities and difference within a community. Second, she suggests that wealth is 'among the most important characteristics that differentiate people within a community' and the 'single most important determinant of [...] family wellbeing'.

In the first chapter of the manual, Grandin suggests that even where the need to examine differences is understood, it is not always easy to identify the households that are poor, partly because it is hard to collect information on wealth. She therefore recommends carrying out a ranking of all the households and making sure that people from all wealth categories are included in any future surveys. While this is being done, the researcher/person in question can learn enough about the area to determine to what extent other differences must also be considered. It is clear that Grandin expects that the person doing the wealth ranking will be conducting it early in their engagement with a community, and will follow it up with a range of other interactions.

Grandin explains that understanding wealth is not only important in itself, but also because it correlates with many other characteristics of poverty. She cites Chambers' description of a 'deprivation trap', which provides an explanation of the links between the different elements of poverty (Chambers, 1983); this supports her statement that wealth ranking is bound to provide an understanding of many elements of wellbeing.

The book is a manual and deals directly with methodological issues, including the following:

- *Local concept of wealth.* This has to be worked out with local people and the local word tested with the informants by asking for some examples of differences between rich and poor.

- *Definition of household as the unit to be ranked.* This also needs to be assessed and the right local word or phrase identified to describe the household, and the variety of forms it can take.
- *List of households to be ranked.* Obtaining this list is described as the *most difficult aspect of wealth ranking* (p.13). Grandin recommends a method of helping local people to identify households by asking them to mentally 'walk' through the area.
- *Informants.* These should be longstanding members of the community and ordinary farmers. Grandin warns against working with community leaders. She suggests that 3–5 informants will be enough because the level of agreement is quite high, but insists that three independent sortings are necessary. She also advises that, while unwillingness to participate is rare in her experience, a different informant should be used if the selected person appears reluctant or ill at ease. The interviews should be conducted in a quiet place and this, in fact, means confidentially.

The manual recommends letting the informants create as many categories of wealth as they want and advises prompting them to subdivide very large piles of cards, especially if any one pile contains more than 40% of the cards. There are several mentions of gender issues relating to wealth, although the suggestion to carry out a ranking of women does not come across very forcefully.

One significant inclusion in the manual is a statistical test showing the very close fit between the results of a wealth ranking exercise and those of a household economic survey. This observation would appear to be an important validation of the method and assumes a greater importance as it has been reported very rarely since the manual was published. The manual became well known almost immediately and publications referring to it appeared almost at once. During the early 1990s, articles were published regularly in the journal *RRA Notes*, and then *PLA Notes*, recording practitioners' experiences using the method, and the 'blue book' is cited by almost all such contributors. Some of these experiences are described in Chapter 4, 'Some practical examples and what users say about wellbeing ranking' (Rowley, 2014).

Robert Chambers (1997)

Robert Chambers published *Whose Reality Counts?* (1997) partly as a follow-up to *Rural Development* (1983), but mostly, it would seem, as a manifesto for participatory approaches based on many observations of the successful use of such methods. At the time, participatory methods were being taken up by many development agencies, given the evident capacity of poor people in poor countries to analyse and describe the complexities of their livelihoods and reach conclusions different to those put forward by development experts. The book contains many references to wealth and wellbeing ranking and may be the first review of the use of the method in development initiatives.

Chambers makes the point that wellbeing ranking can be seen as an alternative to household questionnaire surveys or social cost-benefit analysis, and he makes the point that a wellbeing ranking exercise could be one of many exchanges with people at community level.

Whose Reality Counts? picks up on the question of the level of rapport and trust between the facilitator and the participants. It seems likely that the early users of the method (Silverman, Hill and Grandin), being social anthropologists, had the time to develop good relationships before introducing the ranking exercises. Grandin herself was concerned about this and was slightly apprehensive about using the method when working on a short-term consultancy, but in practice had no difficulty.[2] This experience is also reported by many practitioners who have successfully used wellbeing ranking in situations when there has been little time to build rapport.

Chambers suggests that the method can work well under four conditions: where information is common knowledge; where criteria are commonly held and well understood; where what is ranked is a matter of intense interest; and where analysts do not perceive advantages in giving false or misleading judgements. So far, he adds, these conditions have commonly occurred (p.143).

In fact, the text suggests that the method delivers extremely useful ideas and observations on wellbeing and that the observations from different informants are in strong agreement (p.143). Later in the book, Chambers says that reports of wellbeing rankings note that the method may reveal 10 or more criteria being used, producing multi-dimensional assessments that are complex and dynamic. Financial income, however, is rarely seen as the primary criterion of wellbeing, although it is the main focus of normal economists (p.178).

Chambers finds many weaknesses in the alternative methods, especially in surveys of household income and expenditure based on questionnaires. Among these is that the focus on income and expenditure is too narrow and misses many important aspects of wellbeing. In addition, the use of proxies of wealth is seen as particularly risky in determining the level of wealth or wellbeing. In Chapter 6 (2014), Anton Simanowitz describes some difficulties with using quality of housing as an indicator of wealth. Chambers sums up his examination of the use of proxies by saying that they often 'misfit, miss much and mislead'.

In particular, questionnaires are criticized as being less able to collect information on trends and changes over time and to capture unexpected or surprising findings. Once the questionnaire is drafted, it is hard to introduce new areas of enquiry.

Chambers' assessment of participatory wellbeing ranking is that it is particularly good at drawing attention to areas of enquiry that might be unexpected, invisible assets (like social links and attitudes), and trends over time. This type of observation is common in the reports of practitioners in *PLA Notes*, who described how the method can provide complex multifaceted and nuanced findings, rather than a simple ranking against one or two criteria. The key point that Chambers adds to these observations is that people's values are complex, diverse, and dynamic, and that 'they cannot be known by outsiders without enquiry' (p.179).

Under the title of 'responsible wellbeing', Chambers (1997: 11) acknowledges an important element of wellbeing that Polly Hill had noted, which is that in some conditions the well-off in a community provide support to the least well-off though gifts and other mechanisms that fit within a community-based relationship. This is not to imply that the well-off are necessarily philanthropic or that all their economic links with others in the community are based on generous terms; in fact, some exchanges might be seen as exploitative. The key point is that the wellbeing of a household can depend on a range of factors that are unseen and may not emerge unless the informant is provided with the opportunity to share them. The striking point for anyone who has used wellbeing ranking is that providing people with such opportunities is simple, at once enabling informants to provide a wide range of information and insights, and facilitators to learn.

Chambers mentions the work of Ian Scoones (1995) as supporting the reliability of wellbeing rankings, as the latter's report includes a statistical analysis of the results of a household survey and a ranking and finds them 'highly correlated'. Scoones finds a number of advantages in the wellbeing ranking exercise, including its cost-effectiveness. He also suggests that a wellbeing ranking could be used to set the agenda for subsequent, more detailed and focused studies (Scoones, 1995: 86).

The title of Scoones' paper starts with the phrase 'Investigating difference', which makes the approach and purpose clear. It sets out what had by then become a standard approach, including: work on a definition of household; a search for the right word or phrase in the local language for wealth; the identification of reliable informants (the ranking was done by small groups); and the use of three independent rankings to reach an agreed overall stratification. The only modification from the Grandin approach was to predetermine the number of wellbeing categories that the households could be assigned to. There is a discussion of gender issues, trends that emerge from the findings, and links between the different elements of local understanding of wellbeing. The paper also includes reports of conscientious attempts to avoid imposing ideas or introducing bias, as in the observation that 'no prompting was given' in setting up one of the discussions (p.71).

Adams et al. (1997)

The validity of wealth ranking was directly addressed by Adams et al. in 1997 in a paper that asks in its title *Is it valid?* It comes to the clear conclusion that the theory and idea of wealth ranking ('the construct') are valid, and that the use of the method is a valid way of stratifying households by socio-economic status. The authors carried out a wealth ranking that stratified over 1,600 households in Bangladesh and then carried out a questionnaire survey covering health, demographic and economic variables of the same households. The criteria examined in the household survey included access to health care, income, condition of the housing, material assets, land holding and how prone the household was to crisis. As Polly Hill had found in her work, the variables in this study were found to be significantly different from the wellbeing categories created in the ranking exercise. The paper comments on issues around the selection of informants, the quality of facilitation and other methodological questions, and points out some of the strengths and weaknesses of both methods.

In particular, the paper mentions the potential weakness of wealth ranking that comes from the inability to quantify the differences between components of household wellbeing and the relative importance of the different components in reaching a decision as to which wealth category each household should belong to. Adams et al. also say that the local sensitivity of wellbeing ranking limits its ability to allow cross-regional comparisons. They go on to say that they observed remarkable cross-regional consistency in the selection of indicators, and that conditions in rural Bangladesh might allow comparisons across regions using wellbeing ranking. They say that this finding needs to be tested.

The Homogeneous Blob 1998

Alice Welbourn (IIED/IDS, 1993) described the Homogeneous Blob Syndrome (HBS) in 1993 and this jokey definition of the blindness to difference within communities was picked up by Irene Guijt and Meera Kaul Shah in *The Myth of Community* (1998). These authors were most concerned with the way that HBS hid gender differences, and how even those that emerged during a community appraisal might disappear into averages and a general community development plan, as if a community was a thing that could develop. *The Myth of Community* explores a range of issues about the quality of participatory processes and inadequacies in the definition and understanding of quality at that time. The ladders of participation (as referred to by, for example, Arnstein, 1969 and Pretty, 1994) had not been extensively discussed within the sector and could in any case be limiting, as there are many ways in which participation could be carried out according to the purpose it was intended to serve. The volume mentions the use of wealth ranking in a range of circumstances for several purposes. In *Brides have a Price,* Régine Debrabandere and Arnout Desmet (1998) describe a sequence of participatory exercises that they carried out in Zimbabwe. Unusually, they started with a wealth ranking exercise, and say that it was hugely useful in later exercises to be able to refer back to this and examine how the issues under discussion in the later work related to the different wealth categories identified in the wealth ranking.

The same volume contains two accounts of using wealth ranking to assess differences between men and women. Meera Kaul Shah (1998) describes work in a community in Ghana where the households were identified from a mapping exercise, and the ranking created four or more different categories of wealth. The criteria used by men and women were significantly different and the household was not the functional unit that was being ranked. Importantly, the criteria being used were not those that common perceptions would have predicted; for example, women mentioned marketed crops rather than subsistence crops. Similarly important was the fact that neither men nor women equated wealth with being materially better off. Men initially discussed material wealth, but eventually chose 'god-fearing' as the main criterion of wellbeing, which did not include the richest men by material standards.

Sonja Vlaar and Rhodante Ahlers (1998) report on a wealth ranking in Cambodia. Although the exercise itself was carried out with households, the criteria for assessing households headed by males and females differed significantly. One generally surprising finding for the researchers was that households headed by females occurred in every wellbeing category, whereas it would have been easy to presume that households headed by women would have had a lower wellbeing ranking. In fact, there are a number of criteria that affect the status of a single woman; a widow tends to have higher status than that of other single women and can take on some of the rights of her deceased husband.

Again and again, wealth-ranking exercises provide interesting and useful observations on the different situations of people in the community. Some of these are unexpected, and most of them are the result of subtle interactions of different factors that the people leading the exercises would not have predicted.

Voices of the Poor project (2000)

In a short paper (2000), Narayan et al. summarize the benefits of the use of participatory methods in the poverty assessments that were to help the formulation of Poverty Reduction Strategies. The paper starts with the sentence 'The poor are the true poverty experts'.[3] This sets the approach for the participatory poverty assessments (PPAs) exercise; that is, the objective is to learn from poor people. The benefits are covered extensively in the three volumes of the Voices of the Poor project.

The PPAs make it clear how the use of wellbeing ranking offers a wide range of insights into the nature of poverty. The key observation – that wealth is not the same as wellbeing – is made is several ways, including the number of situations in which material wellbeing appears not to be the key determinant of wellbeing. The model of wellbeing and ill-being contains five elements: power/freedom of choice; security; physical health; social wellbeing; and material wellbeing.

The wellbeing interviews allow the complexity of the interaction between different elements to be brought into discussions of poverty. The method draws out the 'multiplicity of interlocking factors' and the changes over time of important elements of poverty as they are experienced by poor people. These characteristics, and the importance of the psychological issues that make up poverty, are made very clear. Moreover, the way that combinations of issues affect people's wellbeing contributes to a depiction of poverty that represents a dynamic and changing set of complex factors and influences.

Narayan remarks on the importance of behaviour and attitudes for improving relationships between officials and people at community level (2000: 28). This section gives examples of the often poor behaviour of government officials towards people at community level, but also perhaps suggests that the people carrying out the PPA interviews were more respectful, and conducted the interviews with some of the humility of those who are determined to learn.

A comment on power and the PPAs

The use of participatory methods in the work on the Voices of the Poor raised questions about the overall processes as well as the findings. The project put the methods and the processes in international development under scrutiny and produced some important observations. The following paragraphs include comments on power relations from Brock (1999) and comments on the quality of use of methods from McGee and Norton (2000).

Brock adds to the images of poverty that emerge from the PPAs, including descriptions of broad differences according to geographical location and, in particular, differences between experiences of poverty in urban and rural situations. Poverty and vulnerability, she suggests, are context specific and also vary according to the time of year. The analysis of power and a focus on difference helps to build a more complete picture of poverty, including tangible and intangible aspects. As Hill (1972) pointed out and Chambers (1997) describes, interactions between households also change the poverty status of individual households. People in the same community help each other, so relationships matter; assessing a household as if it were an isolated unit will provide an incomplete picture. Crucially, Brock says that the kind of information that comes out of such participatory processes is 'usually marginalised in planning top-down poverty alleviation strategies'. The remark (1999: 24) that the reports of the findings of the complex nature of poverty contain 'little [...] that is new' may also be important.

The difficulties of using and making use of wellbeing assessments seem not to be in relation to the tools but rather to the way they are applied, and to the use to which the results are put. Brock is clear that participatory processes have lost a key link to power analysis, and the 'empowerment' associated with the use of participatory tools no longer applies to the majority of cases.

A comment on quality and standards

In 2000, the Poverty Reduction Strategy Papers (PRSP) process was examined by McGee and Norton (2000). While generally sympathetic to the idea of making the process more participatory, they find a number of concerns about the levels of genuine participation. They also question what makes the process truly representative, which is necessary, they say, as not everyone can participate. They raise the issues of benchmarking (2000: 68) and make a number of suggestions for setting indicators and minimum standards as ways to improve the quality of participatory work in designing PRS. The authors run into the problem of defining the standards and, more importantly, how the standards will be enforced. They continue the argument for higher quality processes, with suggestions for capacity building. The problem that 'much depends on the attitudes and behaviour of key people involved' (2000: 73) is discussed, and the key observation made that the bulk of experience in participatory work lies with the NGO community. The approach and methods have been assimilated to a small extent by the donor community, but to a much lesser extent by governments.

The White and Pettit review (2004)

Almost 10 years after the publication of the Scoones paper (1995), White and Pettit (2004) refer to it in their review of work on wellbeing. It seems important that this simple exercise – comparing the results of two different but potentially complementary approaches to assessing levels of wealth – would appear to have occurred so rarely. There may be several reasons for this. One may be that the methods appeal to people with different views on assessing wellbeing, and neither sees the need to assess their work against a different measure that they have less trust in. Another may be that the difference is at the level of those who fund community-level investigations, so that those who fund economic surveys do not fund wellbeing rankings and vice versa. It may also be that there is an overall lack of rigour in international development processes: that the testing of methods and cross-checking of results is not normal practice. There may be simple economic reasons for this apparent lack of curiosity; it may be seen as profligate to invest in this kind of evidence-checking.

White and Pettit set out to discuss the contribution that participatory methods have made to the definition and measurement of wellbeing. They observe that although participatory methods are normally associated with subjective and qualitative findings, wellbeing ranking provides highly quantitative data, perhaps more so than any other participatory tool. They explore the assessment of wellbeing and describe it as having three components: what people have and don't have; what people do and don't do; and how people assess, judge or feel about the situation and how they make sense of it.

Their paper explores some of the benefits often attributed to participatory work:

- *Economy*. It is simpler and quicker to find out about a community when you use participatory methods.
- *Engagement*. Local people will take part in more democratic processes that enable them to have a greater say in activities that are being carried out in their name.
- *Empowerment*. Participatory methods will bring about a change in power relations and the local people will be able to control more of the work done on their behalf by aid agencies and formal authorities.

The methods are seen as a means to an end in some cases, and in others as an end in themselves. The many expectations put upon participatory methods may help explain the rise and fall in their popularity and use.

White and Pettit provide an assessment of the participatory aspects of the PPAs which, for the first and only time, used a wide range of participatory tools including wellbeing ranking exercises. They report on the broad and varied descriptions of experiences of poverty and the ways that many factors interact to affect people's levels of ill- and wellbeing. In particular, they record the point that when asked to define poverty, poor people talk about a wide range of intangible dimensions of social connections, respect, and inclusion, and the effects of power and powerlessness. However, White and Pettit then rehearse the point made by Chambers (1997) in his review, that this major finding hardly appears in the World Development Report that Voices of the Poor (Narayan, 2000) was supposed to be informing.

White and Pettit observe that where participatory methods fail, it is always in terms of not respecting the principles of good participation. They identify four principles: pursuing genuine facilitation and avoiding bias; being flexible; using visual and interactive tools; and having the analyses done by the participants themselves.

Problems with participation

Problems in the use of participatory methods have been well documented by Cornwall et al. (2001) in a review of Participatory Rural Appraisal (PRA) work carried out in Kenya.[4] The paper presents an inventory of poor practices that go slightly or totally against the principles of a participatory approach. In many cases, the blame appears to lie with donors who want participatory work done according to timetables and procedures that make it impossible to respect the principles of flexibility and shared learning that would normally allow some sharing of control. In other cases, the individuals and institutions carrying out the work seem to be guilty of working in ways that they know are not following appropriate participatory processes. The explosion of demand for participatory work, or at least something called PRA, and an inability to change institutional ways of working to accommodate the necessary flexibility, seem to have put impossible demands on development work. It is possible that donors were, in any case, moving away from working through NGOs and increasingly wanting to work with governments (2001: 21), with the result that their willingness to accommodate NGOs' demands for more time and more flexibility was diminishing.

Cornwall had already expressed these views in a more general way in *Beneficiary Consumer Citizen* (2000) and records predictions of the failure of participation in a 1980 publication by Cohen and Uphoff. They say that 'faddishness and lip service' (p.41) could lead to participation being drained of substance and its 'relevance to development programmes could become disputable' (p.41).

Karen Brock (2003) records her unease at the power relations in the development business and the role of participatory processes. She is somewhat dismissive of the use of participatory methods to help the poor make their voices heard, and puts the word 'heard' in inverted commas to indicate that this practice will alter neither the local nor the international power relations that have made poor people poor in the past, and are likely to keep them poor in the future.

Doubtless there are finer analyses and better descriptions of these processes that have arisen in debates on international development, but these examples are the ones that seem to have emerged from work on wealth ranking.

Q-Squared (2002) – the best of both worlds

In 2002, a conference was held on the use of qualitative and quantitative assessments with a view to exploring ways to use both and get the 'best of both worlds'. The conference led to a publication called *Q-Squared* (Kanbur, 2002). For most of the writers there was no doubt that it was right to seek to obtain the best of both worlds; the notion that participatory methods and quantitative survey methods should be combined was not at question. Robert Chambers writes (Kanbur, 2002: 42) that 'the case for complementarity hardly needs to be made'.

The volume concludes that the two approaches should not be differentiated as quantitative or qualitative, but rather regarded as two different qualities. First, the degree of involvement of the people whose wellbeing is being assessed, which could be active or passive. Second, the degree to which context is important; with qualitative participatory methods, on the one hand, involving substantial local context, and household income and expenditure surveys, on the other, requiring little. This makes comparisons between different contexts easier, whereas participatory methods do not lend themselves so well to comparisons between different places.

The editor Ravi Kanbur (2002: 13) summarizes some of the key points in the contributors' papers and mentions the value of qualitative fieldwork, which, in contrast to quantitative surveys, allows issues to be probed the moment they are observed and allows for any 'surprises' to be incorporated into enquiries.

Chris Barrett (2002) describes a good example of complementarity, in which participatory appraisals and direct observations preceded and crucially informed the design of a questionnaire survey.

Despite the obvious usefulness of combining methods in such ways, *Q-Squared* is full of warnings and unease over whether it is truly feasible to get the best of both worlds. These different worlds are held apart by 'different traditions' and remain in 'separate channels' in many donor agencies (Kanbur, 2002: 20). Almost all the contributors to the report propose that participatory methods can be robust and deliver quantitative data, that questionnaire surveys can deliver qualitative insights, and that the division between them is therefore artificial and unhelpful. Nevertheless, the tone suggests that the division is strong.

Strengths and weaknesses of the questionnaire survey

Appleton and Booth (2001) explored the use of both methods in work in Uganda and reached the conclusion that each method should be seen as being able to enrich and explain the other's findings, but should not be seen as being able to confirm or refute the other.[5] This conclusion is drawn from the view that each method does different things well. The analysis may have been prompted by apparently contradictory findings, where household surveys showed increased food consumption, while wellbeing exercises identified decreased levels of wellbeing.

Appleton (1996) describes some of the difficulties of presuming that household surveys provide robust data. In his examination of a sequence of official household consumption surveys in Uganda, he suggests that there may be discrepancies in a number of areas including, importantly, production estimates, household size and the recall periods of informants. He shows how even small adjustments made to the calculations could lead to a significant change in the apparent results, and concludes that 'estimates of economic welfare from conventional household surveys are more relative than commonly thought'. This is important because, although it seems obvious that there are many ways in which household income and consumption surveys may be well or badly designed, and well or badly implemented, this is not part of the discussion on bringing together the methods in *Q-Squared.*

In *Q-Squared,* Moser (2002: 82) says that it is necessary to change the definition of robustness to make it more inclusive of different methods; she hopes that this will lead to a situation where social issues are no longer 'confined to anecdotal boxes'. The word anecdote has become a wholly derogatory term as the demand for better evidence of impact has grown among the donors in international development.

David Booth (2003) describes the potential for using wellbeing ranking in the PPA in Pakistan to help create focus groups and to form the basis for stratified random samples for questionnaire work. This might seem a good use of wellbeing ranking and a good combination of methods. However he also predicts that the pressure for results that can be 'aggregated upwards in numerical form' will continue to grow, as will the pressure to produce 'bold conclusions and strong policy measures' (p.102). Donors want big numbers and simple statements of impact, and this pressure affects the entire approach of development agencies and the methods they choose to use to design, describe and defend their work.

Simon Maxwell (1999) wrote a briefing entitled *The Meaning and Measurement of Poverty* in which he surveys a wide range of poverty assessment approaches and tools. He explores the issues around using locally relevant relative indicators, and the problems of trying to aggregate them into meaningful national figures and provide the statistics that policy makers desire. He ends by saying that it is 'wise to respect the vision of poverty articulated by poor people themselves' (p.4) because they may have very different priorities. This would lead to a range of different initiatives but, Maxwell goes on, 'Variety of this kind does little to help generate measures of international progress. Does that matter?' (p.4) The question was probably posed rhetorically but seems to have been answered by the donors with a powerful 'Yes!' Donors, it seems, did not want a mixture of results from different places, no matter how interesting or well-founded. Rather, they wanted simple numbers that they could easily aggregate in order to support reports that their funding was reducing poverty.

Hargreaves' tests of consistency

The biggest test of the ability of wellbeing ranking to provide cross-regional comparisons was carried out by Hargreaves et al. (2007a) in South Africa. The methods used in the study are described in detail and are based on the work of Anton Simanowitz and others in Zimbabwe, as described in Chapter 6 (Simanowitz, 2014). It may be useful and interesting to read Simanowitz's chapter to appreciate how Hargreaves' work builds on, and adds to the completeness of, the description of these key pieces of work using wealth ranking. The main point to note regarding the work of Simanowitz and Hargreaves is that they are examples of using wealth ranking over large areas and with very large numbers of households; over 10,000 in the South Africa work. Both appear to have overcome the difficulty involved in using a participatory method to make consistent assessments across different places that allow comparisons between them. Hargreaves examined the findings of the rankings far more intensely than is normal in a wellbeing ranking. He collected all the statements made describing the qualities of wellbeing, in each category of wellbeing, in every ranking exercise. The number of statements ran into the thousands. These were prioritized according to how many times they occurred and then arranged into themes. The first analysis produced 880 statements grouped under 33 themes, which were eventually whittled down to 131 statements arranged under 23 themes for the final analysis. It was then possible to use the statements to assess the nature and extent of poverty in each of five wellbeing categories. These descriptions are of great value in explaining the specific experience of poverty and can be more easily used by policy makers (2007a: 227) in making decisions about the use of resources. The skilful use of a more standardized wellbeing ranking methodology, followed by a range of qualitative and quantitative methods to analyse the results, appears to result in a more useful method of poverty appraisal.

Hargreaves also used wealth ranking in assessing health issues in South Africa (2007b). This work compared wealth ranking with two household survey methods. Correlations between the two approaches seemed disappointingly poor, even though the wealth ranking results were very consistent internally. It may be that some aspects of wellbeing were weighted more heavily by the selected informants than when the components were assessed during the surveys. Hargreaves ends by recommending participatory wealth ranking as a useful method for work in health.

A recent example of wealth ranking 2010

The most recent use of wellbeing ranking that I can find is in work on health issues in Burkina Faso (Souares et al., 2011). The researchers wanted to identify the poorest section of the community in order to offer them financial support in obtaining health care. The normal methodology was modified in that the three informants in each community were brought together after doing their ranking separately to reach an agreed final ranking for the households in the community. The identification of the least well-off was relatively easily achieved, and the offers of financial help with community-based health insurance were apparently accepted, with the result that enrolment rates among the poorest rose from 1% to 11%. It is not at all clear whether this led to improved health, but it is clear that the method for identifying the target population was 'cost and time efficient compared to other methods' (p.363). In 2013, the work was updated (Parmar et al., 2013) by observations that the identification of the poorest households had been effective, but the initiative had not significantly increased their access to health care-evidence, if any were needed, that successful poverty alleviation requires more than good appraisal or assessment tools.

Notes

1. Silverman's work took place in Italy.
2. Barbara Grandin, personal communication to John Rowley, 2013.
3. Similarly, the first principle of the the Participatory Practitioners for Change network in the UK states that local people are experts in their own lives. The principle sometimes needs to be interpreted so that outside practitioners understand that their job is to learn from local people who have knowledge that the outsiders do not have. It is sometimes necessary in training sessions on participatory methods to make it clear that the local people, the insiders, have expert knowledge of their situation, although this does not make them experts in all ways. They know things that other people do not know; for example, through their direct experience of health issues, but this does not make them experts in medicine. That is to say that insiders and outsiders have different types of knowledge about health issues and each can learn from the other.
4. PRA had become a shorthand form for a participatory project appraisal process.
5. This is partly in response to a World Bank document that suggested that the methods should be used to correct each other (Carvalho and White, 1997).

References

Appleton, S. (1996) 'Problems of measuring changes in poverty over time: The case of Uganda 1989–92, *IDS Bulletin* 27: 43–55 <http://dx.doi.org/10.1111/j.1759-5436.1996.mp27001005.x>

Appleton, S. and Booth, D. (2005) 'Combining participatory and survey-based approaches to poverty monitoring and analysis', *Q-Squared* Working Paper No. 14. <http://192.75.12.210/ids/documents/Q2_WP14_AppletonandBooth.pdf>

Arnstein, S. R. (1969) 'A ladder of citizen participation', *Journal of the American Planning Association* 35 (4): 216–24.

Barrett, C. (2003) 'Integrating qualitative and quantitative approaches: Lessons from the pastoral risk management project', in R. Kanbur (ed.), *Q-Squared: Combining Qualitative and Quantitative Methods in Poverty Appraisal*, New Delhi: Permanent Black.

Booth, D. (2003) 'Towards a better combination of the quantitative and the qualitative: Some design Issues from Pakistan's Participatory Poverty Assessment' in R. Kanbur (ed.), *Q-Squared: Combining Qualitative and Quantitative Methods in Poverty Appraisal*, pp. 97-102, New Delhi: Permanent Black.

Brock, K. (1999) *It's Not Only Wealth that Matters – It's Peace of Mind Too: A Review of Participatory Work on Poverty and Ill-being*, Brighton: Institute of Development Studies.

Brock, K. (2003) 'Participation, policy, poverty: where now?' in A. Cornwall and G. Pratt (eds.), *Pathways to Participation, Reflections on PRA*, pp. 32–35, Rugby: Practical Action Publishing.

Carvalho, S. and White, H., (1997) *Combining the Quantitative and Qualitative Approaches to Poverty Measurement and Analysis: The Practice and the Potential*, vol.23, Washington, DC: World Bank Publications.

Chambers, R (1983) *Rural Development: Putting the Last First*, Harlow: Longman.

Chambers, R. (1997) *Whose Reality Counts? Putting the First Last*, Rugby: Practical Action Publishing.

Cornwall, A. (2000) *Beneficiary, Consumer, Citizen: Perspectives on Participation for Poverty Reduction*, SIDA studies 2, Gothenburg: SIDA.

Cornwall, A., Musyoki, S. and Pratt, G. (2001) *In Search of a New Impetus: Practitioners' Reflections on PRA and Participation in Kenya*, IDS Working Paper 131, Brighton: Institute of Development Studies.

Debrabandere R. and Desmet, A. (1998) 'Brides have a price: Gender dimensions of objective-oriented project planning in Zimbabwe', in I. Guijt and M.K. Shah (eds.), *The Myth of Community: Gender Issues in Participatory Development*, pp. 100–109, Rugby: Practical Action Publishing.

Grandin, B. E. (1988) *Wealth Ranking in Smallholder Communities: A Field Manual*, Rugby: Practical Action Publishing.

Guijt I. and Shah, M.K. (eds.) (1998) *The Myth of Community: Gender Issues in Participatory Development*, Rugby: Practical Action Publishing.

Guijt, I. (1992) 'The elusive poor: a wealth of ways to find them. Report on an IDS/IIED seminar on wealth and well-being ranking', *RRA Notes*, 15: 7–13.

Guijt, I. and Cornwall, A. (1995) 'Critical reflections on the practice of PRA', *PLA (Participatory Learning and Action) Notes* 24: 2–7

Guijt, I. (1992) 'A user's note on wealth ranking by cards and list of sources on wealth ranking', *RRA (Rapid Rural Appraisal) Notes* 15: 65–69.

Hargreaves, J.R., Morison, L.A., Gear J., Porter, J.D.H., Makhubele, M.B., Kim, J.C., Busza, J., Watts, C. and Pronyk, P.M. (2007) '"Hearing the voices of the poor": Assigning poverty lines on the basis of local perceptions of poverty; a quantitative analysis of qualitative data from participatory wealth ranking in rural South Africa', *World Development* 35 (2): 212–229.

Hill, P. (1972) *Rural Hausa – A Village and a Setting*, Cambridge: Cambridge University Press.

International Institute for Environment and Development (IIED)/IDS (1993) 'Summary of discussions of PRA and Gender Workshop', 6–7 December 1993; cited in Guijt, I and Kaul Shah, M. (eds) (1998) *The Myth of Community: Gender issues in participatory development*, Rugby: Practical Action Publishing.

Maxwell, S. (1999) *The Meaning and Measurement of Poverty*, London: Overseas Development Institute.

McGee, R. with Norton, A. (2000) *Participation in Poverty Reduction Strategies: A Synthesis of Experience with Participatory Approaches to Policy Design, Implementation and Monitoring*, IDS Working Paper 109, Brighton: Institute of Development Studies.

Mearns, R., Shombodon, D., Narangerel, G., Turul, U., Enkhamgalan, A., Myagmarzhav, B., Bayanjargal, A. and Bekhsuren, B. (1992) 'Direct and indirect uses of wealth ranking in Mongolia', *RRA Notes* 15: 29–38, London: IIED.

Moser, C. (2003) *'"Apt illustration" or "Anecdotal information?" Can qualitative data be representative or robust?'* in R. Kanbur (ed.) *Q-Squared: Combining Qualitative and Quantitative Methods in Poverty Appraisal*, pp. 79-89, New Delhi: Permanent Black.

Mukherjee, N. (1992) 'Villagers' perceptions of rural poverty through the mapping methods of PRA', *RRA Notes* 15: 21–26, London: IIED.

Narayan, D., Chambers, R., Shah, M.K. and Petesch, P. (2000) *Voices of the Poor: Crying Out for Change*. New York NY: Oxford University Press for the World Bank.

Ortiz, S., (1974) 'Obstacle to agricultural growth in Hausaland viewed through a village study', *Economic Development and Cultural Change* 22 (1): 163–168 <http://www.jstor.org/stable/1153150> [accessed 13 May 2014]

Parmar, D., De Allegri, M., Savadogo, G. and Sauerborn, R. (2014) 'Do community-based health insurance schemes fulfill the promise of equity? A study from Burkina Faso', *Health Policy and Planning*, 29 (1): 76–84 <http://dx.doi.org/10.1093/heapol/czs136>.

Pretty, J.N. (1994) 'Alternative systems of enquiry for sustainable agriculture', *IDS Bulletin* 25 (2): 37–48, Brighton: IDS.

Pretty, J., Subramanian, S., Kempu Chetty, N., Ananthakrishnan, D., Jayanthi, C., Muralikrishnasamy, S. and Renganayaki, K. (1992) 'Finding the poorest in a Tamil Nadu village: a sequence of mapping and wealth ranking', *RRA Notes* 15: 39–42, London: IIED.

Rowley, J. (2014) 'Some practical examples and what users say about wellbeing ranking', in Rowley, J. (ed.) Wellbeing Ranking: *Developments in Applied Community-level Poverty Research*, pp. 33–48, Rugby: Practical Action, <http://dx.doi.org/10.3362/9781780448459.004>.

Sarch, M-T. (1992) 'Wealth ranking in the Gambia: which households participated in the FITT programme?' *RRA Notes* 15: 14–20, London: IIED.

Sarkar, A., (1991) 'Wealth ranking in Mahilong, Bihar', *RRA Notes* 13: 81–2, London: IIED.

Schaefer, S.S. (1992) 'The 'beans-game' – experiences with a variation of wealth ranking in the Kivu Region, Eastern Zaire', *RRA Notes* 15: 27–8, London: IIED.

Scoones, I. (1988) 'Learning about wealth: an example from Zimbabwe', *RRA Notes* 2: 12–17, London: IIED.

Scoones, I. (1995) 'Investigating ranking and difference: Applications of wealth household survey approaches among farming households in southern Zimbabwe, *Development and Change* 26: 67–88.

Seeley, J., Nabaitu, J., Taylor, L., Kajura, E., Bukenya, T., Kabunga, E. and Ssembajja, F. (1996) 'Revealing gender differences through well-being ranking in Uganda', *PLA Notes* 25: 14–18, London: IIED.

Shah, M.K., (1998) *'Gendered perceptions of well-being and social change in Darko, Ghana'*, in I. Guijt and M.K. Shah (eds.) *The Myth of Community: Gender Issues in Participatory Development*, pp. 141–151, Rugby: Practical Action Publishing.

Shah, P. (1990) 'Economic classification of a community using locally generated criteria', *RRA Notes* 8: 24–9, London: IIED.

Silverman, S. F. (1966) 'An ethnographic approach to social stratification: Prestige in a central Italian community', *American Anthropologist* 68: 899–921.

Simanowitz, A. (1999) 'Pushing the limits of mapping and wealth ranking', *PLA Notes* 34: 4–8, London: IIED.

Simanowitz, A. (2014) 'Using participatory wealth ranking in a South African microfinance organization: the value of scale', in Rowley, J. (ed.) Well-being Ranking: Developments in Applied Community-level Poverty Research, pp. 71–88, Rugby: Practical Action Publishing, <http://dx.doi.org/10.3362/9781780448459.006>

Souares, A., Savadogo, G., Dong, H., Parmar, D., Sie, A. and Sauerborn, R. (2010) 'Using community wealth ranking to identify the poor for subsidies: A case study of community-based health insurance in Nouna, Burkina Faso', *Health and Social Care in the Community* 18 (4): 363–8.

Swift, J. and Umar A. N. (1994) 'The problem and solution game', *RRA Notes* 20: 138–41, London: IIED.

Tung, L. and Baliña, F. (1993) 'FARMI's experiences on wealth ranking in the Philippines: Different farmers have different needs', *RRA Notes* 18: 60–65, London: IIED.

Welbourn, A. (1991) 'RRA and the analysis of difference', *RRA Notes* 14: 14–23, London: IIED.

Welbourn, A. (1992) 'A note on the use of disease problem ranking with relation to socio-economic well-being: An example from Sierra Leone', *RRA Notes* 16: 86–7, London: IIED.

White S., and Pettit, J. (2004) *Participatory Approaches and the Measurement of Human Well-being,* Research Paper 2004/57, UNU-WIDER, United Nations University (UNU)..

About the author

John Rowley is an international development professional with over 30 years' experience working for national and international NGOs, government agencies, bilateral and multilateral donors and commercial companies in the UK, Africa and elsewhere.

CHAPTER 4

Some practical examples, and what users say about wellbeing ranking

John Rowley

This chapter is a short overview of the immediate reactions of people using wealth ranking. Most of the observations come from issues of RRA Notes, and later PLA Notes, which is the publication aimed at practitioners. I wanted to collect and share these experiences to provide practical and real examples of working with wealth-ranking methods. The chapter begins with observations on the way that people write about their work in PLA Notes and how this may betray a concern about how participatory work is done. It later describes the repeated use of the wealth-ranking method in Vietnam, which shows its potential as a monitoring and evaluation tool. The chapter ends with a section on the heap-of-beans *method, which is the fastest and simplest way of examining differences within a community.*

Keywords: wellbeing, well-being, ranking, interview, methods, evaluation, heap-of-beans

The tone of writing in *PLA Notes*

The journal *PLA* (*Participatory Learning and Action*) *Notes* (formerly *RRA* (*Rapid Rural Appraisal*) *Notes*) is an important publication for sharing learning from participatory work. The articles form a valuable source of ideas on using participatory methods and are usually frank and self-reflexive accounts of practical experience. The tone of the accounts tends to be self-deprecating and, in some cases, gives the impression that the authors feel that they have somehow failed, at least partially, in their work. Articles with a positive tone about important achievements appear quite rare. This may be due to a desire to be self-critical, which is a much-praised virtue in texts on participatory methods. The style seems very different from that found in academic journals or in routine reporting by development agencies which, by contrast, comes across as not only impersonal but almost boastful.

Perhaps the decline in interest in participatory methods observed over the last 10 years is at least partly due to the self-effacing nature of the publications produced on the topic. Sceptical readers might well think that if the supporters of participation were so doubtful about their work, the methods were probably of limited worth.

http://dx.doi.org/10.3362/9781780448459.004

One more practical reason for the self-critical tone may have been practitioners' awareness that such methods are only as good as the person using them. Of course, this is true of all tools and methods, but there is a particular problem in the way that power is managed during interviews that seek to encourage participation. The facilitator, often a stranger in the group, is in a paradoxical situation. Sometimes because the facilitator is a stranger and sometimes for other reasons, they have the power to control the meeting; however, their desire to be genuinely participatory requires them to relinquish that power to the local people so that the latter control the meeting themselves. Participation can be achieved, with different degrees of success, and participatory tools can help. However, no matter how successful they are at handing over power, the sensitive facilitator is often acutely aware of how easy it would be for them to keep control of the meeting from their privileged position. Usually, they will be under pressure to achieve some purpose, which works against yielding power to other meeting participants. They may also be aware of how easy it would be for a less scrupulous facilitator to carry out an interview that is not genuinely participatory at all.

It is easy to say of any method or tool that bad practice is always possible, as a way of excusing the fact that it might not deliver the expected results. In the case of participatory tools, though, this is more than that simple excuse; it is a way of saying that the facilitator's approach and attitude can cause the method to fail. Unconscious bias and domination of the process can prevent an interview from providing an accurate account of the participants' views. Chapter 7 ('Wellbeing ranking, semi-structured interviews and practitioner bias', Heffernan and Misturelli, 2014) includes a detailed discussion of issues associated with the facilitator's performance. To carry out a successful participatory interview, a facilitator needs to have the appropriate self-awareness and attitude, as well as skill and knowledge of how the tool works.

It actually works!

Whenever and wherever I have introduced wellbeing ranking to people carrying out community-level work, I have met opposition, and have been told that the method will not work in the context we are in. When we try it out, what usually happens is that the first observation is that it actually works, in that people are willing and able to sort households into different wellbeing categories. The purpose and method have to be explained carefully and the conditions need to be arranged correctly (for a detailed account of methodological issues, see Chapter 5, 'Methodological Issues in Wellbeing Ranking', Rowley, 2014b), but in the vast majority of cases the local people *can* carry out wellbeing ranking.

The method also works in that a visitor can arrive in a community with little knowledge of the situation of local people, and leave a few hours later with a clear understanding of two things: first, how local people appreciate and understand wellbeing; and second, how they see wellbeing being experienced among the households in the community. This way of putting it emphasizes the learning of the outsiders, because that is how it is most often expressed. This may appear to be emphasizing the extractive nature of the process, which at one time was seen as less honourable, but it may now be seen as good learning.

Wellbeing even works in highly stratified communities, such as those where Ruth Grosvenor-Alsop (1989) tested it in India. Prior to that, she had been uncertain whether it would work in a context where there were strong divisions along caste and religious lines and where it had not been used before.

One reason for reporting the simple fact that wellbeing ranking works is the number of concerns raised by practitioners about working in the highly sensitive area of wealth. They mention the 'extremely delicate nature of the subject' (Ghirotti, 1992: 43); the 'ticklish task' (Sarkar, 1991: 81); and the 'sensitive issue to be approached with caution'; but find that in practice the method turns out not to be threatening, even though it is focused on the 'sensitive issue of poverty' (Welbourn, 1991: 14). I also found this to be the case with middle-class people in the UK whom I know to be very sensitive about wealth, but who were able to carry out the task with apparent lack of embarrassment. It seems that ranking is acceptable in situations where enquiries about absolute wealth would not be tolerated.

It is enjoyable

Practitioners also point out that the process seems to be enjoyable for the participants in many, but not all occasions. A few quotations will make the point: 'there was much shouting, laughter and discussion about how well-off particular compounds were' (Sarch, 1992: 16); 'Unusual and fun' (Schaefer, 1992: 28); 'very enjoyable' (Banliña, 1992: 49); and, 'The more passive role of the team and the more active role of the informants was greatly appreciated and the latter clearly enjoyed the exercise' (Young, 1990: 14).

This kind of reaction is not specific to wealth ranking; many participatory methods bring out the same kind of responses. Perhaps the process is just much easier and more interesting than the more common question and answer sessions. Perhaps the facilitators transmit their own enjoyment of seeing the methods work and having interesting and successful exchanges with local people.

The reports mention a few examples of awkwardness and embarrassment. Janet Seeley (1996) mentions people being uneasy that the results might be used for taxation purposes, although she also records having the same problem with a questionnaire survey when people refused to answer questions on landholding and production. Carrie Turk (1995) records difficulties where participants were asked to talk in front of local officials, and how much easier it was for them to do the exercise some years later when there was no official present. There are stories of difficulties in India where people were angry at being ranked as better-off because they believed that the process might determine who was eligible for project benefits.[1] Ly Tung (1993) and Martin Leach (1994) both found some informants to be embarrassed by the presence of other people during some parts of the ranking exercise. This may have been because they were ranking the people watching them, and reinforces the usefulness of arranging for participants to do the exercise in small groups or individually without others observing. Banlina (1992), however, reports people being quite happy to rank themselves when doing the task, and that has generally been my own experience.

It brings in a huge range of criteria

This is a major area of findings and it would take a long time to record all the interesting and unexpected criteria that were noted by practitioners in their reporting; however, it seems important to share some examples. Reports include mentions of: historical trends and how things have changed for the different wellbeing groups; indebtedness; inexperience; laziness; respect and lack of respect; access to services; and access to commons.[2] The important thing to note is that these examples are invisible and that data might not be asked for in a more conventional household survey. A number of authors in *PLA Notes* point out that the key criteria do not relate to material wealth. For example, 'indicators go beyond income such as education, accessibility to public services, dependency on common property resources, social criteria' (Mukherjee, 1992: 26). Helen Young remarks that 'much hitherto unexpected and unknown information was learnt' (1990: 14). This is repeated in many reports, but is not unique to wealth ranking; many participatory tools seem to prompt the same remark. Discussions sometimes include allusions to ideas of the 'deserving and undeserving' poor (Seeley et al., 1996: 17) and this may relate to the informant wanting to make sure that the facilitator knows which group the informant is in. The fact that wealth ranking allows identification and discussion of invisible intangible aspects of wellbeing seems important, and can occur even where the starting point is material wealth.

It allows identification and discussion of differences

It seems rather unnecessary to point out that ranking draws attention to differences within a community, but it is nevertheless pointed out by practitioners. Differences matter, and understanding these allows practitioners to avoid the problems that follow from treating a community as a unit, or from imagining that there exists such a thing as an average person, or an average household, which would allow for the design of a single initiative suitable to everyone in some equitable way. Alice Welbourn (1991) called this kind of approach the 'Homogeneous Blob Syndrome' (see also Chapter 5, 'Methodological Issues in Wellbeing Ranking', Rowley, 2014b).

A number of reports note that it seems easier during the ranking to identify those households with the highest and lowest levels of wellbeing. It seems more difficult to make distinctions among middle-ranking groups (Banlina, 1992; Carter et al., 1993). In fact, one potential weakness of ranking is that groups in different ranks may not be equal distances apart: group 2 may be much richer than group 3, but just a tiny bit poorer than group 1. The follow-up discussions over the categories should help make this clear. Some discussions do not lead to analysis of underlying causes, where participants do not really know about other people's livelihoods, or where the given explanation of difference is theological.

It provides reliable results

The early users of wealth ranking make the important observation that different ranking exercises within the same community produce extremely similar results. Silverman (1966), Hill (1972) and Grandin (1988) all make the same point. Grandin goes on to say that the case of one informant consistently disagreeing with the others 'has never to my knowledge occurred' (1988: 26). More recent writers find the same, and this may not be surprising if the informants are drawn from the same social group. There are differences between the rankings carried out by women and men (Seeley et al., 1996; Welbourn, 1992; Guijt, 1992). This is mostly because of the use of different criteria, not because of access to different information. It is not as clear that there are important differences where rankings are done by people from different wellbeing groups. Where people know each other extremely well and have done so for a long time, they seem able to rank households very consistently. Consistency may also be increased because many criteria for wellbeing and illbeing are interlinked (Grandin, 1988; Hill, 1972).

It seems better than some alternatives

The publications that I have examined contain a number of somewhat polarized descriptions of the differences between wellbeing ranking and household surveys of income and expenditure (see Chapter 3, 'The history of wellbeing ranking techniques', Rowley, 2014c) for more on this). The practitioners who wrote for *PLA Notes* also have their views on the differences, and they are mostly positive about the quality of understanding that can be gained from the multi-dimensional results of wellbeing ranking compared to simpler assessments of wellbeing. For example, Leach (1994) says that monthly income assessments would be useless for many of the same reasons as Polly Hill (1972) i.e. they vary so much from one time of year to another that making a generalization based on one particular time of year is misleading. Mukherjee (1992: 26) suggests that the official definition of poverty provides only a proxy indicator in terms of income, and concludes that it may not be relevant to translate the diversity and complexity of poverty into a single indicator and arrive at an 'average' picture of poverty.

It requires skills

'Good use of the PRA [participatory rural appraisal] methods is not necessarily guaranteed by the methods alone' write Pretty et al. (1992: 39), stating a concern echoed by many other practitioners and writers regarding participatory methods over the past 30 years. Sharrock et al. (1993: 58), writing about using wealth ranking in Nepal, advise that 'it will be essential to ensure that the philosophy, and not [just] the methods of participatory research are well understood'. The concern over quality is discussed briefly below, but it is clear that there are issues here that are bigger than the observation that 'Bad practice is bad practice, whatever the method' (Barrett, 2000: 95). Of course Barrett is right, and in Chapter 7 Claire Heffernan and Federica Misturelli (2014) discuss some of the issues relating to the management of semi-structured interviews and the bias that tends to be introduced by different personality types and different professional training. However, bias and other aspects of poor practice are not confined to participatory methods. Appleton and Booth (2005) for example, describe some of the dangers in presuming that household surveys by questionnaire are immune to errors introduced by the enumerators. Clearly, the quality of facilitation – which means the qualities of the facilitator – is crucial in all interviews, regardless of the tools used. Elements of an interview, including clearly explaining the purpose, checking on the understanding of participants, and feeding back the results to participants, all seem to be examples of good practice, and some of these can be described in manuals as required steps and stages in the process. There are other qualities that are harder to define in a manual, and harder to insist upon because they relate to personal qualities or personality traits. These include levels of self-awareness and the ability to be self-critical, including the capacity to detect levels of bias even where they cannot be corrected. In addition, an overall attitude of humility will allow the facilitator to learn from the participants and from unexpected and challenging observations.

Intra-household issues

A wellbeing ranking of households does not address intra-household issues. Certainly, a single ranking based on households will not help much in understanding what happens within a household. In *The Myth of Community* (Guijt and Shah (eds), 1998), there are several descriptions of wellbeing-ranking exercises that were carried out with men and women separately, and these obliged the researcher to examine some of the differences between men and women.

In the case of ranking heads of households, a researcher may be forced to acknowledge the importance of gender because of the differences between rankings of households headed by males and females. However, the importance of the difference of gender within a household is not forced on the facilitator by the method itself. If there were no households headed by women it would be possible to continue to ignore gender issues. That is to say, it is necessary to work on gender differences and other differences within households, such as age, from one's own conviction of their importance.

However, a wealth ranking by men on household heads alongside a ranking of women by women would lead to some sharing of insights into differences between the positions of men and women within the household.

One concern that could be raised about wellbeing ranking is that it does not address issues affecting everyone in the community. This is a fine point that would become important if the researcher were unaware of external factors affecting the wellbeing of most people in a community. One example might be a drought, which affects everyone, albeit not necessarily equally. The rankings might remain unchanged, although the wellbeing of everyone would have been depressed by the drought and would increase again if the drought ended. In the experience of users that I have studied, there seems to be plenty of evidence of discussion of external factors that affect wellbeing. It may be that this would be more of a concern if wellbeing findings were being compared between places that had not experienced the same overall impact on wellbeing; in our example, with a place that had not suffered drought. In this case the categories might be mismatched, and the most well-off in the drought-affected community might only have a standard of living equivalent to the second or third category in the community where there had been no drought. However, it remains generally true that the ability to withstand harsh conditions like drought depends to some extent on wellbeing, so the comparisons within the community would remain relatively reliable. The ability to bring in factors affecting the entire community might depend on other sources of information and other discussions; the wellbeing exercises would be just one element of an ongoing process.

It changes outsiders' appreciation

Robin Mearns (1992) writes about an experience in Mongolia where members of the team were initially sceptical about participatory techniques, but became more convinced of their usefulness when they saw the results of exercises on the availability of labour in households disaggregated according to wealth-ranking categories. The exercises provided insight into differences that they had not previously acknowledged.

This kind of impact is not restricted to this particular interview tool. Lots of practitioners talk about the excitement they experience when seeing people suddenly change their understanding of the position and capabilities of poor people. Rachel Percy comments on 'several noting how much they had learned in just a few days of PRA work compared to years of working by themselves in the community',[3] while Cornwall and Guijt (2004: 161) write: 'We both have memories of professionals who experienced quite marked shifts in their perceptions of "the poor" in ways we could not have imagined changing without the field work.' This effect is probably more important than that of people changing their views on the tools.

It helps you find the poor

Smith and Sender (1988) describe work in Tanzania, in which they interviewed households in the richest and poorest wellbeing categories after a wealth ranking, and add that 'locating the richest and largest landowners is [a] much easier task than locating the poorest' (p.20). Other contributors to the *PLA Notes* mention the importance and usefulness of obtaining descriptions of the poorest households separately from other information about a community. Barbara Grandin[4] mentioned during our discussions about this book the ease with which a researcher can point to the piles of cards containing the names of the most poor in the community and ask to be introduced to people in this group.

It provides a good starting point

There are examples of wellbeing rankings being used to form focus groups for more detailed work (for example, to identify the least well-off for credit programmes, or the least well-nourished for supplementary feeding programmes) and as part of a process for identifying development initiatives. The most important result is a better shared understanding of local ideas about wellbeing, and that is a good start for any eventual intervention.

It is only an interview method

Wellbeing ranking is just one exercise that can serve a range of functions. It is like other exercises that may help share ideas or understanding or provide insight or data that can be used as part of a process. This point should not need to be made, nevertheless it is made by Irene Guijt in the issue of *PLA Notes* dedicated to wealth ranking: 'It is not able to overcome all problems of investigating social and economic dimensions of rural life' (Guijt, 1992: 7). There was a need then, and perhaps there is again now, to make it clear that no exceptional claims are being made for a single interview and information-gathering method. The method is potentially effective, powerful and very useful. As mentioned in the previous paragraph, however, it may simply serve as a starting point for the design of other work, and it is likely to be most useful when used within the context of managing development initiatives, which should incorporate repeated exchanges and opportunities for learning.

A classic use of wealth ranking in Vietnam

I am very grateful to Koos Neefjes for showing me the following example (Oxfam HK, 2003) of the use of wealth ranking. It illustrates many of the key characteristics of work involving this method. Wealth ranking was carried out twice, four years apart, and the results are shown in the following table. The numbers in the rows are the numbers assigned to individual households.

First, it gives an understanding of local appreciations of wellbeing, which are clearly focused on food security and means of producing food. Quality of housing is also an indicator, as well as some more invisible characteristics such as education, health and the aptitude for hard work. The work in 2003 seems to be more detailed than the earlier work.

Second, the characteristics of all the households seem to have improved between 1999 and 2003. The hungry period is the key indicator of food

Table 4.1 Wellbeing of households in Na Ca village 1999–2003

	1 (betteroff)	*2*	*3*	*4 (poorest)*
Hhld nos. 2003	1, 16, 22, 29, 30, 37, 44, 49, 51, 53	5, 6, 7, 15, 18, 19, 31, 34, 38, 42, 52	3, 4, 9, 10, 13, 14, 20, 21, 23, 24, 25, 27, 32, 33, 35, 41, 43, 46, 55, 56	2, 8, 11, 12, 17, 26, 28, 39, 40, 45, 47, 48, 50, 54
Characteristics 2003	• 1 month staple food insecure • Have labour • Have 2–3 cows/ buffaloes • Can accumulate money/assets • Good health • Hard-working • Have labour • 4 have tiled roof • 6 have corrugated sheet roofs	• 1–2 months staple food insecure • Firm house • Have labour • Have 1–2 cows/buffaloes • Can accumulate money/ assets • Hard-working	• 6 months staple food insecure • A bit better income than group 4 • Better health than group 4 • Thatched roof	• Up to 10 months staple food insecure • Eat rice (not mixed with cassava) in only 2 months • Thatched roof • No income • Not in good health • Many children • Lack of labour • No assets • Low education
Hhld nos. 1999	1, 16, 22, 29, 30, 37, 44, 49, 53	6, 7, 18, 31, 34, 38, 51*	4, 5* 9, 10, 13, 14, 15*, 19*, 20, 21, 23, 27, 32, 33, 35, 36, 41, 42*, 43, 46, 52*, 55, 56	2, 11, 12, 17, 24*, 25*, 26, 28, 39, 40, 45, 47, 48, 50, 54
Characteristics 1999	• 5 months staple food insecure • Thatched roof • No rice field, only highland rice • Some have 1–2 cows	• 6–7 months staple food insecure • Thatched roof • Some have 1–2 cows	• 7–8 months staple food insecure • Have rice mixed with cassava/sweet potatoes year-round • No cow/buffalo	• Year-round staple food insecure • Thatched roof • Not in good health

Note: The numbers represent nuclear or small-extended households, normally indicated with the name of the head of household. Two households that were ranked in 2003 had not yet been established in 1999.
**Household that changes category between 1999 and 2003*
Source: Eade, D., and Williams, S., 1995

security and all the groups have a shorter hungry period in 2003 than they did in 1999.

Third, there are some families (highlighted) whose situations seem to have improved so much that they have been ranked in a higher category in 2003 than the one they were in four years earlier. Households 24 and 25 were in category 4 in 1999, but have been ranked in category 3 in 2003. There are five households in category 3 that have moved up to category 2. One household (no. 51) has moved up from category 2 to the top category.

There may be a number of explanations for the changes that have occurred. The reasons for the improvement in food security seen by most families, and the fact that some have seen their situation improve more than others, may differ from one family to another. It might be that the project responsible for the work in the village could show that it had worked with the households that have moved up a wellbeing category. It would then have a strong case to claim an impact in poverty reduction and a good focus on working with the poorer households. It might also be interesting to explore whether it is relatively easy to improve the production levels of those in the lowest wellbeing category; it might take a lot longer to achieve the levels of production common in the top category.

The observations that emerge from the wellbeing rankings seem potentially important and useful, and the issues that emerge could be followed up by the agency in question in order to understand more about the situation and the effects of its interventions. It is hard not to wonder why an agency working on poverty reduction at community level would choose not to carry out a wellbeing ranking, given the relatively low resources required and the potential benefits.

Wellbeing groups – the 'heap of beans'

The heap-of-beans method for assessing differences in wellbeing within a community has become one of my favourite and most used tools. It was described by Schaeffer (1992) and has been described many times since. See Annexes ('How to do wellbeing ranking', Rowley, 2014a) for a detailed 'how to' guide.

The method is very simple and very quick. It provides a means of discussing differences within a community in terms of the views of local people, and allows an outsider to pose questions according to their own ideas and needs.

A small pile of beans, grains or pebbles is presented, and the facilitator explains that the beans represent all the households in the village, or another unit as appropriate. It might be the individuals in the community, or more specifically the men or women in that community, or similar. The participants are then asked to divide the pile into subgroups to indicate different levels of wellbeing. They can make as many piles as they like; a small pile represents a small number of households and a larger pile represents a bigger number.

The facilitator will avoid mentioning examples of elements of wellbeing and, when asked what 'wellbeing' means, will reflect the question back to the people doing the exercise.

I have made videos of people doing the exercise and the time taken to create the smaller piles from the initial large pile is usually less than a minute. It seems that the idea is easy to understand and the exercise is easy to carry out.

Once the participants have created the different piles, it is easy to ask many of the same questions as can be asked about the piles of sorted cards in a conventional wellbeing-ranking exercise. For example: the characteristics of households in each category; the ways in which someone from one category moves up to a higher category or falls down to a lower one, and so on.

It is very typical in my work to come across a stratification that creates a tiny group of the elite well-off households; a larger but still small middle group of those who are well-off but not as well-off as the elite; a large or very large group of poor households; and another small group of the poorest, who are ill, very old, alone or otherwise largely dependent on welfare from other households.

It is possible to develop a fairly detailed description of the characteristics of wellbeing in each category and it seems acceptable to repeat the questions about the ways in which people in a particular category resemble each other.

The exercise is then open to deeper probing and/or questions depending on the interviewer's particular interests. The formula that I have found to work well is, 'In which group would you find people who...?' This might be the people who send their children to school, who use the clinic, who borrow money, who take produce to market; or any other aspect of life and livelihoods. It might be the people who own a bed, car, mobile phone, or other element of material wellbeing.

It is also often possible to use the exercise to explore recent changes or trends. The facilitator can ask the participants to repeat the exercise to describe the situation as it was five years ago, or whatever time period is appropriate. Some participants will be happy to do this, although it clearly requires a degree of imagination and the results may contain more guesswork than the exercise focused on the current situation. Nevertheless, the same process can be followed: once the piles of different wellbeing groups have been established, the facilitator can ask about the characteristics of households in each group and explore other aspects of difference within the community. In particular, participants will describe the elements of people's livelihoods that have changed between the given period in the past and the present time. The facilitator will be able to probe on why the changes came about and how the changes have affected people in the different wellbeing categories.

In my own work, evaluating development projects, for example, I often find myself asking 'In which groups would you find people who have taken part in the project?' or 'In which group would I find people who have benefited from the project?' Unfortunately, rather often the participants point to the small group of the most well-off in reply to this question. This does not necessarily mean that the project has failed to bring benefits to the people in the community, but it usually means that the project has failed to match the rhetoric by which donors were persuaded to fund the initiative. If there were promises to reach the poorest of the poor they have clearly not been realized.

One argument for using wellbeing ranking seems to be that a great deal can be learned in return for very little effort and time. This is the economy argument for using a participatory method, which says that project work can be improved through better participation. It is difficult to imagine good reasons why staff running a project at community level would not carry out this kind of exchange with people in that community. The way that I use this method during an evaluation is almost completely extractive, but I take the results back to my clients and question them as to how they will address the various effects the project is having on different wellbeing categories.

I made use of the tool most recently in an area of dryland Africa. The project in question had successfully helped install a dam, which had brought the land downstream into production during the dry season. It was impressive entering a small valley of green crops after travelling for a long time across brown dry land. The heap of beans exercise revealed a fairly typical distribution of wellbeing. The land below the dam, which was now producing crops, was mostly owned by members of the small, elite, well-off category. People in the large poor category obtained some work on the fields of the elite, in an area where previously there would have been no work. My clients seemed very pleased with the results of the tool and and only slightly embarrassed that they had not made the observations on the distribution of benefits themselves. It seemed clear that there were many initiatives they could pursue with the communities below the dam to bring about more equitable sharing of the benefits of the dam, especially if they could describe the differences between wellbeing categories and engage with people of different levels of wellbeing.

Notes

1. These are comments that I have not been able to confirm or source.
2. Commons, or common pool resources, are natural resources such as pasture, woodland, and water bodies that are managed on a communal rather than an individual private basis.
3. Unpublished PhD thesis.
4. Personal communication received from Barbara Grandin, 2013.

References

Appleton, S. and Booth, D. (2005) 'Combining participatory and survey-based approaches to poverty monitoring and analysis', *Q-Squared* Working Paper No. 14. <http://192.75.12.210/ids/documents/Q2_WP14_AppletonandBooth.pdf>

Banlina, F.T. and Tung, L. (1992) 'FARMI's experiences of wealth ranking in the Philippines: different farmers have different needs', *RRA (Rapid Rural Appraisal) Notes* 15: 48–50, London: International Institute for Environment and Development (IIED).

Barrett, C. (2003) 'Integrating qualitative and quantitative approaches: Lessons from the pastoral risk management project', in R. Kanbur (ed.), *Q-Squared: Combining Qualitative and Quantitative Methods in Poverty Appraisal*, pp. 90–96, New Delhi: Permanent Black.

Booth, D. (2003) 'Towards a better combination of the quantitative and the qualitative: some design issues from Pakistan's participatory poverty assessment', in R. Kanbur (ed.), *Q-Squared: Combining Qualitative and Quantitative Methods in Poverty Appraisal*, pp.97–102, New Delhi: Permanent Black.

Carter S., Chidiamassamba, A., Jeranyama, P., Mafukidze, B., Malakela, G., Mvena, Z., Mudhara, M., Nabane, N., Van Oosterhout-Campbell, S., Price, L. and Sithole, N. (1993) 'Some observations on wealth ranking after an RRA looking at soil fertility management in Northeastern Zimbabwe', *RRA Notes* 18: 47–52, London: IIED.

Cornwall, A. and Guijt, I (2004), Shifting perceptions, changing practices in PRA: from infinite innovation to the quest for quality, PLA Notes, 50: 160-169, London, IIED.

Ghirotti, M. (1992) 'A simple method for scoring housing conditions as income proxy in Ethiopia', *RRA Notes* 15: 43–47, London: IIED.

Grandin, B. E. (1988) *Wealth Ranking in Smallholder Communities: A Field Manual,* Rugby: Practical Action Publishing.

Grosvenor-Alsop, R. (1989) 'Wealth ranking in a caste area of India', *RRA Notes* 4: 5–12, London: IIED.

Guijt, I. and Shah, M.K. (eds) (1998) *The Myth of Community: Gender Issues in Participatory Development,* Rugby: Practical Action Publishing.

Guijt, I. (1992) 'The elusive poor: a wealth of ways to find them. Report on an IDS/IIED seminar on wealth and well-being ranking', *RRA Notes,* 15: 7–13.

Guijt, I. and Cornwall, A. (1995) 'Critical reflections on the practice of PRA', *PLA (Participatory Learning and Action) Notes* 24: 2–7

Guijt, I. (1992) 'A user's note on wealth ranking by cards and list of sources on wealth ranking', *RRA Notes* 15: 65–69, London: IIED.

Heffernan, C. and Misturelli, F. (2014) 'Wellbeing ranking: Semi-structured interviews and practitioner bias: Personality traits and participatory narratives', in Rowley, J. (ed.) *Wellbeing Ranking: Developments in Applied Community-level Poverty Research,* pp. 89–110, Rugby: Practical Action Publishing, <http://dx.doi.org/10.3362/9781780448459.007>

Hill, P. (1972) *Rural Hausa – A Village and a Setting,* Cambridge: Cambridge University Press.

Leach, M. (1994) 'Targeting aid to the poorest in urban Ethiopia - is it possible? Rapid urban appraisal', *RRA Notes* 21: 48–55, London: IIED.

Mearns, R., Shombodon, D., Narangerel, G., Turul, U., Enkhamgalan, A., Myagmarzhav, B., Bayanjargal, A. and Bekhsuren, B. (1992) 'Direct and indirect uses of wealth ranking in Mongolia', *RRA Notes* 15: 29–38, London: IIED.

Mukherjee, N. (1992) 'Villagers' perceptions of rural poverty through the mapping methods of PRA', *RRA Notes* 15: 21–26, London: IIED.

Oxfam HK, (2003) 'Poverty reduction in two mountainous districts of Nghê An: Impacts of Oxfam HK, co-funders and local partners on the lives of villagers and the capacities of local leaders and officials in Ký Sơn And Tương Dương districts'. Unpublished.

Pretty, J., Subramanian, S., Kempu Chetty, N., Ananthakrishnan, D., Jayanthi, C., Muralikrishnasamy, S. and Renganayaki, K. (1992) 'Finding the poorest in a Tamil Nadu village: a sequence of mapping and wealth ranking', *RRA Notes* 15: 39–42, London: IIED.

Rowley, J. (2014a) 'Annexes: How to do wellbeing ranking', in Rowley, J. (ed.) *Wellbeing Ranking: Developments in Applied Community-level Poverty Research*, pp. 163–165, Rugby: Practical Action Publishing, <http://dx.doi.org/10.3362/9781780448459.011>

Rowley, J. (2014b) 'Methodological issues in wellbeing ranking', in Rowley, J. (ed.) *Wellbeing Ranking: Developments in Applied Community-level Poverty Research*, pp. 49–70, Rugby: Practical Action Publishing, <http://dx.doi.org/10.3362/9781780448459.005>

Rowley, J. (2014c) 'The history of wellbeing ranking techniques', in Rowley, J. (ed.) *Wellbeing Ranking: Developments in Applied Community-level Poverty Research*, pp. 13–32, Rugby: Practical Action Publishing, <http://dx.doi.org/10.3362/9781780448459.003>

Sarch, M-T. (1992) 'Wealth ranking in the Gambia: which households participated in the FITT programme?' *RRA Notes* 15: 14–20, London: IIED.

Sarkar, A., (1991) 'Wealth ranking in Mahilong, Bihar', *RRA Notes* 13: 81–2, London: IIED.

Schaefer, S.S. (1992) 'The 'beans-game' – experiences with a variation of wealth ranking in the Kivu Region, Eastern Zaire', *RRA Notes* 15: 27–8, London: IIED.

Seeley, J., Nabaitu, J., Taylor, L., Kajura, E., Bukenya, T., Kabunga, E. and Ssembajja, F. (1996) 'Revealing gender differences through wellbeing ranking in Uganda', *PLA Notes* 25: 14–18, London: IIED.

Shah, M.K., (1998) *'Gendered perceptions of wellbeing and social change in Darko, Ghana'*, in I. Guijt and M.K. Shah (eds) *The Myth of Community: Gender Issues in Participatory Development*, pp. 141–151, Rugby: Practical Action Publishing.

Shah, P. (1990) 'Economic classification of a community using locally generated criteria', *RRA Notes* 8: 24–9, London: IIED.

Sharrock G.O'G., Waldie, K. and Joshi, Y. (1993) 'Wealth ranking for agricultural research purposes in the Eastern Hills of Nepal', *RRA Notes* 18: 53–59, London: IIED.

Silverman, S. F. (1966) 'An ethnographic approach to social stratification: Prestige in a central Italian community', *American Anthropologist* 68: 899–921.

Smith, S. and Sender, J. (1988) 'Investigating poverty: an example from Tanzania', *RRA Notes* 2: 18–20, London: IIED.

Tung, L. and Baliña, F. (1993) 'FARMI's experiences on wealth ranking in the Philippines: Different farmers have different needs', *RRA Notes* 18: 60–65, London: IIED.

Turk, C. (1995) 'Identifying and tackling poverty: ActionAid's experiences in Vietnam', *PLA (Participatory Learning & Action) Notes* 23: 37–41, London: IIED.

Welbourn, A. (1991) 'RRA and the analysis of difference', *RRA Notes* 14: 14–23, London: IIED.

Welbourn, A. (1992) 'A note on the use of disease problem ranking with relation to socio-economic well-being: An example from Sierra Leone', *RRA Notes* 16: 86–7, London: IIED.
Young, H. (1990) 'The use of wealth ranking in nutrition surveys in Sudan', *RRA Notes* 8: 10–14, London: IIED.

About the author

John Rowley is an international development professional with over 30 years' experience working for national and international NGOs, government agencies, bilateral and multilateral donors and commercial companies in the UK, Africa and elsewhere.

CHAPTER 5

Methodological issues in wellbeing ranking

John Rowley

This section looks at some methodological issues in carrying out wellbeing ranking. The method is relatively simple although there may be minor variations in the basic steps; this chapter explores such variations and the reasons for choosing one over another. For use at community level, instructions can be reduced to less than a page. Annex 1 (Rowley 2014a) provides an example, as well as a list of references to guides on carrying out wellbeing ranking. The choice of approach depends on the overall purpose of the exercise, and perhaps where it falls in a sequence of interviews. It is good practice to arrange several cycles of learning and conduct a number of ranking exercises so that issues can be addressed as they arise. This helps ensure that conclusions about other people's livelihoods or the design of community-level initiatives are not based on a single set of results. To effectively manage methodological issues, the facilitators must be alert and self-critical; their approach and attitude are more important than the interview tools.

Keywords: well-being, wellbeing, ranking, methodology, interviews, participation, informants, sample size

Introducing the method

First, as in all work at community level, there is the question of how to explain the purpose of the visit and how to introduce interview methods. There seems to be no better answer than to tell the truth and provide local people with a genuine choice on whether or not to take part. It is unlikely that a wellbeing ranking would be the first contact with a community, so there may already be the beginnings of a relationship between the visitors and the local people, which will make this easier. Wellbeing ranking is probably more difficult to introduce than other exercises, because you will need to explain that you will be asking about wellbeing, and this may be misinterpreted.

There are a number of papers in the journal *PLA (Participatory Learning and Action) Notes* that describe cases where the authors expected problems when introducing a method for exploring wellbeing. Indeed, a few problems are reported in community situations, where the local people thought that the findings might be used by tax authorities or that the process might cause difficulties between them. There are some examples of these cases in Chapter

http://dx.doi.org/10.3362/9781780448459.005

4 ('Some practical examples and what users say about wellbeing ranking', Rowley, 2014b). However, in most cases reported the problem turns out to be much less significant than the researchers had feared.

There are likely to be difficulties for anyone visiting a community where they have no previous contacts and where they want local people to engage with them in some exercise or discussions. The visitors have to explain the purpose and possible outcomes, and what is expected or desired. This applies to those wishing to carry out participatory exercises, such as wellbeing ranking, or more conventional enquiries such as household surveys. Wellbeing ranking may be relatively difficult to explain because the method is unusual; or it may relatively easy because it requires only a short amount of time with a small number of people. Whatever the situation, the same need for clarity and honesty applies.

Anyone wishing to carry out interviews about wealth who could potentially be seen as a representative of an organization that might donate funds or other benefits, should be alert to the risks of being offered inaccurate or biased information, and to the potentially serious risk of appearing to intervene in local tensions and inequalities. This concern applies to anyone getting involved at community level regardless of the methods they may be using, and some care is required in being well-informed and sensitive. Wellbeing interviews are no more likely to cause problems than other information-gathering methods, however, and the ability to make use of ranked information rather than absolute assessments of wellbeing may make this method less contentious. Clearly, great care is required where tensions within a community are perceived to be high.

Choosing the words for wellbeing

The phrase wellbeing in English is extremely vague and, until relatively recently, was hardly used. It has become more commonplace and is now the focus of government initiatives and research programmes in the UK. Although there is a general shared understanding of wellbeing, there is no clear agreed definition. This means that starting a wellbeing ranking exercise using the English phrase can allow the interviewee to think fairly broadly about factors that contribute to wellbeing, or that increase or decrease it.

Presenting the phrase wellbeing without offering a definition could be seen to be part of a participatory approach; that is, allowing the interviewee to take more control of the direction and focus of the interview by using their own understanding of wellbeing. Often an interviewee will ask what is meant by wellbeing, and the answer I give is that the interview will help me to understand what they think wellbeing is.

I spend a long time with local interpreters before starting an interview. It is always useful to be clear on roles and how to deal with the common issues that emerge during an interview conducted through an interpreter. In addition, it is often helpful to devote considerable time to discussing how to translate wellbeing. I usually explain how vague the term is in English, and that ideally we will find a phrase that implies material, spiritual, and social wellbeing and any other aspects of wellbeing that are relevant to the participants. Sometimes a word or phrase is suggested after considerable thought, and sometimes it is necessary to change this phrase after testing it on the first few occasions.

At the moment of introducing the exercise and the local word or phrase for wellbeing, there may be a danger in giving an example of a wellbeing factor; it seems easy to influence the direction of thought of the informant.

There are examples in *PLA Notes* of researchers choosing to use the word for wealth, as the notion of wellbeing had not become widespread at the time:

- Banliña (1992), working in the Philippines, uses *pagbana-bana sa kahimtang,* which translates as 'estimates of economic status'.
- Sarch (1992), in The Gambia, gets help from a school teacher to find a Wolof term for wellbeing with each group they work with.
- Anup Sarkar (1991) found that the word wealth needed a lot of explaining in order to ensure it was properly understood.
- Seeley et al. (1996) used the Luganda word for 'riches' or material wealth in Uganda, and later used a phrase that was translated as 'the conditions of day-to-day life of people' to convey something closer to wellbeing, but this did not seem to make much difference to the outcomes.

In Kenya, Barbara Grandin (1988) used a Maasai word, *emali,* for wealth and, as detailed in Chapter 7 ('Wellbeing ranking, semi-structured interviews and practitioner bias', Heffernan and Misturelli, 2014), Claire Heffernan used the Maasai terms *orkasis* to mean the rich and *olaisenani* to mean the poor. In my own work with Maasai people in northern Tanzania, we used the phrase *dapash enkoriong,* which was translated to me as 'broadbackedness', i.e. having a broad back. Someone with a broad back can stand upright in their community, solve their own problems and help others. All of these terms have a powerful sense of material wealth at their heart. This is important because there is a sense expressed by Chambers (1997) that wealth ranking among the Maasai would depend only on the number of cattle that the head of a household owned or could claim. Wellbeing assessments based on the theme of broadbackedness seem to cover other forms of wealth besides cattle, including various aspects of social capital, and as such seem to be closer to the English phrase 'wellbeing'.

The best word or phrase depends on the ultimate purpose of the exercise, and what the external development agent feels they need to know about. However, as many characteristics of wealth are strongly related, it may be that simply by asking about wealth a researcher will find out about multiple aspects of wellbeing. The usefulness of trying to work initially on wellbeing may be in finding out about anomalies, and opening the process to surprise or unexpected elements and observations.

The unit for ranking

We have described wellbeing ranking of households without defining or discussing what might be meant by the word 'household'. There are a number of definitions, including those who share meals, a living space, or an address. In many cases the word household is treated as synonymous with family, but both words cover a wide range of living arrangements. The definitions of 'head of household' also vary, and include 'head of family'; these terms are sometimes replaced by the word 'householder', which does not seem to add much clarity. In any specific situation, the definition is made clear by the living arrangements in place. Polly Hill (1972) used the farming unit in her work in Nigeria, while Silverman (1966) used 'family'. In most cases, the unit becomes clear in discussions with local people and is likely to be based on the way that living, eating or production is organized. *PLA Notes* includes examples based on the concession, compound, family, head of the foyer (part of a household), and those who eat together. The vagueness of the word household may be helpful in allowing people to define the unit.

Teri Sarch (1992) mentions a moment during her work in The Gambia when it became clear that the compound was the unit being ranked, as participants called out, 'We're not talking about the money under his bed, we're thinking about his family.'

Obtaining a list of names

Wellbeing ranking requires a list of people to be ranked, and the method works easily if the names are on separate pieces of card or paper. The simplest approach, and probably a good starting point, is to obtain a list of the male heads of households.

It does not seem always wise to rely on official lists or censuses. Banliña and Tung (1992) had problems basing their wealth ranking on the list of households provided by the political head of the village. Carter et al. (1993: 47) found that the census lists in Zimbabwe required 'considerable verification and amendments'. Scoones (1988), also in Zimbabwe, found that earlier research had usefully defined the nature of households and provided an accurate listing. Most reports suggest it is rarely this easy.

One approach is to develop a list of households from a mapping exercise, in which houses have been marked on a map of the area. This is relatively straightforward: households can easily be identified; and the participants remember the names of those who live in different buildings shown on the map. It is easy to prompt people by pointing at different places on the map; and the map itself helps people to remember who lives in each building. Participants may also add the names of households that they did not remember at the time of the initial mapping exercise. Aerial photographs and satellite images may make this process easier where they can be obtained. Mukherjee et al. (1992) provide good examples of developing a list of names from mapping exercises.

It is also possible to ask people who know the community well to remember the names of the heads of households without any visual reminder. This process can work well in a relatively small community, but it is very common for names to be omitted and this becomes apparent as they are added later in the process. Where several people are involved they can help each other to come up with a list of names. My experience at village level in Africa is that the list is almost but not quite complete at the first attempt, with some names being added later. Usually there are very few names missing, and sometimes those omissions are because of confusion over the names or nicknames that are being used.

At the same time as establishing the list, it is also necessary to identify the 'community' that will be the focus of the ranking exercise. The most important characteristic and limitation of wellbeing ranking is that it only works well where people know each other fairly well. In an African village setting this is normally the case, as people have been living close to each other and have been involved with each other over generations. The elders in such a community are usually able to carry out a wellbeing ranking with ease. However, even what appears to be a single community at the beginning of an appraisal may contain important divisions. It is always necessary to check on the limits of knowledge of those you are going to work with, as it is these limits that in effect define the community that can be ranked.

Participants should be told that they can choose not to rank a particular household or name if they feel that they do not know them well enough. If there is some hesitation in ranking a card, the facilitator can remind the participant of this, and suggest that they put the card aside if they feel that they do not know enough to rank it accurately. If this happens many times, it may be that the 'community' is too large, or that the participant is not sufficiently well-informed. If a participant puts aside a significant number of cards without ranking them, the facilitator can simply ask them about the difficulties they are having.

It may be necessary to split a large community into smaller units in order to work with people who know enough about the households to be able to carry out a wellbeing ranking. Chapter 6 ('Using participatory wealth ranking in a South African microfinance organization: the value of scale', Simanowitz, 2014) explains how rankings were carried out in very large villages by working separately in different quarters. It becomes difficult to carry out wellbeing rankings when the number of units to be ranked rises above 100 or 150, but the real limit is still the knowledge of the people doing the ranking.

Working with clearly delineated villages that have been stable for generations appears to be the easiest situation in which to use wellbeing ranking. Urban situations are more difficult, mainly because their population is more mobile and there is therefore less shared knowledge.

Leach (1994) reports on efforts to use wealth ranking in an urban setting in Ethiopia. The exercises were completed successfully, indicating that people knew each other quite well in relatively small areas within that setting. It was not easy to arrive at a standard set of criteria of wealth. It is important to note that the work involved a large number of other interview methods and it was potentially the combined results of the different interviews that made it possible to target the poorest.

Norton (1994) describes attempts to use wealth ranking in an urban situation where the concept of 'community' had to be examined, and a great deal of discussion and care employed, in identifying what made up a meaningful sample of people to be interviewed. Social links and networks are also more complicated in an urban setting and this is important because they make up 'a critical element of livelihood and survival' (p 55-56). These complications do not seem surprising, and the comments are made mostly to highlight how much easier it is to explore wellbeing with people in a rural setting. Increasingly mobile populations and increasing urbanization will change the way that community-level research is done with both participatory and more conventional surveys.

A colleague from my time at Oxfam in the UK, Ros David, told me about an attempt to use wealth ranking in an urban area in southern England. The participants were able to rank different households across the area but there were large gaps in their knowledge where they were simply unable to place large numbers of households.

I asked councillors in a town in England to rank streets according to the wellbeing of the people who lived there. This led to an interesting exercise and I was surprised by how easy the participants found it. Obviously, there were potentially significant variations in wellbeing between people living on the same street, but there was an important consensus on the ranking of the street names. The main outcome of the exercise was the sharing of ideas around what constitutes wellbeing and perceptions of different areas of the town.

Who should act as informants?

Grandin (1988) says that informants should represent different levels of wellbeing and suggests a cross-section of the community. The other guides to carrying out wellbeing ranking only say that the informants should be knowledgeable and willing. Silverman (1966) and Hill (1972) both describe their informants as very well informed, lifelong residents of the community; both used three older men.

It is clear that people of different wellbeing categories have different concerns. There are good examples of this in Alice Welbourn's report (1992) in which she explores health issues with different wellbeing groups. She finds that poor people mention eye problems as important, whereas richer women do not mention eye problems at all. Swift and Umar (1994) make similar observations from their work with herders in Kenya. Note that these researchers were able to make these observations because they already had ideas about who was better- and worse-off in the community they were visiting. Janet Seeley et al. (1996) worked with informants (three men and three women) who had been chosen by the leaders in each village to represent different socio-economic groups within their village. They were able to consolidate the results and compare the criteria used by men and women as a follow-up exercise to wealth ranking done earlier.

The informants need to know the households they are ranking and the first ranking need not be the only ranking. It is almost always easier to start work with the high-status males in a community, and then go on to work with women and other informants. The most important point about this and all community development work is for the researcher or community worker to be aware of what they are doing and from whom they are getting information and ideas, so that they can be alert to biases in their work. Each exercise should ideally be part of a cycle of learning so that additional work can be designed based on the findings from earlier work.

Do the participants work individually or in small groups?

The decision to work with individual informants, as done by the pioneers and proposed in Grandin's manual, or to work with small groups, as in the highly successful work of Hargreaves (2007) and Simanowitz (Using Participatory Wealth Ranking in a South African microfinance organization: the value of scale), depends on the overall purpose of the exercise and the social context.

One advantage of a small group working together is that there is a greater possibility of easily identifying each household and ranking it accurately, since the exercise will be based on the knowledge of, say, three informants, who may have different information and experience. The three informants are able to exchange ideas and this cross-checking should make the results more reliable. It makes sense to use a small group where the main purpose is to obtain an overall ranking in order to identify the least well-off and so improve the targeting of a credit programme.

A possible disadvantage of the use of a group is that it makes greater demands on the time of the informants. When using single informants, a complete wellbeing ranking of a community could be achieved by three people each providing about an hour of their time. Using small groups to carry out the same process would require nine person-hours. This does not include the time taken to develop the list of names to be ranked.

The advantages of using interviews with single informants are the potential for higher levels of confidentiality and the lower risk of misunderstanding or conflict. Conflicts can occur where people do not want to be assigned wellbeing ranks that they perceive to be pejorative or that they fear might exclude them from potential benefits. Depending on the case, being considered rich or being considered poor might not suit the person concerned, and they might object regardless of the accuracy of the ranking. Conflict like this seems to be extremely rare and would in any case be avoided if the interviews were done on an individual basis.

All the households or a sample?

Polly Hill (1972) points out that her use of wealth ranking involves all the households in the village, whereas a household survey would only collect information from a sample of the households. She is clear that her method is superior in this way. It probably is more useful to rank all the households, if that can be done, because this may reveal interesting or unusual results. It would also be useful to have a ranking of all the households if the intention is to track changes in wellbeing over time, or to identify all the poorest households for inclusion in a development initiative

Ian Scoones (1995), Parmesh Shah (1990) and Helen Young (1990) all use samples of households in their wealth-ranking work. They are particularly interested in comparing the results of the ranking with other methods for assessing wellbeing, so it makes sense to use a sample; that sample might be determined by the other assessment method, for example a household income and expenditure survey. The degree of correlation between the two methods is likely to be demonstrated by the use of a sample, and larger numbers of households may not make the comparison significantly more robust. Young adds a stage of checking after the ranking had been completed, by asking the informants whether the richest and poorest families ranked in the sample correspond to the richest and poorest families in the whole community (1990: 11).

If the purpose of the ranking is to share ideas and understanding of wellbeing in a more general way then using a sample might be adequate, as well as being slightly quicker to carry out each replication of the actual ranking. However, the informants who know the households in the sample will also know the other households in the community; the time saved in the ranking is therefore unlikely to be significant, because once the ranking starts the informants become quite quick at assigning households to different categories. It does not seem worthwhile to use a sample unless there is a special purpose to the ranking and, indeed, sampling seems relatively rare among the reported cases of use.

A ranking of all the households is close to being a census of the community and can serve a range of functions beyond that of describing wellbeing or monitoring changes in wellbeing. In some cases, the complete list of households can be a valuable resource to a village, which may never have had such a list before. Considerable care should be exercised in how the information is shared, however.

Discussions of wellbeing before the ranking

Grandin (1988) recommends checking the word you are using to mean wealth with the informant, and asking for a couple of examples of differences between rich and poor both in a general sense and in the area that specifically interests you. Hargreaves (2007) and Simanowitz (1999) also suggest including a short discussion of wealth and poverty before the ranking is carried out. In cases where the ranking is done by a small group, some discussion may be inevitable. Irene Guijt (1992), the editor of the issue of *RRA Notes* dedicated to wealth ranking, describes ranking based on social mapping in which there is a 'group discussion on what constitutes wealth and wellbeing and agreement reached on the main criteria'. The households on the map are then assessed according to the criteria and marked, with symbols, so that a visual map of socio-economic difference is created.

In the same issue of *RRA Notes*, Guijt describes the classic card-sorting wellbeing ranking and recommends that facilitators discuss general differences between rich and poor in the area, and general differences between problems experienced by rich and poor. She also suggests discussing the local word or phrase for wellbeing because 'you must have a common understanding of its meaning' (Guijt, 1990: 7).

The work by Hargreaves (2007) and Simanowitz (1999) makes it clear that a general discussion of wellbeing prior to the ranking can lead to highly successful ranking and detailed and nuanced definitions of wellbeing. In these cases, the definitions are sufficiently robust to be applied across large numbers of households in a range of different locations.

Where the main purpose is to share understanding about local views on wellbeing, it may be better not to discuss the meaning of either wellbeing or wealth with the participants before starting the exercise. In Chapter 7 (Heffernan and Misturelli, 2014), Claire Heffernan explores the ways in which personality and professional background can affect the outcome of group discussions; it seems difficult to avoid the danger that a visitor, being 'an outsider', will overly influence the discussions. This might happen simply because the facilitator, as a high-status visitor, appears to agree more with comments on some particular topic or show interest in one specific aspect of wealth or wellbeing.

The principle here is the same as when avoiding giving examples during any participatory exercise for fear of focusing the attention of the informants on the example. In starting a mapping exercise, for instance, it is often interesting to ask participants to mark on the map 'important' places or things, without influencing the selection by giving examples. If the facilitator were to start by asking participants to mark roads and bridges, the participants might think the facilitator were interested in infrastructure; whereas a request to mark fields and pasture might be interpreted as an interest in production. That said, examples may be an acceptable part of later discussions, once ideas have emerged from repeated discussions or from earlier wellbeing ranking exercises. The facilitator may then feel more confident that they are not leading the process or introducing too much of their own bias.

Stephanie Schaeffer (1992) says that her team avoided giving examples of what might constitute a reason to create groups of beans in her description of the 'heap-of-beans' game. She does not explain why, but it seems to follow the participatory line that suggestions might be unfairly leading. Sharrock et al. (1993: 58) see a danger 'that the briefing can bias key informants' responses' and argue that it is important to ensure that the philosophy of participatory research is well understood, as well as the methods themselves.

Silverman was very clear in his approach, saying 'no criteria were suggested' (1966: 904). He allows the informants to develop their criteria as they carry out the ranking, partly because it seems to allow the generation of more ideas and partly because it works. It is possible to launch a wellbeing ranking exercise with a general invitation to rank the units according to higher or lower positions in relation to a vaguely described, multifaceted concept.

This assertion is backed up by observations of behaviour during training courses. I try to teach ranking by getting groups of trainees to do some ranking based on a vague instruction and to use a topic far removed from the focus of the work to be done. For example, when training in Scotland for an appraisal of health issues, I asked a group of trainees to rank national football teams from best to worst. The group explored a range of criteria by which a football team might be assessed, including previous performance in competitions; the skills of key players, and the experience of the coach, and reached a clear ranking of the different teams. The ranking allowed them to work out what the criteria were.

Piles or one continuous ranking?

The practice of asking informants to develop a single line of wellbeing from highest to lowest has probably been entirely replaced by the method that involves putting the different units (usually households) into groups or wellbeing categories. There are great advantages in the use of wellbeing categories and it is not surprising that it has become the preferred method.

First, creating piles is much quicker than setting down a continuous ranking, as the informant can lump together relatively similar households and not try to work out minor differences between them. In any case, knowing the minor differences is probably not useful for the overall purpose of the ranking. There are certain ranking exercises in which it is useful to insist on a single ranking and prevent the participants from putting items at the same level, but this is not the case with wellbeing ranking.

Second, the piles method provides opportunities for powerful probing about the characteristics of households within each wellbeing category. In some ways, it seems that the act of getting the cards sorted into wellbeing categories is just the beginning of the exercise and more important learning occurs in the following part of the interview. In Chapter 2, 'How wealth ranking was developed', Barbara Grandin (2014) says that she wishes she had put more emphasis on the value of interrogating the piles, and it allows a lot of useful probing and learning.

It is possible to ask about the general characteristics of the households in each category and one can learn a great deal from the initial descriptions. This questioning can continue in a simple style asking open questions, for example: What other characteristics do those in this group have? How else do they differ from the people in this other category? One can then ask how people might move between groups, and this often brings into the discussions other characteristics of wellbeing. There is much to learn from how people perceive that it is possible to improve wellbeing, and what causes wellbeing to decrease.

A practical or visual exercise allows for more persistent questioning than a simple face-to-face discussion. This phenomenon is described by Chambers (1997: 150), and although it is frequently observed, I think it is not always accorded the importance it deserves. It is much easier to continue to discuss the same point when there is a visual tool involved. One can persist with a line of questioning while pointing to piles of cards in a way that would quickly become intolerable if one were simply repeating the same question without any prompts, and with nothing to reduce the intensity of the interaction between the interviewer and the interviewee.

After establishing the characteristics of households in each wellbeing category and the various means by which people could move from one category to another, it is then possible to ask very specific questions that may relate to other specific areas of enquiry. At this point the interviewer is moving from a purely enquiring role to a more directive one. The questioning can follow the general pattern: 'In which pile would I find people who...?' This might be people who own a mobile phone, who send their children to school, or who take part in a particular project, as appropriate. The questions can be followed up with more discussion of how and why the people might behave in the ways they do or are able to do the things they do. Again, this allows more ideas to emerge and is often a rich source of learning about local perceptions of wellbeing.

It is also possible to cross-check against a household survey at this point, if the interviewer is aware of the questions in the survey questionnaire. It might be interesting to know, for example, in which category of wellbeing one might find people who own a bed, table, bicycle or radio, if these things are being asked in the survey. Combining the findings from a participatory wellbeing ranking and a household survey should be a very useful exercise. It should indicate how local people interpret the ownership of certain items and the pursuit of certain activities. It should also be valuable to know the relative positions, as determined by the wellbeing ranking, of the households that were included in a survey sample. There are, however, very few examples of household surveys and wellbeing ranking exercises being used in tandem (see Chapter 3, 'The history of wellbeing ranking techniques', Rowley, 2014c) for a discussion on combining qualitative and quantitative methods).

Can you preselect the number of categories?

This question seems important but the answer probably depends on the overall purpose of the wellbeing ranking exercise. It seems more obviously participatory if the informants can have as many categories as they like. This is the approach followed by Silverman (1966) and recommended in the manual by Grandin. Grandin (1988: 18) also suggests that the more piles there are, the more accurate the ranking will be. This was also the procedure followed during the Voices of the Poor Participatory Poverty Assessments in 1999–2000 (Narayan et al., 2000).

However, some of the most successful uses of wellbeing ranking have specified the number of categories to use. This was the case with the work by Scoones (1995) and then by Simanowitz (see Chapter 6/, Simanowitz, 2014) and Hargreaves (2007), who followed the same methodology throughout and offered the informants, who worked in small groups, four categories of wellbeing into which to distribute households known to them within the community. This methodology was developed after lengthy testing, during which four categories were developed by participants over many repeated rankings and were found to be appropriate in almost all cases. The results seem highly reliable across the huge number of issues that were analysed according to the statements made describing the households in each category.

The advantages of having a fixed number of categories include greater ease in calculating overall wealth ranks from the three ranking events in each community, and greater ease in training staff and following up on consistency.

Parmesh Shah (1990) also reports on using four categories in wellbeing ranking with the Aga Khan Rural Support Programme (AKRSP) in Gujarat, India. The categories seem to be appropriate for issues relating to health, education, asset ownership, cash wealth, land ownership, employment and quality of housing. It was interesting to the project to find out in which categories Ismaili families were found, and a clear poverty bias emerged, with 232 of the 249 families appearing in the bottom two categories. Shah reports two other useful observations: first, that the ranking exercise led to useful discussions about possible initiatives in the community regardless of religious affiliation; second, that there was a significantly large and gradually widening gap between the top two categories of wellbeing and the bottom two categories. In most cases, ranking only provides a sequence in order, and it is not clear if the gaps between the items being ranked are similar or different; this is perceived as a weakness of the method.[1]

Conducting the interview – privacy

Irene Guijt (1992) mentions that ensuring privacy for the ranking exercise is not as important as it first seemed, and suggests that the delicacy around talking about wealth was more of a preoccupation for researchers than for participants. Scoones (1995), on the other hand, is concerned about wealth being a sensitive issue and suggests that 'it is perhaps advisable to stick to private discussions and leave the group debate for later…'. This may mean waiting until relationships and mutual understanding have strengthened.

Silverman (1966) and Grandin (1988) are both clear that the interviews with individual informants should be in private. Privacy can be important if the people doing the ranking could be embarrassed by the presence of people they are ranking. Carrie Turk (1995) reports on difficulties with ranking exercises when these were observed by state officials who accompanied the researchers wherever they went. Privacy is a different issue when the ranking is being done by a group, but again it seems likely to work best if the informants are allowed to do the ranking without observers. In any case, it seems that the simplest approach is to adopt privacy as the default process for interviews until it is found to be unnecessary.

Getting started

Teri Sarch (1992) suggests an interesting way of getting started to get the informant 'into the swing' of the process. This involves taking two cards from the set of names and asking the informant to say which has a higher level of wellbeing, and then placing the cards in different places. The cards are returned to the set and the ranking exercise then starts for real. It is probably necessary to start by suggesting that one side, or end, of the space in front of the informant implies a higher level of wellbeing and the other end a lower level. Then ask them to place the first card. In fact, the process gets going as the second and third cards are placed and the facilitator asks repeatedly 'Where should this one go? Above this one? Below that one?' When the first tie occurs – that is, when the informant places a card on top of another, thereby putting them in the same group – it is probably wise to check and ask, 'Are you sure they're the same? Should this one be a bit above or a bit below the first one?' It may be helpful to remind the participant that they can create a new category if they are finding it hard to place one of the cards. Some skill is required in doing this, but it is the routine skill of a good facilitator to offer options without unduly influencing the informant. As soon as the first few cards are placed, the exercise usually goes smoothly and rapidly. This is an important observation: once the participants have got going on the ranking it often goes very quickly; the total number of units (usually households or individuals) to be ranked is not a determinant for how long the process will take.

The final list – confidentiality

Although the need for privacy during interviews may not be as important as had been anticipated, it remains important to keep the final ranking confidential. Although the contents will be common knowledge within the community, it might be unhelpful if the list containing the names of the heads of households were to be used by local government or tax officers to put pressure on people who appear at the top or bottom of the rankings. Irene Guijt (1992) warns that great care should be taken about how the results are recorded and stored. This is because any misuse of the results will lead to a loss of trust in the people who have taken part. The same caution probably applies to the management of any sensitive information; household surveys, for example, would pose the same risk. Often the data can be made anonymous where it is not necessary to identify the specific household, and this is why the households are numbered at the start of the exercise. Sometimes a printed list of the names of household heads can be a valuable resource for a village. I have often provided such lists, not in the order of the wellbeing ranking but rather in alphabetical order or in the order they were provided by the community.

Do the participants rank themselves?

It is normal not to oblige the informant to rank their own household when this card turns up in the ranking process. In fact, neither Grandin nor Guijt nor Pretty et al. (1995) mention this procedural step. It seems right that the informants should have the option not to rank themselves or their own household, and this should be made clear at the start of the exercise. This may seem unnecessary and I have rarely encountered individuals who are unwilling to rank their own household when doing the exercise privately, but the informant should have that choice.

The issue of informants ranking themselves is different when the exercise is done in small groups. In this case, if the groups were allowed to avoid ranking their own households it would mean missing out a larger number of households from the overall ranking. If the informants have high status in a community this might mean omitting key elements that make up high wellbeing. However, difficulties only seem to occur where there are onlookers; there seem to be few problems when the group doing the ranking is working with some privacy. I have clear memories of people doing a wellbeing ranking in a group and appearing embarrassed when their household or name came up, yet choosing to continue with the ranking even when I suggested that they could skip their own household. The case remains strong for either group or solo ranking to be carried out without onlookers. This may be difficult to achieve when there are many people about, or if it is a quiet time of day and the work with the strangers looks interesting. Nevertheless, a quiet place or a quiet time of day should be chosen whenever possible. This is easier to achieve when doing interviews with individuals, which should probably be the default approach unless the facilitator is sure that group interviews are appropriate to the aims of the work and accepted by the participants.

Checking the piles

It is important to check the piles when they have been created by the informant. Read the names on the cards in each pile and ask if the informant is happy that they all fit in a coherent group with similarities or if some of them are wrongly placed. Banliña and Ly Tung say (1992), in common with many people's experience including my own, that the informants, 'in fact, did make changes transferring cards from one pile to another'.[1]

Interrogate the piles

The discussions over the characteristics of people in each wellbeing category are usually very rich. Grandin writes in this book that one thing she might want to do differently if she were writing her manual again would be to include more on this area of work. 'There is so much that can be discussed and learned in asking about the situation of people in each pile.' (see Chapter 2 / Grandin, 2014: p. 12).

These are the same questions as can be asked about the subgroups in the 'heap-of-beans' game (see Chapter 4 / Rowley, 2014b). First, a range of open questions can be posed about the characteristics of the households in each pile of cards. The question can be repeated in various ways: for example, how households in a pile resemble each other; or, alternatively, how they differ from households in other piles. These questions usually throw up a range of different qualities, including items that make up material wellbeing and intangible and invisible things that make up other aspects of wellbeing, such as social links and personal attitudes.

Another round of probing questions on wellbeing can be based on historical circumstances, in which participants might be asked how the piles might have been different in the past, for example, a few years ago. This line of questioning may reveal general trends that have affected most households or sometimes only the less well-off. It can also reveal specific changes that have affected particular households and not others.

More ideas about differences between households in the different piles can be explored by asking how households could move from one category to another. Could a household in this pile move up to that pile? Could someone in this group find themselves in a lower category? Stephanie Schaeffer (1992) mentions other possible questions: who will seek assistance/credit with whom? Which groups can intermarry? Which group employs members of the other groups for what sort of work? Clearly, different questions will be appropriate in different contexts.

Silverman (1966) was particularly interested in this issue and how families might move from one pile of 'prestige' to another. He considered it an important discovery that the changes that might allow a family to move between groups were highly variable. Changes that might move a family from, say, category 3 to category 2, were quite different from the changes necessary to move from, say, category 2 to category 1. This is one of the findings that confirms that wellbeing is not the same as wealth. If the two were the same, one might imagine that a household would be able to move up from low wellbeing to high wellbeing simply by accumulating more material wealth. Scoones (1995: 17) says about his experience with wealth ranking in Zimbabwe that when placing a household in a wellbeing category, 'a complex interaction of factors was used to come to the final decision'. Perhaps wealth never exists entirely separately from social issues and other aspects of people's lives.

Analysing the results

Calculating and summing up the ranks given to each of the ranked households has been made much easier thanks to the use of spreadsheets. It is not necessary to convert the scores to percentages, but the computer can calculate the value of each ranking and then sum the values from each ranking exercise. There is a need to take care not to use automatic summing up where some households have been ranked a different number of times, but this is easy to see on a spreadsheet.

The list, when sorted in order of the sum of the different rankings, makes it easier to see where different wellbeing categories could be created. Usually there are households that have been ranked in the top category by all informants, and these will have a small aggregate score. At the other extreme there will be households that are all ranked in the lowest category and will have a score of 1 from each informant. In between, the eye may spot significant gaps where a break in category can be placed with some confidence.

The spreadsheet can show up anomalies where a household may have been ranked differently by different informants. This is sometimes easier to see after the households have been sorted by their overall ranking. An unusual aggregate score may be because of one informant ranking the household very differently from the other informants. It is probably acceptable to ignore differences in rankings if they span only one wellbeing category, but a difference of two categories is likely to imply a difference in understanding or a mistake in identity. There is more on dealing with anomalies below.

Dealing with anomalies

When recording the results of the ranking it is common to find a large majority of households ranked very consistently by the different informants, regardless of how many categories of wellbeing they each chose. This particularly applies to the most and least well-off; there may be more difficulties with households in middle-ranking positions.

Sometimes the anomalies are not interesting and it turns out that the informant was making a simple mistake in identifying the household in question; for example, by mistaking one brother for another. Sometimes, formal names may be used on the cards, though people more commonly refer to each other by nicknames (Banliña and Tung, 1992: 50). At other times, the anomalies provide interesting insights into how wellbeing is being assessed, with one characteristic considered more important by one informant than by others. Presenting the results back to the informants can lead to useful discussions, and often the final ranking position of a single person or household does not change the overall usefulness of the process.

In the UK, I once went back to an informant who had scored one person very high, whereas two other informants had scored them very low. After some thought, the informant said that they were not quite sure about the subject's level of wellbeing, but they had ranked them very highly because they wore Italian shoes. This indicator of material wealth was perhaps not important for the other informants.

Can you decide where to make a break if no obvious break appears?

Where a ranking has been carried out in order to understand and share ideas on wellbeing, it may not be necessary to go on to create wellbeing categories from the rankings. However, it is usually simple to divide a single ranking into wellbeing categories where this is useful to the purpose of the ranking exercise. The aggregate scores are listed in order and there are often clear breaks between some of them, indicating where the researcher can safely create a break between the overall wellbeing categories. The aggregate scores will form a column of figures from smallest to largest. Some of the scores will be the same and there will be small graduated changes, but here and there, there may be larger jumps between the scores where it may be acceptable to make a break and create a new category. There are good examples of how to do this in Pretty et al. (1995: 253). Grandin says that the researcher should not create more categories than the average used by the informants, and that fewer than three categories is probably not very helpful (1988: 30).

Occasionally there does not seem to be a natural break in the aggregate scores and the researcher is faced with a choice as to how to proceed. Fielding et al. (1998) urge caution in this process, which is a subjective decision by the researcher, but most of the advice for overcoming it does not seem to relate well to the problem. One idea is to do another ranking with another informant, which might change the aggregate scores to create a more obvious break point. Manipulating the ranks and calculating means or percentages is strongly opposed (Fielding et al., 1998: 5). The solution probably lies in the original purpose of the ranking. Fielding quotes Chambers in saying that the ranking is not done as 'an end in itself'; if the purpose was to understand local attitudes to wellbeing and get a rough idea of its distribution within a community, then the final categorization may not even be necessary.

The break line above the lowest category of wellbeing is very important for the work described by Anton Simanowitz in Chapter 6 (Simanowitz, 2014), because the prime purpose of the ranking was to identify those households most in need and likely to benefit from microcredit initiatives. It was a targeting exercise. It is important to note that identifying a precise cut-off point usually worked very well for the organization in question, even though the staff sometimes had perverse incentives to increase the numbers found to be in need. The health work in Burkina Faso described in Chapter 3 (Rowley, 2014: pp. 13–32) was intended to identify the poorest 20% of the population, so identifying the cut-off point in that case was a simple matter of counting.

Intra-household differences

It is important to remember that there are always differences in wellbeing within a household. A common concern about using the household as a unit is that it ignores differences within the household, which may be extremely important. Gender may be the most important of the intra-household differences and ranking can be done to assess some of these indirectly. It is often very useful to ask women to carry out a wellbeing ranking of women in a community, as a separate exercise from asking men to rank the heads of households in that community.

I remember being surprised by the results of a wellbeing ranking done by women in a village in northern Nigeria, in which one of the wives of the chief was given a very low level of wellbeing. I might have guessed that the wife of a chief would be ranked highly, but it was explained to me that she was relatively young and newly arrived from a distant town, and therefore lacked the links and support networks that make up key elements of wellbeing for women in that context.

Failures

There are very few publications that record instances of failure and *PLA Notes* is remarkable for being one of them.[2] This is probably because it is very unusual for people to want to publish their failures, even when there are interesting things to be learned. There is one example of a failure to carry out a wealth ranking (Carter et al., 1993), which mostly comes down to the fact that the first respondent, an older man, was unwilling to take part, and the second, a younger woman, ran out of time to take part. It seems that the team also ran out of time to find alternative potential informants. It should be noted that the same team had carried out a very successful wealth ranking in another community before running into these difficulties in this second community.

I have only experienced a couple of failures, which were in fact only delays, and in both cases there was time to sort out the difficulties. In the first instance, in Sudan, an older man began to do the exercise and started to place all the cards in a single pile. I called the exercise to a halt and asked how he found the exercise. He explained that everyone in the community was poor so it was necessary to put them all in a single category. This seems a reasonable response when the informant wants to make that point; they might think the exercise is related to the delivery of support or aid, and that people in higher wellbeing categories will be excluded and the total amount of aid reduced as a result. We went back over the purpose of the visit and discussed the usefulness of the exercise. I was prepared to abandon the exercise, but the informant insisted in having another go, and proceeded to carry out the exercise in a thoughtful way, creating four wellbeing categories.

In the Republic of Congo, I carried out a wellbeing ranking in a number of different communities that were likely to be affected by a mining operation.

A wide range of issues were beginning to emerge and wellbeing rankings had been carried out successfully in 10 of the 11 communities. The biggest community had to be divided into four quarters for the rankings, but most communities were small enough to be done as a single unit. There were important issues relating to different ethnic groups and questions over which communities had been the first to settle in the area. The team that went to the eleventh community came back saying that the exercise had failed and that they had encountered an unwillingness to do the ranking. The following day, in apparently identical conditions, the exercise worked well. It gave rise to an interesting occurrence whereby informants from one ethnic group categorized all the people of another ethnic group in the lowest wellbeing category. Such findings were important for two main reasons: because they alerted the mining company to local ethnic issues; and because getting, and losing, paid work in the company were important issues in determining wellbeing, and needed to be monitored as part of the impact the company was having on local people.

Chapter 7 of this publication (Heffernan and Misturelli, 2014) provides examples of participatory methods failing partly because the facilitators were unconscious of bias being introduced into the discussions. There are other ways that participatory interviews can fail to deliver good and true results, although the instances seem rare according to published material. Time pressure is one problem that is cited; the pressure to produce a report, proposal, or completed community appraisal, rather than follow a good learning process, also tends to lead to poor practice. Successful participatory work depends on the respect of certain principles, the design and use of a good learning process, and good selection and use of participatory interview tools. The methods alone are both easy to use, and easy to use poorly. As Jules Pretty et al. (1992: 39) say: 'good use of the [participatory] methods is not guaranteed by the methods alone'.

Creating a good process by which the earlier findings inform the later exercises, through repeated cycles of learning, seems to be the most difficult thing to achieve in much development work. Surveys are often commissioned and are expected to consist of an information collection phase during which findings are obtained through one-off enquiries. The learning reported by Jules Pretty (1992: 4) is mostly about getting the process right: 'Finding the poorest had not been easy, but the most important lessons we learned related to using sequences of methods and ensuring we do not give up too early.'

Notes

1. It is easy to rank gold, silver and iron in that order according to their value, although the gap between silver and iron is much greater than the gap between silver and gold.
2. *Baobab*, the publication of the Arid Lands Information Network, is the only example I know of that had a regular feature in which members shared ideas of experiences that had not worked. It was a very popular feature.

References

Banliña, F.T. and Tung, L. (1992) 'FARMI's experiences of wealth ranking in the Philippines: different farmers have different needs', *RRA (Rapid Rural Appraisal) Notes* 15: 48–50, London: International Institute for Environment and Development (IIED).

Carter S., Chidiamassamba, A., Jeranyama, P., Mafukidze, B., Malakela, G., Mvena, Z., Mudhara, M., Nabane, N., Van Oosterhout-Campbell, S., Price, L. and Sithole, N. (1993) 'Some observations on wealth ranking after an RRA looking at soil fertility management in Northeastern Zimbabwe', *RRA Notes* 18:47–52, London: IIED.

Chambers, R. (1997) *Whose Reality Counts? Putting the first last*, Rugby: Practical Action Publishing.

Fielding, W.J., Riley J. and Oyejola, B. A., (1998) 'Ranks are statistics: some advice for their interpretation', *PLA Notes* 33: 35–39, London: IIED.

Grandin, B. E. (1988) *Wealth Ranking in Smallholder Communities: A Field Manual,* Rugby: Practical Action Publishing.

Grandin, B. (2014) 'How wealth ranking was developed', in Rowley, J. (ed.) *Wellbeing Ranking: Developments in Applied Community-level Poverty Research*, pp. 9–12, Rugby: Practical Action Publishing, <http://dx.doi.org/10.3362/9781780448459.002> [accessed xx xxxx 2014]

Guijt, I. (1992) 'The elusive poor: a wealth of ways to find them. Report on an IDS/IIED seminar on wealth and well-being ranking', *RRA Notes*, 15: 7–13.

Guijt, I. and Cornwall, A. (1995) 'Critical reflections on the practice of PRA', *PLA (Participatory Learning and Action) Notes* 24: 2–7

Guijt, I. (1992) 'A user's note on wealth ranking by cards and list of sources on wealth ranking', *RRA Notes* 15: 65–69, London: IIED.

Hargreaves, J.R., Morison, L.A., Gear J., Porter, J.D.H., Makhubele, M.B., Kim, J.C., Busza, J., Watts, C. and Pronyk, P.M. (2007) '"Hearing the voices of the poor": Assigning poverty lines on the basis of local perceptions of poverty; a quantitative analysis of qualitative data from participatory wealth ranking in rural South Africa', *World Development* 35 (2): 212–229.

Heffernan, C. and Misturelli, F. (2014) 'Wellbeing ranking: Semi-structured interviews and practitioner bias: Personality traits and participatory narratives', in Rowley, J. (ed.) *Wellbeing Ranking: Developments in Applied Community-level Poverty Research*, pp. 89–110, Rugby: Practical Action Publishing, <http://dx.doi.org/10.3362/9781780448459.007> [accessed xx xxxx 2014]

Hill, P. (1972) *Rural Hausa – A Village and a Setting*, Cambridge: Cambridge University Press.

Leach, M. (1994) 'Targeting aid to the poorest in urban Ethiopia - is it possible? Rapid urban appraisal', *RRA Notes* 21: 48–55, London: IIED.

Mearns, R., Shombodon, D., Narangerel, G., Turul, U., Enkhamgalan, A., Myagmarzhav, B., Bayanjargal, A. and Bekhsuren, B. (1992) 'Direct and indirect uses of wealth ranking in Mongolia', *RRA Notes* 15: 29–38, London: IIED.

Mukherjee, N. (1992) 'Villagers' perceptions of rural poverty through the mapping methods of PRA', *RRA Notes* 15: 21–26, London: IIED.

Narayan, D., Chambers, R., Shah, M.K. and Petesch, P. (2000) *Voices of the Poor: Crying Out for Change*. New York NY: Oxford University Press for the World Bank.

Norton, A. (1994) 'Observations on urban applications of PRA methods from Ghana and Zambia: participatory poverty assessments', *RRA Notes* 21: 55–56, London: IIED.

Pretty, J., Subramanian, S., Kempu Chetty, N., Ananthakrishnan, D., Jayanthi, C., Muralikrishnasamy, S. and Renganayaki, K. (1992) 'Finding the poorest in a Tamil Nadu village: a sequence of mapping and wealth ranking', *RRA Notes* 15: 39–42, London: IIED.

Pretty, J., Guijt, I., Thompson, J. and Scoones, I. (1995) *Participatory Learning and Action: A Trainer's Guide*, London: IIED.

Rowley, J. (2014a) 'Annex 1: How to do wellbeing ranking', in Rowley, J. (ed.) *Wellbeing Ranking: Developments in Applied Community-level Poverty Research*, pp. 163–165, Rugby: Practical Action Publishing, <http://dx.doi.org/10.3362/9781780448459.011> [accessed xx xxxx 2014]

Rowley, J. (2014b) 'Some practical examples and what users say about wellbeing ranking', in Rowley, J. (ed.) *Wellbeing Ranking: Developments in Applied Community-level Poverty Research*, pp. 33–48, Rugby: Practical Action Publishing, <http://dx.doi.org/10.3362/9781780448459.004> [accessed xx xxxx 2014]

Rowley, J. (2014c) 'The history of wellbeing ranking techniques', in Rowley, J. (ed.) *Wellbeing Ranking: Developments in Applied Community-level Poverty Research*, pp. 13–32, Rugby: Practical Action Publishing, <http://dx.doi.org/10.3362/9781780448459.003> [accessed xx xxxx 2014]

Sarch, M-T. (1992) 'Wealth ranking in the Gambia: which households participated in the FITT programme?' *RRA Notes* 15: 14–20, London: IIED.

Sarkar, A., (1991) 'Wealth ranking in Mahilong, Bihar', *RRA Notes* 13: 81–2, London: IIED.

Schaefer, S.S. (1992) 'The 'beans-game' – experiences with a variation of wealth ranking in the Kivu Region, Eastern Zaire', *RRA Notes* 15: 27–8, London: IIED.

Scoones, I. (1988) 'Learning about wealth: an example from Zimbabwe', *RRA Notes* 2: 12–17, London: IIED.

Scoones, I. (1995) 'Investigating ranking and difference: Applications of wealth household survey approaches among farming households in southern Zimbabwe, *Development and Change* 26: 67–88.

Seeley, J., Nabaitu, J., Taylor, L., Kajura, E., Bukenya, T., Kabunga, E. and Ssembajja, F. (1996) 'Revealing gender differences through well-being ranking in Uganda', *PLA Notes* 25: 14–18, London: IIED.

Shah, M.K., (1998) *'Gendered perceptions of well-being and social change in Darko, Ghana'*, in I. Guijt and M.K. Shah (eds.) *The Myth of Community: Gender Issues in Participatory Development*, pp. 141–151, Rugby: Practical Action Publishing.

Shah, P. (1990) 'Economic classification of a community using locally generated criteria', *RRA Notes* 8: 24–9, London: IIED.

Sharrock G.O'G., Waldie, K. and Joshi, Y. (1993) 'Wealth ranking for agricultural research purposes in the Eastern Hills of Nepal', *RRA Notes* 18: 53–59, London: IIED.

Silverman, S. F. (1966) 'An ethnographic approach to social stratification: Prestige in a central Italian community', *American Anthropologist* 68: 899–921.

Simanowitz, A. (1999) 'Pushing the limits of mapping and wealth ranking', *PLA Notes* 34: 4–8, London: IIED.
Simanowitz, A. (2014) 'Using participatory wealth ranking in a South African microfinance organization: the value of scale', in Rowley, J. (ed.) *Wellbeing Ranking: Developments in Applied Community-level Poverty Research*, pp. 71–88, Rugby: Practical Action Publishing, <http://dx.doi.org/10.3362/9781780448459.006> [accessed xx xxxx 2014]
Smith, S. and Sender, J. (1988) 'Investigating poverty: an example from Tanzania', *RRA Notes* 2: 18–20, London: IIED.
Souares, A., Savadogo, G., Dong, H., Parmar, D., Sie, A. and Sauerborn, R. (2010) 'Using community wealth ranking to identify the poor for subsidies: A case study of community-based health insurance in Nouna, Burkina Faso', *Health and Social Care in the Community* 18 (4): 363–8.
Swift, J. and Umar A. N. (1994) 'The problem and solution game', *RRA Notes* 20: 138–41, London: IIED.
Tung, L. and Baliña, F. (1993) 'FARMI's experiences on wealth ranking in the Philippines: Different farmers have different needs', *RRA Notes* 18: 60–65, London: IIED.
Turk, C. (1995) 'Identifying and tackling poverty: ActionAid's experiences in Vietnam', *PLA (Participatory Learning & Action) Notes* 23: 37–41, London: IIED.
Welbourn, A. (1991) 'RRA and the analysis of difference', *RRA Notes* 14: 14–23, London: IIED.
Welbourn, A. (1992) 'A note on the use of disease problem ranking with relation to socio-economic wellbeing: An example from Sierra Leone', *RRA Notes* 16: 86–7, London: IIED.
Young, H. (1990) 'The use of wealth ranking in nutrition surveys in Sudan', *RRA Notes* 8: 10–14, London: IIED.

About the author

John Rowley is an international development professional with over 30 years' experience working for national and international NGOs, government agencies, bilateral and multilateral donors and commercial companies in the UK, Africa and elsewhere.

CHAPTER 6

Using participatory wealth ranking in a South African microfinance organization: the value of scale

Anton Simanowitz

Participatory methods are typically applied in localized contexts, focusing on flexibility and responsiveness to local needs and priorities. This chapter explores the challenges and value of using a particular participatory method – Participatory Wealth Ranking (PWR) – at scale, with a South African microfinance organization that has conducted PWR in rural and peri-urban communities covering some 800,000 households or 4 million people over the past 15 years. Rigour, efficiency and reliability are key factors. The chapter also explores how results from PWR can be benchmarked and compared between communities and regions and over time. A high level of rigour and internal consistency can be achieved where the process is well designed and managed. The credibility of the dataset generated through rigorously using PWR at this scale also creates the opportunity to analyse poverty at a macro-level and to examine changes over time.

Keywords: wellbeing, well-being, ranking, microfinance, participation

Participatory methods are typically applied in localized contexts, focusing on flexibility and responsiveness to local needs and priorities. This article explores the challenges and value of using a particular participatory method – participatory wealth ranking (PWR) – at scale.

Part One discusses the rationale for the use of PWR as opposed to a proxy indicator method to assess poverty.

Part Two addresses the methodological issues in achieving the standardization and consistency necessary to integrate PWR as a poverty-targeting tool into the operations of a specific microfinance organization: the Small Enterprise Foundation (SEF). SEF reaches over 80,000 women in rural South Africa, building operational self-sufficiency through a focus on high productivity levels (around 350 members per field agent) and low operating margins. Rigour, efficiency and reliability are therefore key. Over the past 14 years, SEF has conducted PWR in rural and peri-urban communities in three South African provinces (Figure 6.1 'Map of SEF operations showing areas where PWR has been conducted') covering some 800,000 households or 4 million people.[1]

http://dx.doi.org/10.3362/9781780448459.006

In Part Three, I use the experience of SEF to explore the scope of applicability of participatory methods, exploring how results can be benchmarked and compared between communities and regions and over time. In addition to the much discussed value of local knowledge, context and timeliness of information, I highlight the high level of rigour and internal consistency that can be achieved where the process is well designed and managed. The credibility of the dataset generated through rigorously using PWR at this scale also creates the opportunity to analyse poverty at a macro-level and to examine changes over time. This is particularly interesting in the South African context, where there has been an intense focus on poverty reduction through one of the most ambitious social protection programmes worldwide. Preliminary analysis of PWR data over time provides a very different picture to national survey-based poverty data, and suggests there might be a role for large-scale data, generated through participatory methods, to feed into national policy processes.

Part One: PWR compared to physical proxies for poverty and wellbeing

This section draws on the experience of SEF in developing and operationalizing two different poverty-targeting systems. The first, based on an 'outsider's'

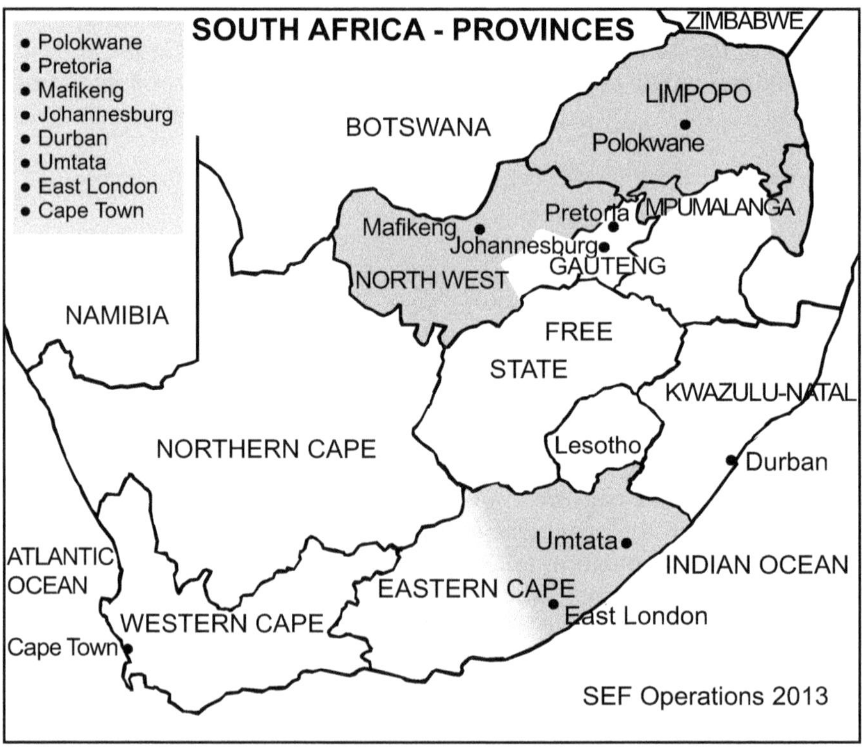

Figure 6.1 Map of SEF operations showing areas where PWR has been conducted

perspective, used a Visual Indicator of Poverty test (VIP), based primarily on external housing conditions. Failures within this system led to the development of PWR, which takes an 'insider's' perspective and is based on villagers defining their own concepts.

SEF aims to ensure that no women who could usefully use its services are unnecessarily excluded. Experience has demonstrated that in practice a large proportion of poorer women exclude themselves through fear or lack of confidence, or are excluded owing to the biases of other clients and staff members. SEF therefore requires the use of a poverty targeting tool, and carefully monitors its outreach to, and the progress of, the poorest people in the community. Although SEF benchmarks its outreach to the international US$1.25 and US$2.50 per day poverty lines using a poverty scorecard developed for South Africa (Grameen Foundation, no date), in practice it relies on the self-perception and definition of poverty of members of the community who participate in the wealth-ranking process.

Prior to the use of PWR, SEF used a VIP developed in Malaysia by a microfinance organization called Cashpor and adapted it to the South African context. The VIP was designed to 'allow a field agent to make an educated guess about the income of a household', based on the appearance of their housing from the outside. Indicators included the physical condition, size, type of roofing, and type of construction of houses. Field agents scored the external conditions of the house according to a checklist. Using this method, those people living in houses constructed from mud bricks, with poor-quality thatch roofing, small windows, and in a general state of disrepair, tend to be selected as the poorest, whil those with cement bricks, zinc roofing, larger windows, a pit latrine, and generally better constructed housing, do not qualify to benefit from the programme.

The VIP can be criticized in that it takes a static 'snapshot' and limited spatial view of households. It does not take into consideration changes that occur in household welfare over time; for example, the loss of a job, or the main earner dying or deserting the household. Changes in circumstances may therefore result in a household being misclassified as well off, when in fact it is very poor. Similarly, household mobility may affect the VIP classification, in that a household may move to a new area and initially live in very poor-quality accommodation. Many households in South Africa have multiple residences located in different areas, so a poor-quality home in one village may be only a minor residence, whereas the household may have a much better quality home in another location, such as in town. A further criticism of the VIP is that it does not take into account the wider construct of household livelihoods in terms of household resources, household activities, resource flows, social networks and other obligations and entitlements. It is therefore a very one-dimensional view of the characteristics of poverty. Thus, although it is acknowledged that housing plays a significant role in household expenditure, and is one of the main ways of spending additional income, the use of this single criterion is open to many distortions.

In practice, SEF received many complaints from clients and from field staff regarding 'exceptions' who were seemingly misclassified by the VIP. There were many instances of potential beneficiaries being excluded from the programme who gave detailed reasons as to why they were, in fact, poor – in some cases bringing the field staff into their homes to show them that a good structure on the outside was in reality empty inside. A pilot comparison between PWR and VIP corroborated the weaknesses of the visual indicators. Like the VIP, PWR identified some physical characteristics such as poor-quality or small housing as a significant factor in determining wealth. However, the PWR differed in that a number of anomalies were identified by participants that in a ranking based on visual criteria, would result in inaccuracies. These included households where the person providing the main income had recently died. In other cases, participants ranked as wealthy a household with a poor-quality house, as they knew that the family also owned a house in town. The PWR also identified many characteristics that are not visible as determinants of wealth, such as diversity and security of income, whether children attend school regularly, and the quality and sufficiency of food (see Table 6.1).

Table 6.1 Pile statement scores and frequency of statements made during participatory wealth ranking in rural South Africa, in descending order of pile statement score

Pile statements		*Theme*	*Statement*	*General statements – No. of times said*			
Pile statement score	No. of times said			Very poor	Poor but bit better off	Doing OK	
0.0	7	Food	Don't have soup	10			Very poor ↓
0.0	6	Health	Mental illness	4			
0.0	22	Family and household	Orphanhood/no parents	24			
0.0	8	Employment	Widows/ deserted wives without jobs	5			
0.4	39	Food	Beg for food	33			
0.8	24	Need	Needy	4			
0.9	16	Societies and *stokvels*	Not in societies	10			
1.1	85	Begging	Begging	49			
1.8	11	Family and household	Widow	15			
2.8	28	Dirtiness	No soap	15			

Pile statements		*Theme*	*Statement*	*General statements*			
				No. of times said			
Pile statement score	No. of times said			Very poor	Poor but bit better off	Doing OK	
3.1	4	Societies and *stokvels*	Unable to join burial society	7			
3.1	134	Food	No food	137			
3.2	41	Housing	Not got shelter	33			
3.7	58	Employment	No one is working	34			
5.2	101	Schooling	Doesn't go to school	39			
5.6	73	Clothing	No clothes/ do not have clothes	73			
5.7	199	Employment	Not got job(s) unemployed	113	4		
5.8	22	Food	Sleep without food	17	15		
6.2	10	Housing	One room	7			
6.3	20	Housing	Has no place to sleep	11			
6.4	82	Money	Don't have/earn money/income	49			
7.7	14	Food	Going to school without eating	7			
8.3	100	Schooling	Unable to/can't afford to go to school	66			
9.0	67	Housing	Not got housing	65			
9.6	37	Schooling	Can't afford/ does not pay school fee	18			
11.9	23	Clothing	Tattered/torn/ poor clothes	20			
13.3	53	Housing	Mud housing	10			Very poor↑
14.4	76	Housing	Shacks	18	15		Poor↓
15.0	51	Housing	No proper housing/shelter	18	6		
15.3	11	Self employment	Dig toilets		4		
15.5	19	Survival skills	Have survival skills		9		
15.8	26	Clothing	Do not have proper clothes	14			

SEF felt that the level of inconsistency in the VIP was sufficient to warrant a change to PWR. Costs for PWR and VIP are similar in terms of staff time (see Table 6.12) , although PWR requires a more intensive input at one time and is more challenging in terms of the staff skills and management systems (see Part Two). SEF found, however, that the communication effect of PWR built a good understanding of the organization in the community, and acceptance that it was targeted only to certain people. This helped significantly in supporting growth and operations in new villages, and was therefore seen to be more cost-effective than the VIP survey.

Part Two: Methodological challenges in scaling PWR

Adapting PWR for scale and rigour

SEF took the traditional wealth-ranking tool, commonly applied in a fairly ad hoc way on a small scale, and sought to transform it into a poverty targeting tool that could be operationalized in a microfinance organization that has grown around 20% per year and now has over 300 staff and 80,000 clients.

Essentially, wealth ranking involves two stages: mapping households in a community and writing the household names onto cards; and then asking a small group (reference group) of community members to define characteristics of wellbeing, wealth or poverty, and then use these to rank the cards of community members by comparing households and using local knowledge to sort them into piles defined by characteristics (see Box 6.1).

A number of methodological adaptations were necessary to adapt the PWR to the scale of communities in South Africa, which consist of up to 1,000 households. The key lesson was to break down the process into manageable pieces, with communities being mapped in commonly recognized sections, and any sections larger than about 120 households being split during the ranking process.

Additional steps were added to make the ranking process more rigorous: a minimum of three reference groups to allow for triangulation; and strict rules defining acceptable levels of correlation between these.

Table 6. 2 Staff time required for PWR and VIP (for a village of 500 households)

Participatory wealth ranking	*Visual indicator of poverty scorecard*
Preparations; contacts with village structures	Preparations; contacts with village structures
Day 1: 2 staff mapping, 0.5 days = 1 person day Day 2: 2 sections (each approx. 100 households) = 2 person days Day 3: 2 sections = 2 person days Day 4: 1 section = 1 person day	1 or 2 staff mapping and scoring in village
TOTAL: 6–8 person days	TOTAL: 6 person days

Box 6.1: PWR process

Mapping

Step 1. Mapping: A community meeting is set up involving representatives from all areas of the village where the programme will be established. After introductions and explanations, a participatory mapping exercise is facilitated. A village map is drawn either on the ground with a stick, or on the floor of a building using chalk. If the village is large (over 100 households), it is divided into recognized sections. A household list is generated from the map, with participants writing down the commonly used name for each household (i.e. not necessarily the household head), and these names are written onto cards. There is one card written for each household in the area.

Reference groups

Step 2. Setting up reference groups: Three reference groups are set up for each section that has been mapped, with 3–5 members of the community in each group. If there are not enough people present, those who are present are asked to invite additional people to the groups.

Step 3. Card sorting/Wealth ranking: Each reference group meets separately and sorts the household cards into piles according to wealth, along a continuum of high to low. The number of piles generated is determined by the participants, but at least four piles should be made. During the process of card sorting much information is gained about the participants' perceptions of wealth and poverty, and there is opportunity for discussion. A staff member facilitates the process and monitors whether the ranking is done openly, with good participation of the group.

Analysis

Step 4. Triangulation: The results of the ranking are triangulated by using a minimum of three reference groups. The numbers given to each household from each reference group are then totalled. Consistency between the groups verifies the results. If more than 10% represent either gross inconsistencies or households with missing data, then an additional reference group is required.

Step 5. Scoring: Piles are scored using the formula [100 divided by the number of piles, then multiplied by the pile number], so that the poorest pile always scores 100. For example, with four piles the poorest pile would score [100/4 x 4 = 100]; the next [100/4 x 3 = 75]; the next [100/4 x 2 = 50]; and the wealthiest [100/4 x 4 = 25]. With five piles the scores would be 100, 80, 60, 40, and 20. The final score of each household is the average of the ranks it was given by the three reference groups. For example, if the three reference groups had scored it 100, 75, and 80 respectively, its final score would be [(100+75+80)/3 =] 85.

Step 6. Selecting the poorest: By this time, field staff have collected information about the poverty characteristics of the households in each pile during the reference group sessions. This information is analysed and compared with a standardized checklist of poverty characteristics drawn up from the information given in a number of rankings. The ranking score that corresponds to these characteristics is taken as the cut-off point. The selection of the poor who can be included in the programme is done on the basis of this cut-off score.

For the sake of cost-effectiveness, SEF sought to strike a balance between the level of accuracy required in targeting and the resources required to achieve this. Thus a key question in the operationalization of PWR is to find the point of 'optimal ignorance', thereby reducing the time and resources required to a minimum.

PWR very rapidly builds up consistent results for the vast majority of households. The few remaining inconsistencies, however, require that repeat reference groups are conducted to achieve close to 100% consistency. Practice has demonstrated that it is rare that more than about 10% of households are not consistently ranked after three reference groups. Accepting a margin of error – particularly for those who obviously do not rank among the poorest – allows the number of reference groups to be kept to three (or four in exceptional circumstances where the levels of inconsistency are higher, or where one reference group is discarded as unreliable). This reduces the time required for the process; it is expected that one field agent would complete the process for at least one section of the village (approximately 100 households) in one day.

For those households where there is a gross inconsistency between results (defined as a difference between the highest and lowest scores of 50 or greater), *and* where there is one score placing the household among the poorest, a visit would be made to the person's house to verify their true situation. Thus, those households that are not considered among the poorest by any reference group are discarded and effort is focused on the very small number (often zero) of inconsistencies where the household might be amongst the target group.

External academic studies have demonstrated the high level of rigour in SEF's PWR approach. James Hargreaves, an epidemiologist who has written a number of articles drawing on data from SEF's wealth ranking (see, for example, Hargreaves et al. 2007a and 2007b), writes in correspondence: 'SEF's TCP procedures are remarkably reproducible ... i.e. the level of agreement between the three reference groups on "poverty level" of households is amazing in my view. I believe when well conducted – as is most often the case through SEF's procedures – PWR participants know on what they are ranking households and do so very effectively, more effectively in my view than a survey-based tool like an asset index (though this is difficult to prove because if the two approaches differ in their ranking of households, how do you decide what is "right"?)'.

Implementing PWR presented a number of practical problems in terms of training and supervising staff to use the method in a consistent and cost-effective manner. With a view to ensuring that the process was clearly defined and could therefore be instructed, assessed and managed, an iterative process was used to document key points in the process where mistakes might be made. These were used as learning points for the training; evaluation points for assessment; and a checklist to guide management supervision of the process.

A training methodology was developed, with field staff trained in theory and then supervised facilitating the PWR process. An assessment PWR was then set up for another date and trainees observed the facilitation of the mapping exercise and at least two reference groups. A high standard of facilitation, adhering to the checklist, was required for qualification.

Experienced PWR facilitators could apply to become supervisors, undergoing additional training and tests.

Also key to the scaling of PWR is the ability to standardize the decision-making process relating to the poverty categorization of the ranked people. During each ranking, information is captured about why people are sorted into each group and the common characteristics of each pile emerge. Interestingly, data generated during the early implementation of PWR showed remarkable consistency between the characteristics used by the reference groups in different rankings in different villages. This allowed SEF to develop a standardized set of criteria by which to judge the cut-off line for entry into the programme (see Table 6.3).

Management challenges

Although PWR as developed by SEF has proved itself to be a rigorous methodology, and qualified facilitators have demonstrated their ability to achieve very high levels of consistency between three reference groups in the same community, significant challenges have been experienced in managing PWR over time.

In the 12 years that PWR has been in operation in SEF there have been huge social and economic changes in South Africa. The government has invested heavily in rural infrastructure and has set up one of the largest welfare grant systems in the world. A large proportion of rural South Africans now receive child-support grants, disability allowances or pensions. Changes have not all been positive and, at the same time, despite economic growth, there has been a restructuring of the economy away from labour-intensive activities, leading to large numbers of low-skilled workers being retrenched. This has hit the precise target population of SEF. At the same time the population has become more mobile, with the ending of apartheid-era restrictions on movement and a lot of younger and more skilled people moving out of rural areas. Thus, although there have been overall reductions in poverty in South Africa, the changes in SEF's operating areas are less certain.

The perception among staff is that there have been significant changes – particularly in terms of a reduction in the number of very poor people. This is seen to be the main driver of a change in the cut-off line used by SEF: the original line targeted those who 'have nothing' and who 'have a little' – the bottom two categories; the new line extends the scope of the programme to include those that 'have basic necessities' (see Table 6.3 for details of cut-off line).

This shift has led to a significant increase in the percentage of people qualifying: from 40–50% in the past, to 70–80% now. The analysis of distribution of poverty levels by Hargreaves et al. (2007a: 223) demonstrates the high number of people close to the poverty line, and the significant impact on the numbers qualifying by moving the cut-off line:

> '24.4% were deemed "very poor" by PWR participants. A further 7.8% might simply be described as "poor", covering the scores relating to

Table 6.3 Cut-off line table for PWR; updated 2011 (columns 1–3 qualify)

	1. Have nothing	*2. Have a little*	*3. Have basic necessities*	*4. Doing OK*	*5. Well-off*
Income and dependents	Unemployed, no regular income or grants with many dependants, orphans	Rely on grants and piece jobs; many dependents; hawking	More income or fewer dependents; pensioners with few dependents; rely on temporary work, small business; more regular income	Multiple regular income sources or formal employment; pensioners with only themselves to look after	Professionals and/or business owners with smaller families; earn company pensions
Food	Begging; eat once a day; go hungry to bed	Struggle to get food; some get food parcels from government; food doesn't last a long time/ the whole month; eat once or twice a day	Enough but not good food; eat meat once a month/ pension day only	Always have enough food; sometimes eat meat, drink tea, etc.	Regularly eat luxury foods e.g. bread with margarine
Housing	Poor quality, mud; too small for members of the household; cannot afford water and electricity	2 rooms; poor quality; sometimes *rondavel*[2]; not enough space for all household members	2–3 rooms; government house	Larger, better-quality house; enough space for all household members	Large house; bricks, carpets, tiles, fence
Education	Kids often miss school or don't go at all	In public school, but not regularly; children have one/poor school uniform; children don't have school shoes; no lunch money	Kids at public school (primary and secondary); can afford to buy uniforms but cannot afford tertiary education	Kids at school, sometimes pay for college or private education; children have pocket money	Kids go to private schools and universities, *Technikons*[3]
Assets/ Health	No assets; dirty, torn clothes; no shoes; no ID/birth certificate; no burial society; children are sick	A few assets such as basic clothing; cheap, second-hand, poor quality; no livestock	Basic assets; second-hand/old furniture; few livestock (chicken, goats); small gardens to cultivate can afford to buy new clothes once a year (Christmas)	Some luxury assets, e.g. DVD, stereo; good quality, labelled clothes; more livestock (various); sometimes a car	Many luxury assets, e.g. car, satellite television; children have expensive clothes; rent out rooms; have domestic workers; lots of livestock and land

statement scores split between "very poor" and "poor, but a bit better off". We suggest in this analysis that both of these groups of households should be considered below the poverty line. Following this comes a large group of households (48.2%) who are described as "poor, but a bit better off". This is followed in turn by another small marginal group (termed "a bit better off" here, and encompassing 7.8% of all households), before a final group of households that are "doing OK" (14.1%).'

The shift in numbers of people qualifying mean that the net effect of the PWR effort is to exclude the top 20–30% of people; previously SEF was excluding 50–60%. There is therefore less value in the activity, leading managers to question whether there might not be a more cost-effective way to achieve this goal.

Managing the quality of PWR results is challenging. There are strong disincentives against maintaining quality for both field agents and field managers. The ability to do PWR well does not mean that it is done well. PWR takes several days and is hard work. Where PWR is done well, there is usually high consistency between reference groups, therefore it is very tempting for facilitators to conduct just one reference group and then 'make up' results for the others. This in itself may not have a significant impact on the quality of results if it is done by a good facilitator, but it is a significant lapse in the quality of the system. A bigger risk is the tension between targeting and growth. SEF is a 'social business' that imposes high productivity targets on its staff; this is necessary to ensure the financial viability of the organization. Staff are incentivized to increase the numbers of clients they reach, and know that having more people qualify will increase the pool of potential people for them to recruit. There is therefore an incentive to have more people qualify in PWR and a risk that field staff will 'adjust' the figures to ensure that a higher percentage of people do so.

Branch managers who supervise the PWR process, and are responsible for ensuring that results are not manipulated by field agents, also have a performance target for growth linked to a financial incentive; this means it is in their interest to ensure that the pool of potential clients is as large as possible. Spot-checking cannot therefore be left to branch managers alone and there is a need for several levels of checks. The quality of implementation has thus proved to be hard to manage effectively over time. A re-examination of the system in 2010 highlighted a number of instances of manipulation of results by staff and highlighted weaknesses in the management system. There was no evidence that this was happening systematically, but managers recognized that some supervision systems would need to be significantly strengthened.

After exploring the use of a survey-based poverty targeting tool, such as the Progress Out of Poverty Index (PPI)[4], in 2012, the SEF Board recommitted the organization to the use of PWR based on a belief in its robustness and validity compared to other methods. SEF is currently strengthening its PWR management systems.

Part Three: Scaling understanding using participatory methods – comparing poverty between communities, regions and over time

Participatory methods are commonly used at a localized level. In SEF's case, however, results in individual villages are benchmarked and demonstrate a remarkable level of internal consistency between communities, regions and over time. Through repeated rankings, the characteristics commonly mentioned by communities were collated and used to develop a cut-off line table (see Table 6.3). This has been updated over time, but the characteristics within the five broad categories have remained remarkably similar, the main change concerning access to government child benefit and disability grants. This allows the results to be benchmarked and compared, rather than having to interpret them as a perception of poverty that is only locally relevant.

SEF's on-the-ground experience has been verified through a large-scale academic study. Hargreaves et al. (2007a) conducted a rigorous analysis of PWR results from almost 10,000 households, doing so with strong management and supervision to ensure data quality. They looked in detail at the statements made by participants in the ranking process used to determine the ranking position (pile selection). This work supported SEF's experience that there is a remarkable commonality between the subjective definitions of poverty used by different communities (within the same geographical area). During the ranking process, notes were taken on the statements made by participants to explain their reasons for categorizing households as having a particular level of wellbeing. Nine characteristics accounted for over 87% of statements made during the ranking process: formal employment; schooling; housing; food; self-employment; clothing; family and household; money; and pensions. Strikingly, money was mentioned in less than 5% of statements (See Table 6.4).

As SEF has expanded its operations to cover the whole of Limpopo Province, and has started operations in two neighbouring provinces, this consistency in perceptions of poverty has been maintained, thus allowing the same cut-off line table to be used. Remarkably, in recent years SEF has expanded into a new province on the other side of the country: the Eastern Cape. Although the area is culturally and economically different – with a higher proportion of people farming and fewer business opportunities – the PWR results continue to demonstrate very similar priorities in terms of poverty definitions. The challenges in applying PWR in the Eastern Cape have been operational: very dispersed sections within the same village leading to poor turnout for the mapping exercise; and relatively high levels of poverty leading to very high percentages of people qualifying.

The key comparability is the ability to benchmark an individual section's ranking result. Households from two different sections and with different scores may actually be at the same poverty level. For example, the characteristics of a household in one section with an average ranking score of 85 may be the same as one with an average score of 73 in another section. The qualitative understanding of how people define poverty (as gained during the ranking

Table 6.4 Themes raised in discussions of poverty during participatory wealth ranking conducted in rural South Africa

Theme	*General statements*		*Pile statements*		*Total*	
	N	*%*[a]	*N*	*%*[a]	*N*	*%*[a]
Employment	577	14.5	2,236	21.3	2,813	19.4
Schooling	557	14.0	1,.351	12.9	1,908	13.2
Housing	559	14.0	1,229	11.7	1,788	12.3
Food	506	12.7	921	8.8	1,427	9.9
Self employment	380	9.5	922	8.8	1,302	9.0
Clothing	399	10.0	755	7.2	1,154	8.0
Family and household	146	3.7	781	7.4	927	6.4
Money	162	4.1	535	5.1	697	4.8
Pensions	100	2.5	499	4.8	599	4.1
Cars	177	4.4	297	2.8	474	3.3
Begging	91	2.3	134	1.3	225	1.6
Towns	0	0.0	216	2.1	216	1.5
Need	10	0.3	96	0.9	106	0.7
Dirtiness	42	1.1	60	0.6	102	0.7
Water	28	0.7	49	0.5	77	0.5
Survival skills	11	0.3	65	0.6	76	0.5
Societies and *stokvels*	34	0.9	37	0.4	71	0.5
Other assets	34	0.9	35	0.3	69	0.5
Health	31	0.8	31	0.3	62	0.4
Furniture	24	0.6	24	0.2	48	0.3
Livestock	19	0.5	26	0.2	45	0.3
Planning	16	0.4	25	0.2	41	0.3
Fighting	6	0.2	29	0.3	35	0.2
Happiness	16	0.4	19	0.2	35	0.2
Depended upon/ employ …	20	0.5	14	0.1	34	0.2
Telephones	8	0.2	25	0.2	33	0.2
Employ home help	3	0.1	23	0.2	26	0.2
Position within society	3	0.1	20	0.2	23	0.2
Electricity	11	0.3	11	0.1	22	0.2
Crime	10	0.3	5	0.1	15	0.1
Whites	3	0.1	11	0.1	14	0.1
Land/agriculture	9	0.2	3	0.1	12	0.1
Lifestyle	0	0.0	9	0.1	9	0.1

[a] Reported percentages are as a percentage of all coded statements.
Source: Hargreaves et al., 2007a

exercise) is therefore used to achieve consistency between sections. During the ranking exercise, the facilitator takes notes relating to the statements given by the participants on why people are placed in a particular pile. This generates a set of characteristics for each pile. Following the ranking, supervisors look

Reference Group	Score – qualification status	Score – qualification status	Score – qualification status	Score – qualification status
Reference group 1	100 – yes	83 – yes	67 – yes	50 – no
Reference group 2	100 – yes	80 – yes	60 – ?	40 – no
Reference group 3	100 – yes	86 – yes	71 – yes	57 – ?

at the results for each section and compares these characteristics to the cut-off line table. For each ranking, they determine whether each pile definitely qualifies, definitely does not qualify, or is questionable. They then look at the ranking scores that definitely qualify/definitely do not qualify, and make an estimate as to where the cut-off line is likely to be.

Take the following example, which presents the results from a single section with three reference groups generating 6 piles, 5 piles and 7 piles.

The supervisors review the information and through analysing the qualitative information conclude that all reference groups with a score of 67 and above qualify, and those with a score of 50 and below do not qualify. Those with a score of 57 and 60 are questionable. The cut-off line therefore lies somewhere between 50 and 67.

The next step is to look at the actual results and determine how many households have a score between 50 and 67. These are then reviewed and the actual scores for these analysed to see what specific scores generated the average score. Any households that have scored 67 or above in two reference groups qualify. Any that have scored 50 or below in two groups do not qualify. As the ranking generates discreet numbers, most households can be classified in this way (i.e. in the ranking by group 1, households can score 67 or 50 – both results with a clear yes/no qualification status. In each of the rankings by groups 2 and 3 there is only one score that does not have a definite qualification status, therefore the chances are that this analysis will generate clarity.

Assigning individual households in this way will allow the cut-off line to be more clearly defined; for example, if several households with average scores of around 60 are shown to qualify, then the cut-off line will be closer to 60. This will help in determining whether any remaining questionable households should qualify. Where there is lack of clarity – a very occasional occurrence – households are given the benefit of the doubt and classed as qualifying. Note that, in the case of field staff feeling that a potential client should qualify despite the PWR classification, SEF also has an appeals procedure involving a household visit.

It is the combination of a standardized cut-off line table based on scientific evidence of comparability of results, and a rigorous process to benchmark specific results to this table, that enables SEF to claim comparability of the minimum poverty level of its clients across its operations.

The internal consistency of PWR should, in theory, allow analysis of SEF's PWR data to track changes over time. Since the democratic elections in 1994, considerable effort has been made to address poverty (though not inequality) in South Africa. Most notable was the introduction of social grants, which now reach around one in three households. Although this has been coupled with economic restructuring, leading to increases in retrenchment and unemployment (especially in the rural areas where SEF works), the social grants, in theory, significantly reduce extreme poverty (though there is academic debate about whether this is the case; see, for example, Meth, 2009). If this were the case, then it would be much harder for SEF to limit its outreach to the poorest people. This seems to correspond with the operational reality, where in practice the cut-off line had moved from including the first two piles – 'have nothing' and 'have little' – to include the third pile, 'have basic necessities', as well. To test this hypothesis, SEF conducted an analysis of the community poverty profile using 29 quality PWRs from 2000 and 73 quality PWRs from 2010 (covering approximately 3,000 and 7,500 households, respectively).

Data from 2000 had been subject to rigorous supervision and therefore SEF was confident that the data were of good quality. To ensure comparable data quality for 2010 data, SEF's Research and Development department selected only data from PWRs conducted by qualified and experienced supervisors.

The results (see Figure 6.2) were surprising, and seemed to demonstrate that poverty levels for the very poor (PWR score of 90–100) had remained

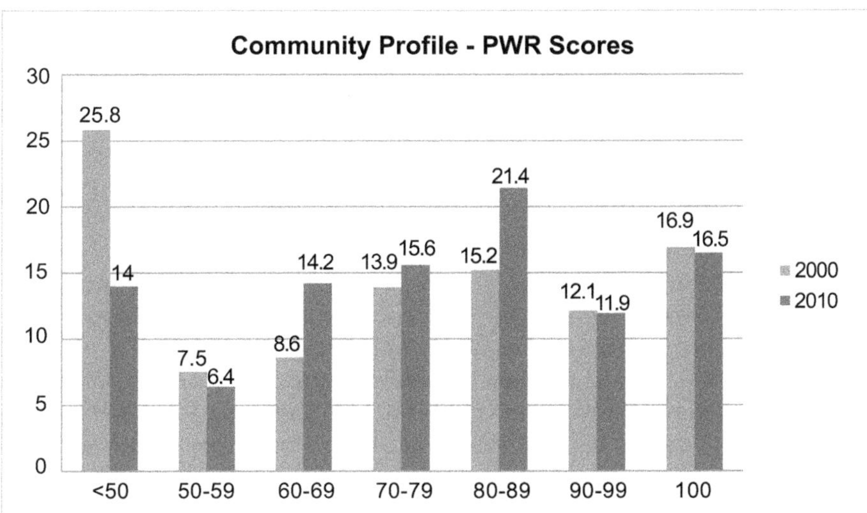

Figure 6.2 Community profile of PWR scores, 2000 and 2010

constant, whereas poverty levels for the better off (PWR score >50) had increased significantly.

More careful consideration of the data highlighted that the analysis did not control for comparable villages ranked, and the 2010 data included a significant number of rankings from a new operational area (KwaZulu-Natal), which has a higher poverty incidence than the 2,000 villages, which were all in Limpopo Province. The data, however, did demonstrate that there are as

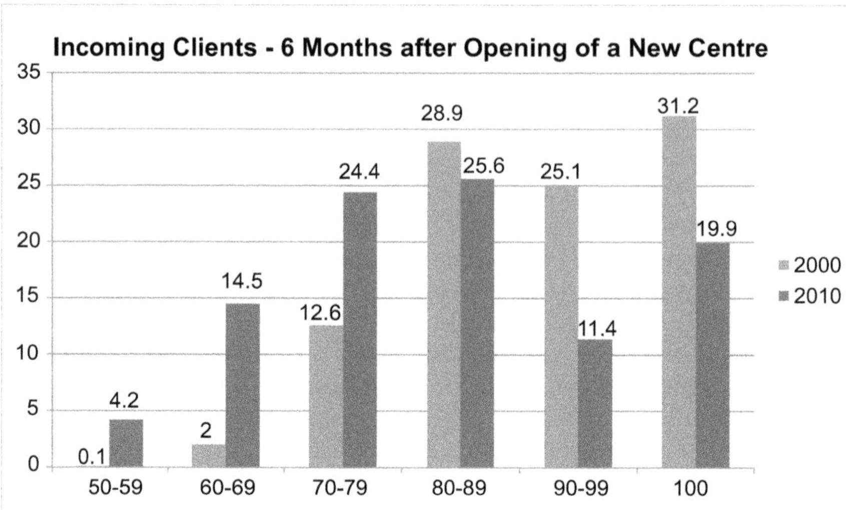

Figure 6.3 PWR scores of incoming SEF clients, 2000 and 2010

many very poor people in the villages SEF is working in now as there were in the villages where SEF worked in 2000. As this comparison was made using consistent definitions of poverty, the shift in cut-off line reflects a real change in the characteristics of people targeted.

A second analysis, using the same data, looked at the proportion of very poor clients (with PWR scores of 90–100) joining the organization. This showed a drop from 56% in 2000 to 31% in 2010 (see Figure 6.3).

This seemed to confirm the shift in clientele, and raised concerns at management level about mission drift and the declining numbers of very poor people being reached. Again, further discussion revealed a different picture. In 2000, SEF had a policy that the first 15 clients in any new target village had to have PWR scores of 90–100 (i.e. they had to be among the poorest). This ensured a rapid intake of very poor clients in the first few months of operations. This policy was removed around 2005 in order to assist operations staff in growing the portfolio. Operations staff argued that, over time, very poor women would still join the programme and that the eventual number of very poor people benefiting from it would not differ significantly.

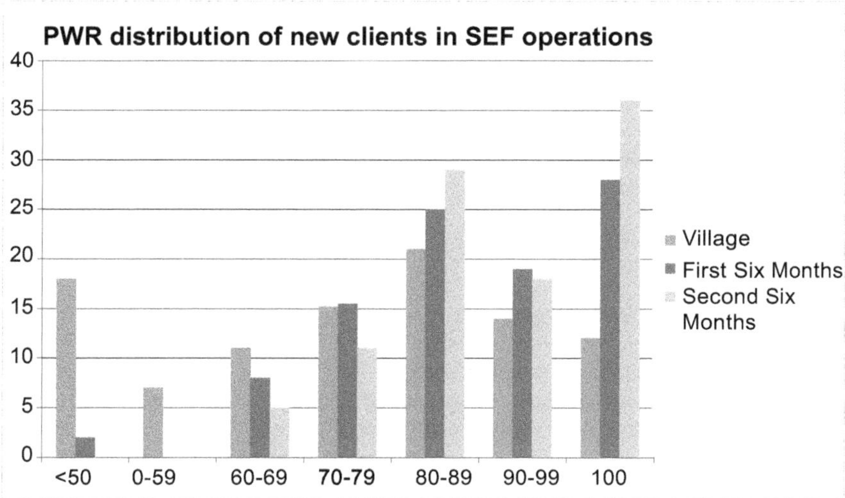

Figure 6.4 PWR distribution of new clients in SEF operations

Further tracking of the PWR scores of SEF clients confirmed this belief (see Figure 6.4).

Conclusions

The experience of SEF over 13 years, ranking households totalling over 3 million people, represents a vast – and largely untapped – source of experience and data. SEF has successfully demonstrated how a methodology normally perceived as subjective, labour intensive and small scale can be scaled up to be a powerful, practical and cost-effective tool. Considerable challenges have been encountered, but the recent commitment of the Board to re-adopt this approach validates its efficacy.

Beyond the methodological considerations, the vast amount of data generated by the tool provides an opportunity to analyse community perceptions of poverty across time and space, and has the potential to be a fascinating source of information for national poverty data analysis. Although beyond the means of an organization focused on service delivery, it would be relatively easy to benchmark SEF data to national poverty surveys, allowing for more meaningful analysis of changes in poverty status within communities or regions, or between regions.

Notes

1. Estimate given during detailed discussion with SEF managing director and chief operating officer.
2. A traditional mud-brick and thatched roof building.
3. Before 1993, Technikons were separate from universities as polytechnics but many now have merged with universities or have become Univerisities, of Technology.

4. The Progress out of Poverty Index (PPI) is a poverty scorecard developed and marketed by the Grameen Foundation USA. This allows for relatively robust data on poverty, benchmarked to national and international poverty lines to be collected quickly and reliably. It uses indicators from national income and expenditure surveys that have a strong correlation with national poverty data and can be easily and constantly collected by relatively unskilled field staff as part of their routine work.

References

Coren, M.J. (2011) 'When communities identify their own poor, aid has the most effect', Fast Company [website] <www.fastcompany.com> (posted 29 August 2011) [accessed 23 April 2014]

Grameen Foundation (no date) *Progress Out of Poverty Index* [website] <www.progressoutofpoverty.org> [accessed 02 May 2014]

Hargreaves, J.R., Morison, L.A., Gear J., Porter, J.D.H., Makhubele, M.B., Kim, J.C., Busza, J., Watts, C. and Pronyk, P.M. (2007a) '"Hearing the voices of the poor": Assigning poverty lines on the basis of local perceptions of poverty; a quantitative analysis of qualitative data from participatory wealth ranking in rural South Africa', *World Development* 35 (2): 212–229.

Hargreaves, J.R., Morison, L.A., Gear, J.S.S., Kim, J.C., Makhubele, M.B., Porter, J.D.H., Watts, C. and Pronyk, P.M. (2007b) 'Assessing household wealth in health studies in developing countries: a comparison of participatory wealth ranking and survey techniques from rural South Africa', *Emerging Themes in Epidemiology* 4: 4 <http://dx.doi.org/10.1186/1742-7622-4-4>

Meth, C. (2009) *Unemployment and poverty halved by 2014?* Working Paper No 56, School of Development Studies, Durban: University of KwaZulu-Natal.

Simanowitz, A. (1999) 'Pushing the limits of mapping and wealth ranking', PLA Notes 34: 4–8, London: IIED.

Simanowitz, A., Nkuna, B., and Kassim, S. (1999) 'Overcoming the obstacles of identifying the poorest families', Paper prepared for the Microcredit Summit Meeting of Councils in Abidjan, Côte d'Ivoire, 24–26 June 1999. www.microfinancegateway.org/gm/document-1.9.25808/1578.pdf

About the author

Anton Simanowitz is a socio-economist with 20 years' experience in participatory/action research, evaluation, impact assessment, poverty-focused methodology development and innovation, and microfinance. Following roles with the Small Enterprise Foundation, South Africa, the Institute of Development Studies at Sussex University, UK, and Dutch social investor Oikocredit, he is now working freelance. Contact: antons@pkrc.co.uk

CHAPTER 7

Wellbeing ranking, semi-structured interviews and practitioner bias: personality traits and participatory narratives

Claire Heffernan and Federica Misturelli

Semi-structured interviews are a core component of participatory methods generally, and of wellbeing ranking more specifically. While historically practitioners were cautioned to avoid 'bad practice', in which the 'voices of the poor' were filtered/ distorted, and encouraged instead to be critically self-reflective, in practice it was unclear how practitioner bias could be measured or assessed. Therefore, in the following chapter the authors explore the role of the personal characteristics of the practitioner on the narratives produced in semi-structured interviews. Three main elements of the interviews are analysed: the level of communicative competence between practitioner and participant; the use of key themes; and the influence of core personality traits of the practitioner on the depth and quality of the interview.

Keywords: wellbeing, well-being, ranking, participatory methods, practitioner bias, data analysis

Notions of wealth and of wellbeing are notoriously difficult to measure among communities of the poor. Therefore, the advent of wealth ranking (Grandin, 1988) and the subsequent evolution of wellbeing ranking were perceived as important tools to address this gap. Nevertheless, over the course of the last 20 years the fortunes of the tools have waxed and waned. The heyday of participatory approaches is widely attributed to the early 1990s, with the demise of the paradigm a decade later. Latterly, however, there has been a renewed interest in participatory approaches, particularly in the health and environment sectors (Ali et al., 2008; Beyer et al., 2010; Catalani and Minkler, 2010; Balansky et al., 2011; Macauley et al., 2011).

Yet in the resurgence of interest in such approaches, the wider narrative of participation is both cautionary and illuminating. The core tenet of Participatory Rural Appraisal (PRA) was to empower communities by 'putting the last first' and allowing the former 'objects' of development to participate fully in decision-making processes (Chambers, 1983; Nelson and Wright, 1995). Thus, along with the new approach, new tools were needed to both better understand local realities and ensure that the voices of the people were heard and acted upon. During the 1980s, traditional methods such as

http://dx.doi.org/10.3362/9781780448459.007

formal surveys began to come under increasing criticism (Casley and Lury, 1981; Bulmer and Warwick, 1983; Mukherjee, 1993; Chambers, 1983, 1992, 1997). The structure and limited flexibility of questionnaires were viewed as an inhibitor/barrier to dialogue. More problematic, such approaches were often viewed simply as an expression of the dominant, external (i.e. Northern) cultural paradigm (Bulmer and Warwick, 1983; Mukherjee, 1993). The format of the interview and the jargon deployed often excluded the poorest and most marginalized community members. Consequently, it was argued that formal surveys misrepresented the opinions of the communities and individuals involved. Participatory methods, on the other hand, used tools and techniques that were intended to overcome the above constraints. Issues of reliability were dealt with simply: information should be triangulated or cross-checked using an array of additional participatory methods, such as semi-structured and key informant interviews, focus groups, etc.[1] Equally important to the approach was the new construct of the development worker. Researchers and practitioners were discursively portrayed as direct participants, as opposed to their former role as 'outsiders' imposing their reality on passive recipients. In this manner, actors had a new role as facilitators, sharing experiences and enabling community members to express local needs and knowledge via their own unique narratives (Cornwall and Jewkes, 1995).

Nevertheless, the stress on practitioners' behaviour had both methodological and theoretical implications. Indeed, it may be argued that over the years, a discursive divide built up between the facilitator and the methods. Such a division implied that participatory approaches themselves were neutral, and that the introduction of bias was the domain of the practitioner. Therefore, in response to criticisms of the tools themselves, the distinction between 'good practice' and 'bad practice' arose. In this manner, the participatory literature appeared to acknowledge the presence of *reflexivity* bias (the influence of the researcher practitioner's own subjectivity) (de Munk and Sobo, 1998). Yet, across the PRA literature, very little attention was accorded to the personal characteristics of the researcher/practitioner, which may create the conditions associated with 'bad' or 'good' practice; nor to the specific impact of such conditions on data derived. It was unclear how the 'behaviour' of the practitioner could be measured or assessed, or indeed who set the rules of conduct. The extent to which a practitioner could intervene without imposing his or her subjective reality was never clarified.

This chapter explores the role that the personal characteristics of the practitioner play on the narratives generated in a participatory setting. A single tool is the focus of the analysis: semi-structured interviews (SSI). SSI are a core component of wealth/wellbeing ranking. The approach is often used either to derive the criteria or components of wellbeing (prior to a public forum) or to corroborate the results (following a public forum). In cases where wealth and income have been deemed sensitive subjects, making privacy an issue, SSI have often functioned as the main method of wealth or wellbeing ranking.

Two areas of the interview process are explored: first, the level of interaction between practitioner and participant; and second, the role of specific personality traits on the interview process. A cross-sectional analysis further explored the role of cultural orientation, i.e. 'outsider' vs. 'insider' perspectives, and the role of gender on the narratives produced.

To assess the impact of practitioners' personal characteristics on interview narratives, SSI were carried out among a sample of 30 communities across three countries: Bolivia, Kenya and India. The analysis proceeded on three levels.

First, the frequency of 'non-responses' was evaluated. The issue of non-responses in formal surveys has been discussed at length by authors such as Martin and Beerten (1999) and McCarthy and Beckler (1999). However, few studies have examined the topic in qualitative research. Clearly, during an interview, the enumerator has the power to make decisions, and these decisions could ultimately influence the response rate. The practitioner can, for instance, rephrase the question, add explanations, or give examples that may help the respondent in interpreting the question (Foddy, 1993; Wengraf, 2001). As such, rather than controlling the manner in which the questions were asked, the study explored the overall rate of non-responses as a means of evaluating the communication dynamics between practitioners and clients. Second, to establish biases in question formulation or delivery, responses were analysed for the presence of patterns or themes. Third, to assess whether the personality of the enumerator had an influence on the outcome of an interview, a psychometric test (Appendix 1) was devised to identify practitioner personality predispositions or traits that could potentially influence an individual's performance in an SSI. The analysis also explored whether gender-matching (e.g. male enumerator/male respondent; female enumerator/female respondent) had an influence on the resultant discussions and narrative produced.

Methods

In total, SSI were performed with 258 individuals across three countries: Bolivia, India and Kenya (see Table 7.1).

Table 7.1 Study participants

Country	*State*	*SSI (n)*
Kenya		58
Bolivia		70
India		
	Pondicherry	70
	Tamil Nadu	60

Prior to the analysis, in each country, practitioners were broadly divided by geographic origin, i.e. local vs. non-local. Table 7.2 sets out the composition of the practitioner teams across the three countries.

Table 7.2 The practitioners

Country	*Gender*	*Local (n)*	*Non-local (n)*
Kenya	Men	2	1
	Women	0	3
Bolivia	Men	5	1
	Women	3	3
India	Men	10	1
	Women	7	3
Total		27	12

Data analysis

Frequency of 'non-responses'

The level of non-responses was explored in relation to three open-ended questions regarding the criteria for poverty/wealth (and thereby wealth ranking) in the communities involved:

- What is the difference between rich and poor people in your community?
- Are there differences between the rich and the poor that are not easily noticed?
- What are the reasons for being poor?

Establishing bias in question formulation or delivery

As noted above, to explore bias topics and themes were disaggregated across the responses. Thematic analysis derives from the socio-linguistic method of content analysis (Huckin, 2002), which identifies, codes and categorizes primary patterns in spoken and written language (Patton, 1990; Silverman, 2001). For example, in the following narrative offered by a Bolivian farmer exploring the differences between rich and poor people, four topics were identified:

> The rich people in my community have a car [Topic 1: car] and big land [Topic 2: land]. The ones in the middle have either cattle [Topic 3: livestock] or land [Topic 2: land]. The poor has one or two cows [Topic 3: livestock], does not have land [Topic 4: no land] and works outside the community [Topic 5: type of job].

The topics were subsequently collated into themes. In the above example, topics 1, 2 and 3 were coded under the theme 'assets'. Topic 4 was categorized as 'lack of asset', whereas Topic 5 was coded under 'activities'. The patterns of topics and themes across the interviews were evaluated to detect the dominance of particular topics or themes across the responses derived by an individual practitioner, which could indicate bias.

Influence of practitioner personality

The psychometric test (Appendix 1) was utilized to identify specific personality traits in the practitioner that may influence an individual's reaction to any given situation, in this case an interview. In general, psychologists believe that people can be categorized according to the likelihood of their behaving, feeling or thinking in a particular way (Pervin and John, 1997). Hence, core traits have been identified, known as 'the Big Five', which constitute the basic dimensions of personality: neuroticism (also referred to as emotional stability), extraversion, openness, agreeableness, and conscientiousness (Goldberg, 1990). Three of the traits are considered particularly relevant to the collection of data in the field and to the overall success of an interview: extraversion, openness and agreeableness. Extraversion includes a number of components such as talkativeness, assertiveness, energy and boldness (ibid.), which determine the ability of the person to relate to other people, and to feel at ease in unknown environments. Openness measures the willingness of the person to be exposed to new experiences, and their level of empathy towards the situation of others. Finally, agreeableness measures empathetic concern for others among other factors.,

The test was divided into two parts, each aiming to measure the three traits listed above. The measurement of extraversion and agreeableness or in this case empathy [*E*] was based on seven questions with attributional scores ranging from + 2 to -2. Therefore, the range of possible scores was +14 to -14. Openness [*O*] was measured via four questions and scores ranged from +8 to -8. From the 12 questions, a total additive score [*TS*] was derived. Openness scores were weighted (*w*) in the final total.

$$TS = [E] + w\ [O]$$

Individual test performance was then compared to the quality of the information/narrative derived in the interviews. Responses were rated on three broad criteria: the *quantity, quality* and *appropriateness* of the information on offer. Quantity [Q] was evaluated by summing the number of topics identified across the three questions. Using the totals, interviews were then categorized across a 7-point scale: -3 to +3.

To assess the quality of an interview, three criteria were examined: the depth of information covered; the level of personalization (likes, dislikes, etc.); and finally, how appropriate the responses were to the initial query. Interviews were then accorded a depth [D] and personalization [P] score on a scale of -1 to +3. For example, a score of 1 was given for basic information lacking descriptive detail, whereas a score of 2 was given to responses that included personal details/the opinions of the interviewee. A score of 3 was accorded to richly detailed responses that contextualized the insights offered. The appropriateness of responses [A] was scored as follows: a score of -1 was given when the practitioner failed to obtain a response. No points, or a score of 0, were given when the response was inappropriate. Full points (1) were provided where responses were appropriate.

$$TQ = [Q] + [D + P] + [A]$$

In total, for each practitioner, 25 interviews were chosen at random for further analysis. To lower inter-rater bias, the interviews were scored by a single researcher. In the final portion of the analysis, *TS* and *TQ* scores were compared across the subset of interviews.[2]

Results

Measuring communicative breakdown: the level of non-responses

The following table explores the number of non-responses among the different practitioners, across the total number of responses related to the three questions in Bolivia, India and Kenya (see Table 7.3). As the table demonstrates, responses varied depending on the gender/geographic origin of the practitioner and the gender of the participant.

Table 7.3 Total number of 'non-responses' across target questions by practitioner group[3]

Total responses	*Gender participants*	*Local practitioners (women)*	*Local practitioners (men)*	*Non-local practitioners (women)*	*Non-local practitioners s(men)*	*Total*
Kenya (n=174)	Men		13	4	7	24
	Women		10	7	5	22
Bolivia (n=210)	Men	36	13	9	16	74
	Women	12	8	10	13	43
India (n=390)	Men	21	25	30	31	107
	Women	10	13	22	20	65

In Kenya, non-local practitioners tended to have higher response rates than their local counterparts. In Bolivia, the lowest level of communicative competence was between local women practitioners and male farmers. Here, local and non-local men tended to achieve high response rates from women participants.

In India, local women generally outperformed local men and non-local practitioners. Interestingly, foreign practitioners, who recorded higher levels of communicative competence than locals in Kenya and Bolivia, fared less well in India. Given the non-response rate, more fluid communicative exchanges appeared to occur with women study participants (39%) than their male counterparts (61%).

Key themes

In Kenya, when asked to describe the differences between the rich and the poor, responses were categorized into 15 themes, as listed in Table 7.4.[4]

Although assets and attitudes were the most common themes elicited by both groups of practitioners, major differences were discovered in relation to physical appearance, capabilities, the role of external factors and vices. On first inspection, it appears that non-local practitioners were most frequently informed about the external characteristics of poverty, or those factors 'that were most easily noticed'. Local practitioners, on the other hand, obtained more nuanced information associated with the 'personalization' of poverty, such as factors relating to the capability of the household or 'vices' such as gambling and alcoholism. Yet the vagaries of life, such as bad luck and external events such as droughts and/or raiding, were also raised more frequently with local practitioners. One possible explanation may be that, in the eyes of the interviewee, a non-local practitioner may be considered less knowledgeable about poverty and is therefore given a less detailed explanation. Interestingly, laziness was an attribute more frequently described to non-local practitioners. At least ostensibly, this may be a form of reactivity bias, i.e. if there were a possibility of future aid, the respondent might have identified themselves as part of the 'deserving' poor (see Misturelli and Heffernan, 2009; 2010).

Table 7.4 Kenya: Themes by practitioner

Themes	*Local practitioner*	*Non-local practitioner*
Assets	24%	27%
Attitudes	9%	20%
Luck	7%	2%
Behaviour	2%	6%
Capabilities	16%	1%
External conditions	10%	2%
Physical appearance	3%	11%
Power	2%	1%
Vices	10%	3%
Activities	4%	9%
Education	1%	5%
Age/disability	0%	3%
Family composition	0%	3%
Appearance of livestock	1%	1%
Laziness	3%	9%

Interestingly, the information yielded when local terms were used to define poverty was not as rich as when these terms were not employed. This finding was particularly surprising given that one of the recommendations when doing field research in developing countries is to use local terms as much as possible, in order to achieve the same referential meaning (Bulmer and Warwick, 1983; Devereux and Hoddinot, 1992). Indeed, identifying local terms for wealth and poverty is a core part of wealth and, latterly, wellbeing ranking. However, there is always a degree of unperceived discrepancy between the referents (Wengraf, 2001). In other words, the meaning of a local term may not be entirely accurate once translated. One such example of differing referential values was identified among the interviews collected in Kajiado, Kenya, among Maasai pastoralists.

One of the practitioners in Kenya, an anthropologist, obtained from key informants the Maasai words for 'poor' and 'rich' and descriptions of what the terms entailed. Three main classes were listed: the *orkasis* (the rich), who were defined as people who owned either land and/or livestock and had many daughters; the *ilkirikoi*, former pastoralists, who became poor through mismanagement of their herds; and the *oleisenani*, people who never owned livestock, e.g. orphans and the disabled. As data collection progressed, the definitions of the terms became more specific, as demonstrated by the following examples:

> *Orkasis* [the rich] with many sons or daughters, because of the dowry and you have more relatives. *Oleisenani* [the poor] not many children, the family was poor, they don't have livestock.
> The rich [*orkasis*] must have more than 50 cows.
> The number of cattle: the rich have more than 50 cows.

When the responses were averaged, practitioners who did not use local terms for poverty obtained almost three times more indicators (n=11) than the practitioner who did (n=4). The responses suggest that the use of the local terms may have unintentionally restricted the range of criteria by which the poor and the rich were identified, as illustrated by the following examples:

> [The difference between the rich and the poor] is in his clothes, personal health and the appearance of his livestock.
> The appearance and number of livestock, the appearance of the *boma* ([translation of boma]), or homestead], the number of wives and children, and also the number of children in school.
> Poor people sit at the back of meetings and leave early as they are hungry.

The data appear to suggest that the semantic meaning of local terms may encompass more than one conceptualization of the rich and poor. The original meaning of the terms focused on the number of livestock and sons, the traditional forms of wealth for the Maasai (Talle, 1988). However, as Maasai society is currently undergoing rapid social change, it seems that the terms *orkasis* and *oleisenani* have not similarly expanded their semantic meaning. In the context of the research, the practitioner obtained the traditional explanations of the terms; while using the words during his interviews, he inadvertently restricted responses to this historical context. Thus, the responses that he obtained reflected only part of the reality, and as such offered an inaccurate description of local perceptions and conceptions of poverty. Language is dynamic and the nuances of local terms and conceptions may be missed when applied by outsiders.

In Bolivia, as in Kenya, the practitioners were divided into 'local' and 'non-local' and the dominant themes in the responses identified. Table 7.5 explores the variation in the themes mentioned in response to the question regarding the differences between the rich and the poor.

As the table demonstrates, the themes with the largest differences between the local and non-local practitioners were 'assets', 'attitudes' and 'behaviour'. Unlike in Kenya, where local practitioners obtained a more nuanced view of poverty, in Bolivia the reverse was true. The attitudes and behaviours of the poor tended to be stressed to non-local practitioners. Therefore, in Bolivia, the attribution or blame for poverty was clearly depicted to outsiders as being the responsibility of the individual involved. For local practitioners, the economic criteria of poverty, such as those related to assets, livelihood activities, poor agricultural land, or being born into a poor family, represented

Table 7.5 Bolivia: Themes by practitioner.[5]

Themes	*Local practitioner*	*Non-local practitioner*
Assets	41%	21%
Attitudes/behaviour	22%	38%
Activities	6%	1%
Capabilities	13%	14%
Lack of work	1%	2%
External constraints	3%	3%
Old age/disability	1%	0%
Physical characteristics	1%	5%
Productivity	4%	3%
Born poor	4%	2%
Education	1%	2%
Powerless	0%	1%
Laziness	1%	2%
Vices	1%	1%
Cooperation	0%	2%
Others	3%	6%

the bulk of responses. As in Kenya, one potential explanation is that the findings may simply be a form of reactivity bias. Aid in Bolivia is frequently delivered via non-governmental organizations, and communities may have viewed local practitioners as future providers of aid, stressing those signs of poverty that were easiest to address accordingly.

When responses were divided by practitioner (three social scientists, an agricultural scientist, and three practitioners with no formal academic discipline), two main differences were noted. First, the number of themes elicited varied widely across the group. Second, large differences in the thematic patterns emerged, particularly with regard to the theme 'assets'. For example, for two of the non-local enumerators, 'assets' was the most frequent theme mentioned (26% and 21%). Conversely, for the third practitioner, who had a degree in psychology, 'assets' were mentioned in only 6% of instances, whereas 'attitudes' dominated responses.

The analysis of the response pattern and the identification of topics in Bolivia highlighted major differences between local and non-local practitioners. First, the topics reported by local practitioners tended to relate to agriculture. Particularly with reference to the reasons for being poor, the local agriculturist obtained a number of responses that outlined how crop production was poor because of lack of rain or poor-quality inputs such as fertilizer. The overall distribution of topics among local practitioners revealed a strong tendency to report land and livestock as indicators of wealth. The non-locals, on the other hand, recorded a wider variety of criteria, such as material possessions and/or the external appearance of a family's house. Table 7.6 illustrates the topics recorded by practitioners with regard to the theme 'assets' and the frequency with which they were mentioned.

The choice of indicators reflects the agricultural production system, because the major livelihood activities are related to agriculture and livestock. However, the fact that the local practitioners emphasized agriculture-related topics portrays a bias towards those indicators. Similarly, the thematic pattern detailed above (see Table 7.5) suggests that the 'outsiders' also tended to receive responses that matched their own background or interest. The high

Table 7.6 Bolivia: Topics identified for the theme 'assets', by practitioner

Topics	*Social scientist I*	*Social scientist II*	*Social scientist III*	*Local agriculturist*	*Local I*	*Local II*	*Local III*
Land	6	4	0	18	16	11	11
Livestock	16	4	0	18	6	10	6
Material possessions	14	10	2	8	3	3	3
Irrigation	0	0	0	1	–	–	1
Appearance of house	4	0	0	0	–	–	1

percentage of 'attitudes' and 'behaviour' themes reported by the social scientists, compared to the local enumerators, suggests that the responses they received were equally biased.

Table 7.7 explores the differences in the themes for the question regarding the differences between the rich and poor in India among a subsample of 60 study participants from Tamil Nadu State.

As in Bolivia, the theme 'assets' featured highly across responses, particularly among the local team, whereas 'attitudes and behaviour' were criteria largely derived by the non-local practitioners.

Table 7.7 India: themes by practitioner

Themes	*Local practitioners*	*Non-local practitioners*
Assets	39%	29%
Activities	13%	9%
Attitudes/behaviour	6%	17%
Born poor	4%	4%
Capabilities	7%	9%
Education	2%	3%
Unemployment	0%	5%
External situation	8%	5%
Low income	2%	2%
Physical appearance	7%	12%
Vices	1%	3%
Other[6]	11%	2%

When the pattern of topics obtained by individual practitioners was investigated, large differences emerged (see Table 7.8), suggesting that some

Table 7.8 India: topics identified for the theme 'assets', by practitioner

Topics	*Local Vet I*	*Local Vet II*	*Local Vet III*	*Non-local Vet*	*Non-local Social Scientist*	*Non-local Animal Scientist*
Land	7	5	7	9	3	14
Appearance of house	1	3	4	–	–	3
Livestock	–	3	2	2	1	–
Irrigation	–	2	1	2	1	–
Income	–	–	2		–	–
Material possessions	1	2	1	14	7	11
Money	–	–	–	4	2	6

practitioners had a preconceived idea of what poverty was or should be, or that responses were guided. The local team in Tamil Nadu comprised recently graduated veterinarians, while the non-local group included a veterinarian with an additional background in the social sciences, a social scientist, and an animal scientist.

Land was, overwhelmingly, one of the most important indicators of poverty, followed by material possessions.[7] However, while the non-local responses tended to emphasize material possessions such as clothing, jewellery and cars as poverty differentials, the local group tended to obtain responses that focused on external appearance and land ownership, as the following responses illustrate (Local Vet I):

> Who has land is rich. The casual labourers are poor. (Mr Chandra Kuppan, Sivanathapuram, Tamil Nadu)
> The rich are landlords, they have a house made of concrete. Poor are landless and casual labourers. (Mr Arjun Kumar, Sivanathapuram, Tamil Nadu)

Although other indicators were sometimes included, the majority of responses obtained by Vet I were focused around land ownership. This finding suggests practitioner bias. To further evaluate the impact of the practitioners' discipline on the data, additional analysis was performed on the interviews conducted in the Indian states of Tamil Nadu and Pondicherry, where the local research team was composed of newly graduated veterinarians.

Practitioner bias: Veterinarians vs. non-veterinarians in India

The exploration of practitioner bias focused on the part of the interview during which the veterinarians were likely to feel most comfortable: animal health. Households were asked to describe and discuss those livestock diseases that were most problematic (with regard to frequency or severity) for their herd.

Subsequent analysis compared the lists of diseases obtained by the veterinarians and non-veterinarians. Surprisingly, across both states, the number of diseases listed by the veterinarians was consistently lower than the number obtained by non-veterinarians. For example, in Pondicherry the veterinarians listed 13 diseases, as opposed to 30 listed by the enumerators of other disciplines. Similarly in Tamil Nadu, the veterinarians listed 17 diseases, whereas the non-veterinarians listed 31. Furthermore, large differences were noted in disease reporting even among the veterinarians, as detailed in Table 7.9.

As the table demonstrates, there is a recognizable trend in the identification of the diseases, which raises questions regarding the influence of practitioners on responses. It is not only the number of times a certain disease has been reported by the practitioner that is relevant, but also the differences in the types of disease reported. For example, one of the veterinarians in Pondicherry reported 'indigestion' as a problematic disease in 19 separate instances. As the disease was not reported by her colleagues, the finding suggests the practitioner had a heavy influence on responses.

Table 7.9 Variation in disease reporting, by veterinarian

Livestock disease	*Vet I (Tamil Nadu)*	*Vet II (Tamil Nadu)*	*Vet III (Tamil Nadu)*	*Vet IV (Pondicherry)*	*Vet V (Pondicherry)*
Foot and Mouth Disease (FMD)	5	1	6	31	9
Fever	–	1	5	37	9
Haemorrhagic Septicaemia (HS)	4	–	1	5	2
Pox	–	1	–	–	1
Diarrhoea	1	2	3	10	7
Ticks	–	–	–	1	2
'Indigestion'	–	–	–	19	–
Lack of appetite/ anorexia	–	–	2	8	–
Dystocia	–	1	–	2	–
Bloat	–	–	2	2	–
Infertility	–	–		1	–
Mastitis	1	–	2	1	–
Wounds	–	–	1	1	–
Anthrax	2	–	–	–	–

However, the background of the practitioner is only one element that could impact the quality of participatory narratives. The next step is to examine whether personality characteristics play a role in generating participatory dialogues.

Personality traits and participatory narratives

To explore whether specific personality traits influenced the communicative exchange, a personality test was administered to a subset of local and non-local practitioners involved in the study. As noted above, the objective of the test was to measure the interviewer's extraversion, coping response, agreeableness and openness, and to evaluate the impact these traits had (if any) on the narratives generated. Three factors were considered. The incidence of non-responses was compared to the degree of extraversion and coping response that each enumerator displayed. As extraverts enjoy interaction with people (Pervin and John, 1997), it was predicted that practitioners with a higher degree of extraversion would encounter fewer non-responses or communicative breakdowns during the interview. Meanwhile, an assessment of coping response would reveal the practitioner's ability to adjust to what might be perceived as difficult conditions in the field. A low score in coping response would suggest a relative inability to deal with uncooperative informants, or unfamiliar/ uncomfortable situations. In these cases, the expectation was that the quality of the interview would be lower, with a higher frequency of non-responses.

Responses to questions that were considered particularly sensitive, such as those regarding income, social structure and social relationships, were assessed, by measuring practitioners' scores in relation to openness and agreeableness or in this case empathy. Sensitive questions generally require greater effort on the part of the practitioner to relate to participants on a more personal level, a characteristic which is believed to be stronger among empathetic personalities. A higher degree of openness tends to correlate with curiosity and broad interests/understanding. Therefore, if a practitioner scored highly on openness it was assumed this would facilitate their handling of sensitive questions.

As Table 7.10 demonstrates, across the sample, the extraversion trait displayed a high degree of variability (8 to -5). In comparison, coping response and openness presented lower variability (5 to -3). Empathy had the narrowest range of responses (1 to -1). According to the hypothesis outlined above, a practitioner who obtains a low or negative final score is likely to have weaker communication skills, and this should result in poorer quality interviews. On the contrary, enumerators with a high score should find it easier to interact/engage with study participants, and conduct better quality interviews. Table 7.11 displays the result of the comparison between the percentage of non-responses and the personality traits of practitioners.

As the table demonstrates, there was no clear association between the incidence of non-responses and the total personality score. For example, in Kenya, while Practitioner 5 fitted the theory, with a low personality score and a high percentage of non-response, in India practitioners with even lower total scores had very low levels of non-responses. Individual personality traits also appeared to have a mixed impact on the non-response rate. For example, extraversion seemed to influence the ability to obtain a response in some cases, but not in others. Similarly, a high score with regard to coping or empathy did not appear to significantly impact the non-response rate. The results suggest that additional factors may be at play.

Table 7.10 Results of personality test

Practitioner	*Extraversion*	*Coping response*	*Openness*	*Empathy*	*Total*
Kenya	–	–	–	–	–
Practitioner 1	8	5	4	1	18
Practitioner 2	7	6	–1	1	13
Practitioner 3	7	2	3	1	13
Practitioner 4	7	–3	5	–1	8
Practitioner 5	3	–1	1	2	5
India	–	–	–	–	–
Practitioner 6	1	–3	–3	–1	–6
Practitioner 7	7	3	–2	2	10
Practitioner 8	–5	4	–3	1	–3

Table 7.11 Personality traits vs. non-responses

	% Non-response	*Extraversion*	*Coping-response*	*Openness*	*Empathy*	*Total*
Practitioner 5	10%	3	−1	1	2	5
Practitioner 4	4%	7	−3	5	−1	8
Practitioner 2	3%	7	6	−1	1	13
Practitioner 1	2%	8	5	4	1	18
Practitioner 6	2%	1	−3	−3	−1	-6
Practitioner 8	2%	−5	4	−3	1	-3
Practitioner 3	0%	7	2	3	1	13
Practitioner 7	0%	7	3	−2	2	10

To further explore the relationship between SSI narratives and the personality of the practitioner, the relationship between the level of openness and the quality of the responses was analysed. The hypothesis was that the degree of enumerator openness and empathy would influence the frequency with which more 'sensitive' themes were addressed. The analysis therefore focused on the discussions generated by question 1: 'What are the differences between rich and poor people?' The responses were analysed to establish how frequently respondents mentioned the theme 'vices'. This theme was chosen as it tended to display the personalization of poverty for the individuals involved. References to vices generally described family or household members with problems such as alcohol, gambling or drug addiction. Figure 7.1 compares the frequency of the theme with practitioners' openness score.

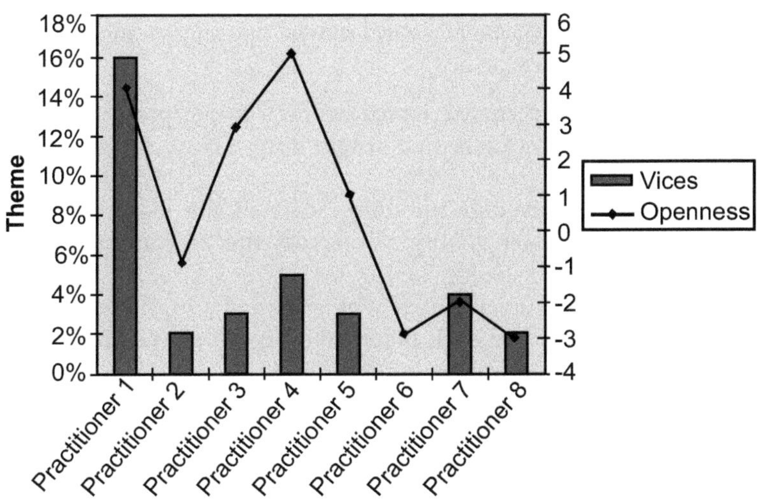

Figure 7.1 'Vices' vs. practitioner 'openness'

As the figure illustrates, the incidence of the theme 'vices' and the openness trait broadly followed the same trend. Practitioners with a low openness score tended to receive fewer responses related to this theme. Openness proved to be similarly relevant in other sections of the interviews. Practitioners who displayed a higher degree of openness tended to conduct a more uniform interview, whereas enumerators with a lower openness score performed better in those sections of the interview that matched their own interests, or those that required fewer interpersonal skills. Thus, the findings suggest that the personality traits of the practitioner may broadly influence the information obtained, particularly in relation to sensitive topics.

Finally, the narratives of the interviews were examined. Personal information that expressed the feelings or expectation of the informant was considered to be a factor that added value to the interview and enriched the narrative. For example, when asked about the causes of poverty in Kariobangi, an urban area in Nairobi, a widow offered the following:

> Land grabbing is a problem... if you are poor you are cheated by the rich. The rich person takes the land and offers to build you a house somewhere else. Then he tells you to pay the expenses, which is a lot of money that you can't afford. Next, you go to court and the rich '[person]' pays you a little money and you are left in poverty. (Margaret Mutoni, Kariobangi, Kenya)

Joseph Kimbwuisi, also in Kariobangi, explained his aspirations for the future:

> I want to start another project alongside this one with the chickens. I want to start a recycling garbage business to make fertilizer. You tie the cabbages in a plastic bag and after 15 days it has become manure, and you can sell it. I want to ask the chief of the area, and maybe he can give me a small plot where I can keep the bags.

In both examples, participants were sharing their hopes/problems with the facilitator, as well as offering additional insight into wider social and economic issues.

Table 7.12 offers the average interview score of the eight practitioners who participated in the personality test across the 25 randomly selected interviews.

As the table illustrates, practitioners who obtained a high overall score in the personality test tended to elicit better narratives than facilitators whose final personality score was lower or negative.

However, two exceptions were noted. First, Practitioner 5, whose personality score was not particularly high at 5, yet elicited narratives that offered a unique insight on the life and values of study participants, as the example below illustrates. Significantly, this practitioner had the highest score in empathy (2).

Table 7.12 Quality vs. personality total score

	Mean quality score [TQ]	*Personality score [TS]*
Practitioner 1 (n=25)	4.2	18
Practitioner 2 (n=25)	3.9	13
Practitioner 3 (n=25)	4.4	13
Practitioner 4 (n=25)	3.2	8
Practitioner 5 (n=25)	4.8	5
Practitioner 6 (n=15)	2.9	–6
Practitioner 7 (n=25)	2.3	10
Practitioner 8 (n=25)	3.0	–3

> I was married, but now I am divorced and I live alone. My children died in 1963 and my wife blamed me for that, she said I am not good and she left. Only one son survived and he is living with me... I came to Kiamaiko in 1953 and I left in 1960 for three years. But my sons got ill, all five died. After burying one, I went home and the other was sick and so on. I don't think it was poisoning, I think it was witchcraft... Now my wife comes to visit the son, but she cannot come to see me...During the emergency time, we were allowed to have 15 goats, but we had to mark them, otherwise the authorities would have taken them away... (Josephat Ndirangu, Kariobangi, Nairobi)

Conversely, Practitioner 7 attained a high personality score (10), but a low grade in the overall quality of the interviews (2.3). Indeed, although the practitioner managed to answer the majority of the questions appropriately, the narratives were lacking in detail and tended to be generic and neutral in nature, as in the following example:

> A rich person is well dressed, has jewels, a big house, many cows and land. A poor person has a shabby appearance, and work in the land of the rich. Rich people do not respect the poor, because of caste and appearance. (Indra, Pondicherry, India)

It appears clear that the practitioner did not explore areas of potential interest, such as the influence that caste had on the behaviour of the rich, losing any insight into local social divisions and the individual's perspective on such matters.

While the test demonstrated the importance of specific personality traits in achieving good interviews, it appears that those traits alone are not sufficient to explain the differences in practitioners' performance. For example, with regard to the percentage of non-responses, it was evident that the personality traits explored were not the only factors influencing the results. More revealing was the analysis of the different personality traits in relation to the type of information obtained. Openness, in particular, appeared to be a key trait capable of influencing the exploration of sensitive topics.

Discussion

The outcome of the analysis of non-responses raised a number of interesting issues. The results largely challenged the 'outsider' vs. 'insider' dynamic that so often dominated early participation discourse (see Chambers, 1983; 1997). It was also clear that the question itself really mattered to communicative competence. Not surprisingly, the topics respondents were less keen to discuss varied from country to country. In Bolivia and India, the percentage of non-responses was higher when identifying the less visible features or descriptors of poverty; whereas in Kenya study participants found it equally difficult to discuss the root causes of poverty. The variations may be because of dissimilar cultural perceptions of poverty. Or the responses may simply reflect differing notions of what is considered conversationally acceptable with 'outsiders', both local and non-local.

The identification of the thematic patterns in responses also proved to be a useful tool in highlighting the influence of practitioners on participant responses. Across the three countries, these patterns seemed to suggest that the educational background of the practitioner influenced the outcome of the responses, although the finding was not universal. For example, in Kenya, the practitioner with the least formal education provided exceptionally detailed narratives, whereas in Bolivia, local practitioners found it difficult to elicit detailed narratives regardless of their educational background. In India, the local practitioners offered good insight into the lives of the informants, but their responses often appeared to be 'limited' by their preconceptions, particularly when the questions focused on their specific area of expertise, as in the part of the interview regarding livestock disease. The findings have clear implications for wealth ranking, in that the practitioner can be just as important as the community in prioritizing poverty indicators. Clearly both local and non-local practitioners brought different strengths and biases to the process, and these varied from country to country.

On a broader level, it may be argued that the two groups of practitioners brought different forms of bias to the interview process: 'expertise' bias and 'exposure' bias. For the non-local practitioners, their area of expertise tended to heavily influence responses; for example, the psychologist detailing attitudes and the anthropologist focusing on traditional but less relevant conceptions of poverty. Local practitioners often had preconceived notions regarding the problems and issues of the poor, which may have coloured responses. Thus 'expertise bias' may be defined as an influence on responses that directly relates to a practitioner's field of expertise. 'Exposure bias', on the other hand, may be defined as an influence on responses that relates to perceptions and understandings gleaned from previous, as opposed to present, exposure to a community.

Finally, while the test demonstrated the importance of specific personality traits in conducting good interviews, it appeared that those traits alone are not sufficient to explain the differences in practitioners' performances. For example, with regard to non-responses, it was evident that the personality traits explored were not the only factors influencing the results. More revealing was the analysis of the different personality traits in relation to the type of the information obtained. Openness, in particular, appeared to be a key trait with regard to the exploration of sensitive topics.

Conclusions

Participatory methods are valid and flexible tools that offer significant insight into the perceptions and realities of the poor. Wellbeing ranking is no exception. However, the process of conducting wellbeing ranking and SSIs, which underpin many exercises, involves complex negotiation and mediation among the many individuals involved. The product of most interviews is a narrative, the interpretation of which is delegated to outsiders. The quality of this narrative, and its associated usefulness, is what ultimately matters in underpinning effective pro-poor praxis. The starting point of this study was to challenge the component parts of wellbeing ranking with the overall goal of deconstructing both process and outcome. With the resurgence of interest in participatory methods, the aim is to support a more critical awareness of the role and impact that a practitioner's particular qualities play in the narratives they derive in this way.

To avoid 'expertise' or 'exposure' bias, there is an urgent need for facilitators and practitioners to be trained in methods and techniques to lower their personal influence on both the process and outcome of participation. As such, better interpersonal and negotiation skills are required. On a broader level, it is time to shift our paradigms of research and development away from the promotion of multidisciplinary teams. Indeed, to alleviate practitioner bias, the focus should now be on creating cadres of multiskilled practitioners with widely varying backgrounds, cultures and interests. In a team of multiskilled practitioners, each individual will lend fewer biases to the overall process of participation, leading to a more nuanced and balanced outcome. That said, it is clear that some forms of personal influence are not negative, and that a 'good' SSI is one that involves an equal exchange of information between individuals. Indeed, practitioners with higher scores for extraversion and openness generally performed better, demonstrating that the personal characteristics of the practitioner cannot be ignored. While quantitative research has historic tried to remove the practitioner's influence, participatory methods have embraced it. This should not be interpreted as negative per se; however, it is clear that without concerted efforts, the unequal power dynamics of facilitator: group, or facilitator: individual, interaction will continue to allow practitioner bias to flourish.

Notes

1. One of the obvious difficulties of triangulating information using different participatory techniques is that the methods deliver information in a variety

of forms and are derived in differing contexts. As Mason (1996) suggested, the use of different methods and data sources are likely to clarify different phenomena, rather than confirm a specific finding.

2. 'Inter-rater' in this context simply refers to the interviews being scored (rated) by more than one person.
3. *n* represents the total number of interviews per country, multiplied by the three questions, to obtain the total number of responses that could be achieved.
4. Where the theme of 'assets' included reference to land, livestock, vehicles, tractors, etc. Personal and physical characteristics included comments on the external appearance of the person such as being badly dressed, thin etc. Meanwhile, 'attitudes' included such attributes as being happy, working hard, being proud/arrogant, etc. The theme 'capabilities' included all of the things that rich people could obtain easily and that the poor could not, such as educating a child or having a secure livelihood. Additional themes included behaviour, luck, external situations (such as drought, poor prices for livestock, etc.) vices (mainly alcoholism and gambling), and power.
5. The theme 'powerless' referred to the lack of power that the poor perceived. For example, sentences such as 'the poor does not count' and 'poor are always below the rich' were coded under the theme 'powerless'. The theme 'productivity' referred to scarcity of harvest and agricultural products. 'Cooperation' takes in all the topics that allude to the relations between rich and poor and within the two social groups. For example, 'the poor help the children of the poor, the rich don't want to help other people'. Finally, the theme 'other' comprised concepts such as 'lifestyle', 'knowledge', and 'charity'.
6. Themes that were mentioned less frequently, such as 'forward planning', 'God's will', and 'laziness', 'place of living' and 'no help', were grouped under 'other'. Examples include: 'The rich think a lot about the future and plan for the future. Poor person cannot think about the future, because his daily income is not sufficient for daily needs', and 'God only decides who is poor'.
7. The topic 'material possession' included indicators such as cars and bicycles, TVs, refrigerators, etc.

References

Ali, R., Olden, K. and Xu, S. (2008) 'Community-based participatory research: a vehicle to promote public engagement for environmental health in China', *Environmental Health Perspectives* 116 (10): 1281–1284.

Balansky, E., Cutforth, N., Chavez, R., Waters, E. and Bartlett-Horch, K. (2011) 'An adapted version of intervention mapping (AIM) is a tool for conducting community based participatory research', *Health Promotion Practice* 12(3): 440–455.

Beyer, K. and Comstock, S. (2010) 'Disease maps as context for community mapping: a methodological approach for linking confidential health information with local geographical knowledge for community health research', *Journal of Community Health* 35 (6): 635–644.

Bulmer, M and Warwick, D. (eds) (1983) *Social Research in Developing Countries: Surveys and Censuses in the Third World*, Chichester: Wiley.

Casley, D. and Lury, D. (1981) *Data Collection in Developing Countries*, Oxford: Clarendon Press.

Catalani, C. and Minkler, M. (2010) 'Photovoice: a review of the literature in health and public health', *Health Education & Behaviour* 37(3): 424–451.

Chambers, R. (1983) *Rural Development: Putting the last first*, London: Longman.

Chambers, R. (1992) *Rural Appraisal: Rapid, Relaxed and Participatory*, Discussion Paper 311, Brighton: Institute of Development Studies.

Chambers, R. (1997) *Whose Reality Counts: Putting the first last*. Rugby: Practical Action.

Cornwall, A. and Jewkes, R. (1995) 'What is Participatory Research?', *Social Science and Medicine* 2 (41): 1667–1676.

De Munk, V. and Sobo, E. (eds) (1998) *Using Methods in the Field: A practical introduction and casebook*, Walnut Creek, CA: Altamira Press.

Devereux, S. and Hoddinott, J. (eds) (1992) *Fieldwork in Developing Countries*, Hemel Hempstead, London: Harvester Wheatsheaf.

Foddy, W. (1993) *Constructing Questions for Interviews and Questionnaires: Theory and Practice in Social Research*, Cambridge: Cambridge University Press.

Goldberg, L. (1990) 'An alternative description of personality: the big-five factor structure', *Journal of Personality and Social Psychology* 59: 1216–1229.

Grandin, B. (1988) *Wealth Ranking in Smallholder Aommunities: A Field Manual*, Rugby: Practical Action.

Huckin, T. (2002) 'Textual silence and the discourse of homelessness', 13 (3): 347–372.

Martin, J. and Beerten, R. (1999) 'The effect of interviewer characteristics on surveys response rates', University of Maryland Joint Program in Survey Methodology [website] [accessed 29 April 2014]

Mason, J. (1996) *Qualitative Research*, London: Sage Publications.

McCarthy, J. and Beckler, D. (1999) 'An analysis of the relationship between survey burden and non-response: If we bother them more, are they less co-operative?', University of Maryland Joint Program in Survey Methodology [website], <www.jpsm.umd.edu> [accessed 29 April 2014]

Macauley, A., Jagosh, J., Seller, R., Henderson, J., Cargo, M., Greenhalgh, T., Wong, G., Salsberg, J., Green, L., Herbert, C. and Pluve, P. (2011) 'Assessing the benefits of participatory research: a rationale for a realist review', *Global Health Promotion* 18 (2): 45–48.

Misturelli, F. and Heffernan, C. (2009) The Language of Poverty: An exploration of the narratives of the poor. *Sustainable Development* 17, DOI: 10.1002/sd.437

Misturelli, F. and Heffernan, C. (2010) The concept of poverty: a synchronic perspective. *Progress in Development Studies*, 10 (1): 35–58.

Mukherjee, N. (1993) *Participatory Rural Appraisal: Methodology and Applications*, New Delhi: Concept Publishing Company.

Nelson, N. and Wright, S. (eds) (1995) *Power and Participatory Development*, Rugby: Practical Action.

Patton, M. (1990) *Qualitative Evaluation and Research Methods*, London: Sage Publications.

Pervin, L. and John, O. (1997) *Personality: Theory and Research* (7th edition), New York, NY: John Wiley & Sons.
Silverman, D. (2001) *Interpreting Qualitative Data: Methods for Analysing Talk, Text and Interaction*, London: Sage Publications.
Talle, A. (1988) *Women at a Loss: Changes in Maasai Pastoralism and the Effects on Gender Relations*, Stockholm: Stockholm Studies in Social Anthropology.
Wengraf, T. (2001) *Qualitative Research Interviewing*, London: Sage Publications.

About the authors

Claire Heffernan is the Director of the Livestock Development Group (LDG), School of Agriculture, Policy and Development, University of Reading. She is a veterinarian by training with a background in the social sciences. She initiated the LDG in 2000 in response to the need for a multidisciplinary approach to global poverty and food security praxis.

Federica Misturelli is a linguist by training with a background in cultural anthropology. Her research interests include critical discourse analysis and other methodological approaches regarding both the perceptions and treatment of poverty across a range of actors from decision-makers to the poor themselves.

CHAPTER 8

Wellbeing assessment in practice: lessons from wellbeing and poverty pathways

Nina Marshall, Sarah C. White, Stanley O. Gaines Jr., Shreya Jha

The concept of wellbeing is gaining prominence in contemporary development policy and practice. However, there is a need for robust measures that clearly, effectively and rigorously enable wellbeing assessment and demonstrate its 'value added' to international development. This chapter presents lessons from Wellbeing and Poverty Pathways, a project developing, validating and applying a model of wellbeing through research in marginalized rural communities in India and Zambia.

Our experiences demonstrate the complexity and tensions that arise in balancing the requirements for statistical measurement and quantification, and the often complex process of assessing wellbeing. This chapter details how we have successfully developed and validated a multi-domain model of wellbeing that is both grounded in theory and adapted and contextualized for use in developing country contexts. What this experience demonstrates is the importance of critical, reflective and flexible attention in the process of developing, administering and interpreting wellbeing assessment tools and the results they generate.

Keywords: wellbeing, well-being, ranking, poverty, policy, practice, happiness

The concept of wellbeing has recently captured the attention of policymakers and practitioners around the world. It is linked in a number of ways to the longstanding trend in international development towards a more 'people-centred' approach, aimed at broadening both development's vision and the range of voices heard. While wellbeing is understood in diverse ways, two general areas of agreement suggest it may open up different ways of both thinking about what matters, and assessing policy outcomes and impact. First, wellbeing encourages a positive emphasis on people's strengths and aspirations, rather than deficits and deficiencies. Second, wellbeing extends the measurement of human welfare beyond objective measures to include some subjective assessment of quality of life. From United Nations (UN) resolutions on the centrality of the pursuit of happiness (UN, 2011) and an OECD World Forum centred on wellbeing (2012), to the incorporation of wellbeing in development interventions and evaluations at the community and local levels,

http://dx.doi.org/10.3362/9781780448459.008

the concept is gaining prominence in contemporary development policy and practice.

However, beyond opening up this space for different reflections and conversations about policy and practice, the critical challenge facing wellbeing is to demonstrate its practical utility to development policy and practice. Demands for high-quality evidence within international development have increased greatly in recent years. Applied to wellbeing, such demands call for robust measures that clearly, effectively and rigorously enable its assessment in development contexts and evaluate the 'value added' it brings. In other words, we must ask how we can assess wellbeing in ways that meet the standards required within development circles, and what, if anything, this adds to existing development indices. Wellbeing may be an appealing concept, but does it make sense on the ground in developing country contexts, and how useful is it?

These questions lie at the heart of ongoing research by Wellbeing and Poverty Pathways, an international research partnership based at the University of Bath. We are working in marginalized rural communities in India and Zambia to test a theory-driven model of wellbeing in developing country contexts. We are doing this by developing a wellbeing survey and using this to generate data about the relationships between poverty and wellbeing. In the process, lessons have emerged; these have helped in refining our own wellbeing survey, but have also highlighted important general issues in developing ways of asking about wellbeing with a view to meeting the standards required of rigorous assessment processes within development.

The chapter begins by outlining our model of wellbeing and how we have developed a survey designed to translate that model into a tool for wellbeing assessment. It then describes and discusses issues that arose in our first round of fieldwork in Zambia, which in combination meant that we were unable to run the statistical tests necessary to validate our model. Subsequent reflection and adaptation have since enabled us to run these tests successfully. We finish by highlighting lessons from both this process and the general project experience to date, relating to the significance of the form, content and context of wellbeing assessment measures.

The wellbeing pathways model of wellbeing

The Wellbeing and Poverty Pathways project aims to develop and test a model of wellbeing that is grounded in the South, and is thus closer to the ways that people there think, talk, feel, and act than the dominant models that have been developed by psychologists in the West. We are using this model to explore the relationships between poverty and wellbeing in marginalized rural communities. Running from 2010 to 2013, fieldwork in India (Chhattisgarh) and Zambia (Chiawa) gathered both quantitative and qualitative evidence from around 350 respondents in each location over two rounds of data collection.[1]

In designing this research, a number of difficult questions have emerged from our desire to be responsive to Southern realities, while appreciating the value of work done on wellbeing to date in other contexts and its importance in shaping our thinking. We aim to produce a model that is both responsive to context and enables comparison across contexts. This aspect of comparison is important, given our concern with testing the practical utility of wellbeing assessment for development policy and practice, and meeting the associated requirements. We have therefore chosen to draw on insights from other research and traditions explicitly, while remaining aware of our position in relation to this and the biases it may bring with it. Two aspects of our research stem from this, each bringing their own tensions and risks. First, the model of wellbeing we have developed and are testing is theory-driven, rather than derived solely from the contexts in which we have been working. This is not to say that localization does not play an important part in our research, as discussed extensively below. However, going in with a theory-driven model that draws on concepts considered to be important to wellbeing, and then localizing and testing that model in different contexts, allows us to assess how useful this form of wellbeing assessment could be to development policy and practice in general. Conversely, there is the possibility that the research may fail, and that the theoretically derived model will not hold up when applied in context.

Second, we are testing this model through a wellbeing survey specifically designed to meet the demands for rigorous data generation and analysis that are central to development policy and practice. We want to go beyond a simple description of people's lives, so as to be able to say something about wellbeing assessment and its potential that meets the requirement for statistical rigour. But we recognize that in doing so there is a risk that we could lose sight of the priorities of people in our research communities, and that quantitative concerns could overwhelm qualitative insights. As a project, we are specifically interested in how quantitative and qualitative methods and perspectives can work in combination, and indeed reinforce each other; nevertheless, tensions within this framework are an important consideration.

How have we gone about developing our model and a process for its statistical assessment? We started with a basic definition: 'Wellbeing is experienced when people have what they need for life to be good.' The subjective perspective therefore occupies a central position, as this definition links together people's experience with the needs they identify and the resources they can summon to meet those needs. Individual and family wellbeing are also critically underpinned by the external context in which people are living.

From this starting point, we have developed a model of wellbeing which identifies seven closely interacting domains, located in a broader environment that can enable or constrain wellbeing (see Figure 8.1). This builds on and is influenced by two previous pieces of research. The Wellbeing in Developing Countries Research Group (WeD), based at the University of Bath, identified the *material* (what people have or do not have), the *relational* (what people do or cannot do with it), and the *subjective* (what people think or feel) as

Figure 8.1 The Wellbeing Pathways domains of wellbeing

three interlinked dimensions of wellbeing (see Gough and McGregor, 2007; White, 2010). The Colombo-based Psychosocial Assessment of Development and Humanitarian Intervention (PADHI) introduced a political dimension to wellbeing by highlighting the difference between what constitutes wellbeing (positive achievement in five interconnected domains), what mediates wellbeing (power, influence, identity), and what enables wellbeing (systems and institutions in the wider environment) (PADHI, 2009). White et al. (2012a; 2013) provide more detail on the influences on our model of wellbeing.

Instead of seeing wellbeing as a state that can be achieved, we see it as something that *happens* in the ways that different domains affect each other: for example, how physical and mental health affects and is affected by agency and participation, close relationships, economic resources and so on; in personal and social encounters; or as people interact with the broader environment. The model is thus intended to be seen as dynamic, not static, with constant flow and interchange between its different elements.

As we worked with this model, we realized that a simple contrast of 'subjective' and 'objective' would not work, as there are many different kinds of subjective data. This led us to identify a number of different layers, or levels, which can be used to assess each domain of wellbeing. An example of these layers as related to the economic domain is set out in Figure 8.2.

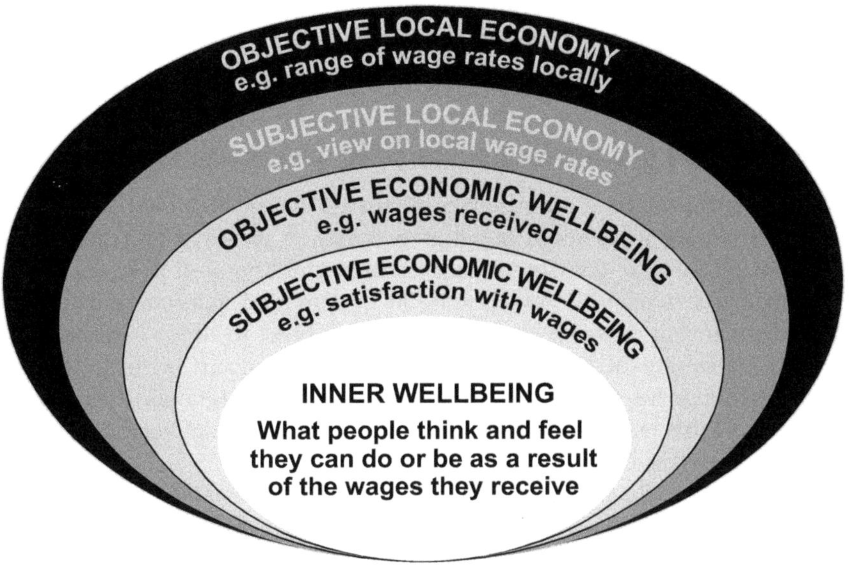

Figure 8.2 The Wellbeing Pathways layers of wellbeing (economic domain)

First, you can ask objective questions about the particular context; for example, in the case of the economic domain, what is the range of livelihoods available locally? The answers to such questions can be determined by observation or by official data, although of course there may be a mismatch between what is claimed on paper and what is actually available on the ground in terms of objective resources. Second, there are people's perceptions of these things: how are the livelihoods available viewed by people? How do they compare to past and future prospects? What quality of living can be gained from them? This is the first level at which you can ask subjective questions. Third, you can ask a further 'objective' set of questions about the extent to which a particular individual or family has access to the resources available locally. Can the individual or family take advantage of the potential livelihood opportunities available? This can lead to a further subjective layer of questioning: what do they think of the livelihood opportunities available to them? How satisfied are they and why?

However, the level that we are ultimately most interested in lies beyond this. We have labelled this 'inner wellbeing'. It describes what people think and feel they can do or be. What do the respondents' livelihoods mean for how they are in themselves? How does it enable or disable them? Some of this is linked to the other levels: a steady job, for example, may give people an inner sense of economic security that frees them from worry and enables them to plan for the longer term. We favour the term 'inner wellbeing' over others because it allows space for different understandings of mind, body and spirit and the relations between these. We think this is important because people in different cultural contexts see these things in quite distinct ways. This model of wellbeing, its origins and influences is set out in more detail elsewhere (White et al. 2012a; 2012b; 2013; White and Jha, 2014).

Turning a model into a measure: designing a wellbeing survey

Developing this model is an important first step in our research, but our focus is also on testing it, to see if it hangs together in the field and how it can be translated into an assessment process that could be used in development policy and practice. While extended and open-ended qualitative interviews are integral to our research, a central task has been to develop a wellbeing survey to generate quantitative data, given the concern with statistically reliable evidence for policy and practice noted above. The main focus of this chapter is on this wellbeing survey, its development and delivery, and lessons emerging from this process.

Our survey translates our model of wellbeing into a research tool to generate reliable and relevant data for wellbeing assessment. As made clear above, we believe objective conditions have a significant effect on the levels of wellbeing people experience, and we aim to test this through the opening and closing sections of our survey. We therefore begin with a series of questions that focus on demographic characteristics such as household members, marital history, children, education, and health. The survey ends by gathering information about economic resources, access to services, and community involvement. It also includes three subjective questions, which ask respondents to reflect on their current standard of living and changes in their economic position over the previous five years, and to assess how happy they feel in general.

However, it is in the section of the survey between these 'objective' sections that we seek to measure what we term 'inner wellbeing': what respondents think and feel they are able to be or do. This section is the most innovative but, as will become clear below, it has also proved to be the most complex to develop. In essence, the items in this section seek to tap into each of the seven domains of wellbeing. As represented in Figure 8.3, the idea is that each domain of wellbeing is made up of a number of different facets, and that each item in the survey captures one of those facets. If the model of wellbeing is constructed effectively, a statistical method known as factor analysis will show that how respondents answer one item in a domain is a good guide as to how they will answer other items within that domain. If this is the case, it confirms that the different items are indeed capturing different facets of a single underlying factor (the domain). Looking across the domains in the same way – in other words, using factor analysis to test whether the way respondents answer one domain is a good guide as to how they answer other domains – should in turn show that the domains also capture different facets of a single factor (inner wellbeing).

Our initial survey explored inner wellbeing through a series of statements, each relating to one item. Respondents were asked to rate their agreement

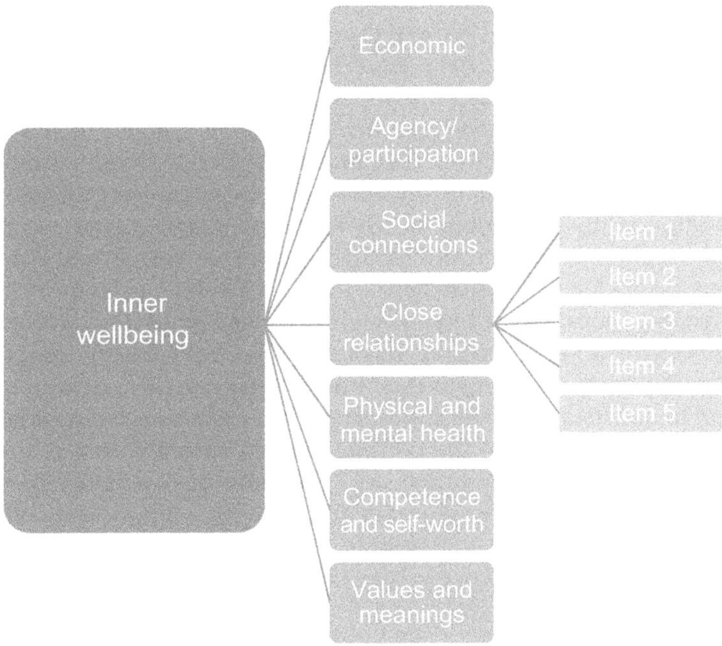

Figure 8.3 Relationship between items, domains and inner wellbeing

with each on a five-point 'Likert' scale, ranging from 'strongly disagree' at one end (scoring 1) to 'strongly agree' at the other (scoring 5). More recently, and in light of learning discussed below, we have switched to using questions instead of statements, and provide a series of carefully graded answers for people to choose from.

Developing items that tap into the domains of wellbeing and, ultimately, inner wellbeing itself, is central to developing a survey that works. What seems like an elegant survey design in the abstract does not necessarily play out as expected in the fieldwork context. Grounding and piloting have therefore been a key source of learning and localization in our research. Our approach centres on a theory-led model of wellbeing rather than seeking to develop a model through, for example, asking people to tell us what matters to them and how important each of those items is. This means we approach our fieldwork with a prior sense of what the important elements of wellbeing are: the domains and layers of wellbeing. But localization is critical to developing survey items that will correspond to these concepts and help us validate the model. Developing items that tap into what values and meanings are significant in a particular context, or that provide a way for people to express the important elements of social connections within their community, for example, requires considerable sensitivity to local context, as well as space to test how appropriate items are.

Our initial survey design arose from an earlier pilot study in Nepal and Zambia (White, 2009) and has evolved throughout the first rounds of fieldwork in Zambia (2010) and India (2011). These also involved significant grounding and piloting processes totalling 10 weeks. They provided valuable space to learn what people in the survey communities thought about in relation to our wellbeing questions, and what they found easy or hard to understand and respond to. By spending time in the communities where we were gathering data and, importantly, by working closely with local people as peer researchers, we gained insights that significantly shaped our survey design, and indeed its later adaptation. Our peer researchers – three in Zambia and four in India – were all recruited locally. They mediated, interpreted and interacted between local respondents and the external team members both during the piloting and fieldwork proper. Listening to their insights was critical to developing the survey and to understanding the kinds of responses we had been hearing. Such learning was not confined to the piloting, but is continued through regular team meetings to share how things are going and discuss issues that arise in survey delivery. These opportunities for ongoing support and collective reflection have been critical not only in ensuring data quality but also in identifying and addressing issues as they have arisen.

Refining survey design: lessons from wellbeing data difficulties

We are conducting two rounds of fieldwork in each location, which means that the learning processes are ongoing. More localization and survey development has been taking place in the interim periods as well as between countries. One significant reason for refining the survey design as a whole is the fact that data from our first round of fieldwork in Zambia in 2010 did not come together as we hoped, so that we were unable to run the statistical tests necessary to validate the model. As we reflected further we realized this was because of a series of issues related to the use of statements, the way people were asked for their responses to these, and external or contextual factors affecting the responses that they gave. It is worth describing these difficulties because they show how complex it is to translate a model of wellbeing into a survey that can generate statistically reliable data. Resolving them can offer valuable lessons to others developing wellbeing assessment measures that seek to meet such requirements.

To describe the problems, when we looked at the data two main issues emerged: first, regarding the distribution of responses within each item; and second, regarding the correlation of responses across different items. In brief, you would expect the distribution of responses within an item to follow a 'normal distribution'curve, with most responses concentrated in the centre and tailing off to either side (see Figure 8.4). However, our data was 'skewed' (see Figure 8.5). For some items, responses were clustered strongly at one extreme (scoring 1 or 5 on our points system), indicating that most respondents were answering in the same way; for others, the distribution was bipolar, where people had selected extreme options rather than those in the centre. Our data also showed what statisticians term 'kurtosis', which is where responses at the level of weak agreement/disagreement (scoring 2 or 4 points) were extremely low: respondents tended to answer at either extreme or neutrally (see Figure 8.6). Taken together, these issues meant that factor analysis did not produce the hoped-for results: the 'skewness' and kurtosis

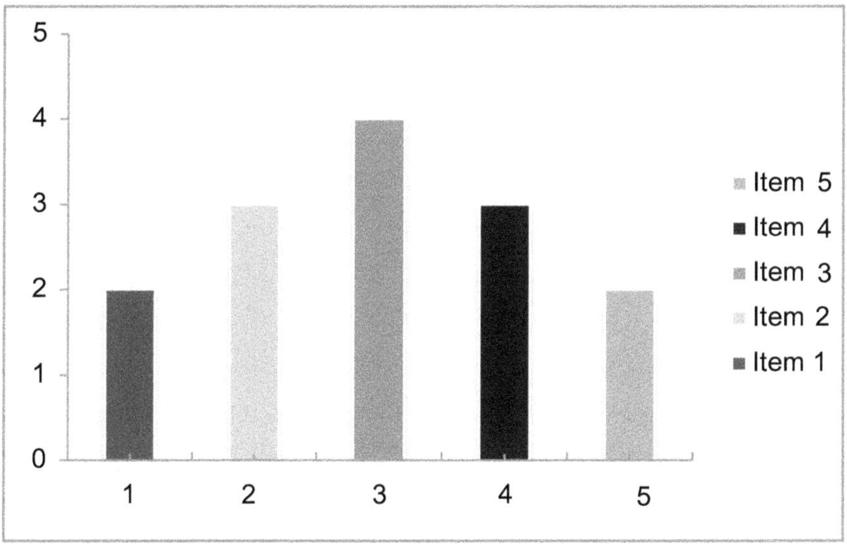

Figure 8.4 Normal distribution

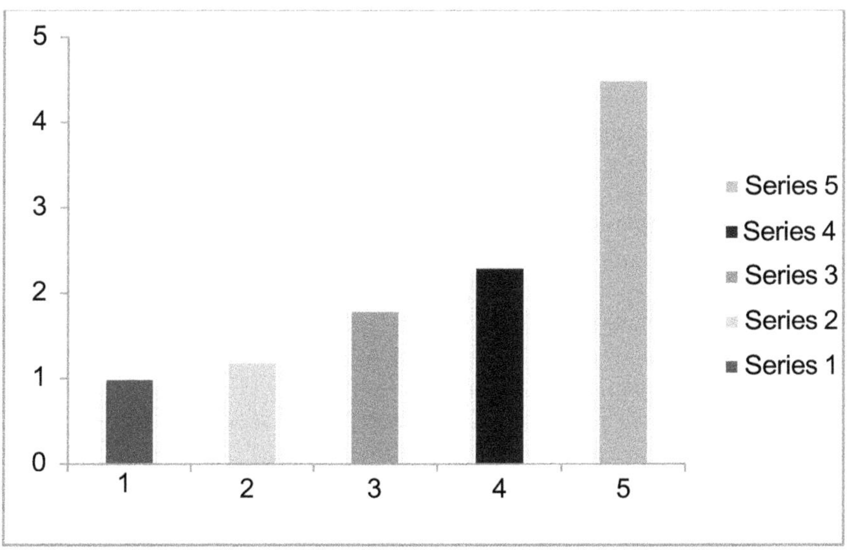

Figure 8.5 Skewed distribution

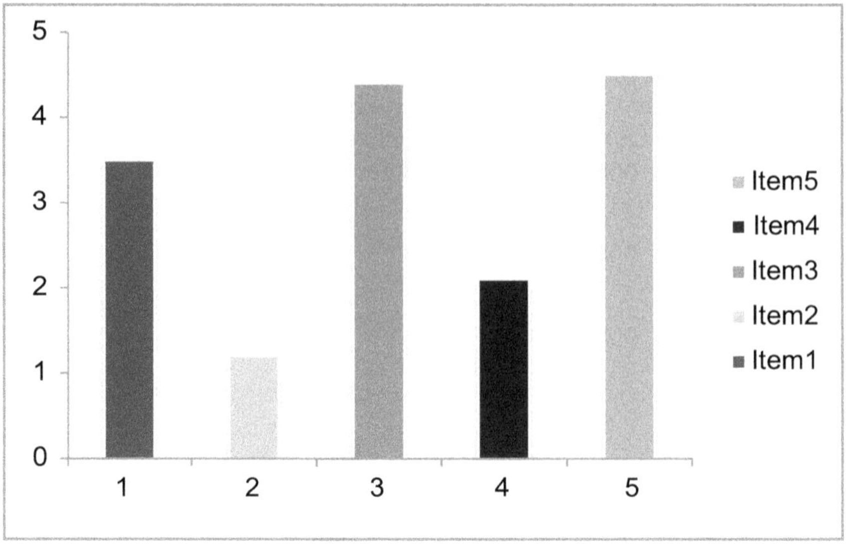

Figure 8.6 Kurtosis

meant we could not validate our model of inner wellbeing by showing the anticipated relationships between items and domains, and between domains and inner wellbeing, illustrated in Figure 8.3.

What all of this meant is that at the end of our first round of fieldwork in Zambia, we were unable to pass the rigorous tests needed for a measurement tool to be deemed statistically reliable and robust. While we were able to learn much from the data, and could report on people's responses on specific items (see White et al., 2012b), we could not make general statements about people's subjective experience of wellbeing or constituent dimensions of this.

This raised the following question: had the testing failed because the model itself was wrong, or was the failure because of other factors? Closer inspection of the results, and reflection on these, showed us that the failure of the statistical tests could be explained by a series of issues related to the questions asked, the way they were asked, and external or contextual factors affecting the way those questions were answered. The refinements we made in light of these insights have paid off: we adapted our approach prior to our first round of fieldwork in India and were able to use confirmatory factor analysis to validate our model of inner wellbeing with the data gathered there. The lessons emerging from this process were not only valuable in resolving our difficulties; they have a broader relevance for others seeking to develop robust and reliable wellbeing assessment measures.

Lesson one: what you ask about matters

Reliable measurement of wellbeing depends on the successful translation of conceptual models into appropriate questions. This is particularly an issue where a theory-led model is being applied, as in our research. However, translating a theory-led model into survey questions is not always straightforward, and the problems with our Zambia data discussed above reflect in part the difficulty of developing questions that tap into different, distinct aspects of wellbeing.

We worked hard in the initial survey design to ensure that phrasing was sufficiently personal to capture how respondents were themselves affected by issues, rather than just general observations. On reflection, however, we realized that some of our inner wellbeing statements actually asked about an external situation, rather than a respondent's inner state. This helped explain why, in some cases, most people had answered a question in the same way. An example of this was the statement about respondents' experience of receiving government assistance. The average score on this was very low (1.59 out of a possible 5), reflecting the real experience for respondents in relation to poor timing in the provision of welfare assistance. However this item was not in fact asking about inner wellbeing, or what respondents felt they themselves were able to be or do. Rather, it asked for a subjective account of an objective experience. For our model of wellbeing, distinctions such as this are important. In subsequent fieldwork we therefore ensured that items like this, where the main referent was external, were removed from the inner wellbeing section. Instead, we expanded the other sections of the survey to cover certain items relating to satisfaction, for example by including questions about the timing of and access to government services. Clarifying those items that were genuinely concerned with inner wellbeing in this way, for later rounds of fieldwork, contributed significantly to improving the reliability of our data and successfully validating our model.

Beyond this, other issues related to the nature of questions asked within a survey, can also impact on how wellbeing assessment is undertaken and the kinds of results it can generate. It is widely recognized that a longer survey is more fatiguing for respondents, reducing data quality. A key principle guiding our survey design was therefore to include only what we thought we would use. Including a question meant we needed to be sure about the work it would do for us. Piloting was critical in this process, in helping us work out the best ways of asking what we needed to know, as well as testing the validity of our inner wellbeing items. This process showed us, for example, how some questions could shift between wellbeing domains when respondents were answering them in a different way to the way we had expected. This enabled us to adapt what we were asking to make sure it tapped into what we wanted. For us, therefore, piloting was not simply a case of 'trying out' the questions, but also involved analysing the responses within and between rounds of fieldwork, leading to further refinement, redesign and testing to ensure the right questions were asked.

We also wanted to avoid asking for unnecessary detail, particularly in the objective parts of the survey, both to prevent the survey from becoming onerous and to ensure we created the kind of interaction appropriate to asking about wellbeing. Accordingly, our survey does not contain the specific detailed questions about income and expenditure common in household surveys.

Ultimately, we felt that the kind of atmosphere conducive to talking about inner wellbeing was not consistent with a forensic-style investigation into a respondent's economic situation. Similarly, we decided to place the inner wellbeing statements in the middle of the survey, because their feel and pace is different to those in the objective sections of the survey. We also felt it would be less taxing for respondents if we varied the style of our questioning in this way. Thinking about the 'wellbeing' nature of the survey itself therefore emerged as an important factor shaping its design and the questions asked.

Lesson two: how you ask about wellbeing matters

This point, about the style of questioning, links to a second theme that emerged from our experiences: the importance of how, both in form and delivery, wellbeing questions are asked.

We realized that the problems encountered with our Zambia data related in part to two issues linked to the form of our wellbeing questions. As explained above, we used a standard Likert scale, asking respondents to score their agreement or otherwise with a statement designed to tap into an aspect of inner wellbeing. Given the low levels of literacy among our respondents, it was clear that we needed to conduct surveys through face-to-face interviews. In line with recommended practice for researchers working with such respondents, we began by reading out the statement and then asking if respondents agreed or disagreed with it. We then asked a follow-up question about whether they dis/agreed weakly (scoring 2 or 4 points) or strongly (scoring 1 or 5 points). However, when asking questions in this way in Chiawa, we found that there was a sociability dynamic in the interview setting in that cultural context which appeared to encourage respondents to be bold and go for the emphasized response. This resulted in the bipolar response pattern of people tending to answer with 1 and 5.

A second issue was the strong relationship in our Zambia data between the loading of a statement – positive or negative – and the scores given. This problem of 'acquiescence bias' – the tendency to agree with statements – is widely recognized. We had taken it into account by designing a survey with a roughly equal number of positively and negatively worded statements. However, the degree of bias we found in our Zambia results was striking: 19 of the 20 positively phrased statements had a positive average score, and 17 of the 22 negatively phrased statements had a negative average score.

Thus in both aspects – scoring and acquiescence – we experienced difficulties, despite having designed our survey in line with recommended practice. What we have ultimately found to work when asking about inner wellbeing is to request responses to questions rather than statements, and to develop a set of carefully graded answers appropriate to the questions. Questions were easier for people to understand and respond to than statements, and did not carry the same tendency to lead answers in a particular direction. As an example, in Zambia, we had asked for dis/agreement with the statement 'I can work with others to bring change to my community'. In India this became 'How confident do you feel that (along with others) you will be able to bring change to your community?', with potential answers 'I never feel confident; I rarely feel confident; I sometimes feel confident and sometimes not; more often than not I feel confident; I always feel confident.'

Lesson three: context matters for both questions and answers

The above discussion highlights how we have needed to adapt standard reporting and survey methods. A third lesson from our research experience is the significance of context. While we are concerned with ensuring we generate the kind of data required to validate our model, our aim is for that model to be grounded in Southern perceptions and ways of being. Throughout the project we have remained committed to paying attention to the way local people – both our research respondents and the peer researchers discussed above – think and talk about their lives. On the one hand, we need our survey questions to tap into the concepts and processes central to our model; on the other, we need to ensure an interview atmosphere conducive to the discussion of wellbeing. For us, this includes making sure there is space for stories and explaining answers, to help us get a deeper sense of what is really going on for people.

In practice, this has meant trying to carry out the survey in as conversational a way as possible, and letting go of our desire to work systematically through all the layers of wellbeing. In designing the survey we have tried to order the questions in a way that flows naturally, and in conducting the interviews we have taken time at the start to introduce ourselves and put respondents at their ease. We have also found that when it comes to the inner wellbeing items, in both India and Zambia, respondents' most common reaction is to ask for a context or an example of what we mean. While we don't want to lead answers in a particular direction, we have found it is very difficult for respondents to answer without an example, so we have agreed as a team on examples for each item should clarification be requested. Sometimes these examples are drawn from what early respondents used as illustrations of their answers, and sometimes they draw on insight from the peer researchers. So, for example, in India, asking the question, 'If official decisions are made that affect you badly, do you feel that you have power to change them?' led respondents to mention a local example relating to a (successful) campaign against government appropriation of some village land. In contrast, for the question, 'Do you know the kind of people who can help you get things done?' we used the example of dealing with issues around official documents.

This experience made us reflect on the assumptions built into this kind of research. Western academics and respondents are used to dealing with questions at a relatively abstract level, which is required by statistical methods such as factor analysis, which look across responses to get at underlying factors. For village people in India and Zambia, however, questions are much easier to answer if they are specific and tangible. In part, this is because of the structure of language: English is relatively direct and abstract; Hindi, in comparison, is much more indirect and concrete. In addition, our respondents not only have relatively little schooling – in Zambia more than 70% of respondents have either had no schooling, or only a primary level, and in India the same percentage have not passed any formal education level at all – but they are also unused to this mode of questioning. As a result, we find that more time than expected is spent in settling on responses with respondents and providing them with examples. In this there is clearly a balance to be struck between the need to conform to standard approaches required for statistical analysis, and the contextual needs of respondents. Indeed, the skewness and kurtosis evident in our data from Zambia may in part be because in such contexts, it is particularly hard to generate responses that conform to 'normal' patterns and that meet the demands of standard levels of reliability.

One reason underlying those results is the impact of 'socially approved' answers; in other words, we realized that responses tended to bunch together when there was one perceived 'right' answer. This was particularly the case in the 'close relationships' domain, where people tended to want to present a good face to the world, even when the reality they experienced was less positive. So, for example, while we know that there is a good deal of domestic violence in our research community in Zambia, our carefully worded statement, which tried to get a measure of this in a sensitive way, still scored very highly, indicating that most people claimed there was no violence in the home. The lack of fit here between our quantitative and qualitative data suggests that people may respond differently when approached through a survey than when talking in a more open-ended interview or conversation (see also Camfield et al., 2009). While we worked hard to find questions that would avoid such bias, we had ultimately to accept that this was not possible. The combination of strong social norms, which encourage people to present a positive picture of family, with the use of a survey questionnaire to gather responses, resulted in consistently high quantitative scores for the close relationships domain across both India and Zambia.

Context also matters regarding the extent to which respondents may answer in ways we would not expect. For example, in India many issues around inner wellbeing are not matters people would normally speak directly about themselves, but rather would indicate and imply through more general statements or exclamations: 'The life of a woman!' In addition, while many studies hold that aspirations are important for wellbeing, in both India and Zambia we have found that questions about future prospects invite the response, 'Who can tell what the future will hold?' Many of the statements about the self are also difficult for respondents: negative statements may be feared in case they somehow attract bad luck; comparisons with others may be seen as invidious; professing pride in one's own achievements may be seen as inappropriate. We do not suggest that these would not be issues in other contexts, or that they are uniquely Southern, but having a sense of how local sensibilities and habits of speech may impact on responses enables the development of survey items that are more likely to generate the kinds of findings required for statistical validation.

Conclusion

As the introduction to this chapter made clear, there are many different levels at which a focus on wellbeing is being advocated in international development: from statistical measures of national progress to project-level processes of monitoring and evaluation. The ambition is both to provide a more comprehensive measure of what matters to people, and to capture something of people's own perceptions and values. In this chapter we have focused on the local level: describing some of the challenges we have encountered in developing an approach to wellbeing that both draws on wider learning in international development and reflects local people's own perspectives; and that respects the quality of people's experience yet aims to produce measures that can represent this in quantitative terms. What we have found through our research process to date is that it is indeed possible to develop, apply and statistically validate a multi-domain model of wellbeing that is grounded in theory, but adapted and contextualized for use in developing country contexts. That said, in our experience this has been far from easy. There can be a real tension between the demands of statistical packages for data that conform to certain norms, and the experience of sitting with people and seeking to understand something of the way they view their lives.

Notes

1. This chapter focuses on lessons from the research process, rather than the data themselves. For more information on the findings generated through our first rounds of fieldwork, see White et al. (2012a) and White et al. (2012b).

References

Camfield, L., Crivello, G. and Woodhead, M. (2009) 'Wellbeing research in developing countries: reviewing the role of qualitative methods' *Social Indicators Research* 90: 5–31.

Gough, I. R. and McGregor, J.A. (eds) (2007) *Wellbeing in Developing Countries: New Approaches and Research Strategies,* Cambridge: Cambridge University Press.

Psychosocial Assessment of Development and Humanitarian Intervention (PADHI) (2009) *A Tool, a Guide and a Framework: Introduction to a psychosocial approach to development,* Colombo: Social Policy Analysis and Research Centre.

University of Bath (no date) 'Wellbeing and Poverty Pathways: An Economic and Social Research Council/Department for International Development project' [website] <www.wellbeingpathways.org>[accessed 29 April 2014]

White, S.C. (2009) 'Bringing wellbeing into development practice', Wellbeing in Developing Countries Research Group (WeD) Working Paper 50 [online resource] <www.welldev.org.uk/wed-new/workingpapers/workingpapers/WeDWP_09_50.pdf> [accessed 29 April 2014]

White, S. C. (2010) 'Analysing wellbeing. A framework for development policy and practice', *Development in Practice* 20 (2): 158–172.

White, S. C., Gaines Jr. S., Jha, S. and Marshall, N. (2012a) *Wellbeing Pathways Report: India Round 1*, [online resource] <http://wellbeingpathways.org/images/stories/pdfs/working_papers/indiatime1report.pdf> [accessed 29 April 2014]

White, S.C., Gaines Jr. S., Jha, S., Marshall, N. and Graveling, E. (2012b) *Wellbeing Pathways Report: Zambia Round 1*, [online resource] <http://wellbeingpathways.org/images/stories/pdfs/working_papers/zambiatime1report.pdf> [accessed 29 April 2014]

White, S.C., Gaines, Jr. S., Jha, S. (2013) 'Inner wellbeing: Concept and validation of a new approach to subjective perceptions of wellbeing – India', *Social Indicators Research* 1–24 <http://dx.doi.org/10.1007/s11205-013-0504-7> [accessed 13 May 2014]

White, S.C. and Jha, S. (2014) 'Inner wellbeing: The wellbeing pathways approach', in White, S.C. and Abeyasekera, A. (eds) *Wellbeing Assessment: A Practical Guide*, Rugby: Practical Action Publishing.

About the authors

Nina Marshall is the Research Communications Officer for Wellbeing and Poverty Pathways. She recently completed doctoral research on disability and international development policy, and has an interest in exploring connections between disability and wellbeing in Southern contexts. Nina has a background in journalism and experience working in research communications with international development projects.

Sarah White is the Director of Wellbeing and Poverty Pathways. She came to study wellbeing through an interest in the significance of culture and social identities in international development. She has researched wellbeing in South Asia within the Economic and Social Research Council (ESRC) Research Group on Wellbeing in Developing Countries (WeD) 2002–07 and the DFID-funded Religion and Development programme (RaD) 2005–10. Her new edited book, *Wellbeing Assessment: A Practical Guide*, is to be published by Practical Action Publishing in 2014.

Stanley Gaines is the Deputy Director of Wellbeing and Poverty Pathways. He has written extensively in the fields of ethnic studies and close relationships, authoring the book *Culture, Ethnicity, and Personal Relationship Processes* (1997, New York, NY: Taylor & Frances/Routledge). His current work is branching into development studies and cross-cultural psychology.

Shreya Jha is the Research Officer for Wellbeing and Poverty Pathways. She is a development researcher and practitioner based in New Delhi, India. She has previously worked in the area of mental health and psychosocial interventions in India which, in turn, has led to her interest in the area of wellbeing.

CHAPTER 9

Wealth ranking to wellbeing: where next for development?

Roger Williamson[1]

In moving from Barbara Grandin's work on wealth ranking (1988) to current approaches to understanding wellbeing, this wide-ranging chapter moves from the village level to the global village. A key challenge currently is to find better ways to quantify and compare wellbeing within and across societies. The following approaches are presented: the Human Development Index; the Basic Capabilities Index; the Millennium Development Goals; Wellbeing and Development; the Multidimensional Poverty Index; the Sarkozy-Sen-Fitoussi Commission; Bhutan's initiative at the United Nations; and the World Happiness Report. This chapter provides some comments on a set of central challenges, and emphasizes that the process of struggling to achieve wellbeing is unavoidably political. The key issues stress that wellbeing is more than happiness; welfare economics cannot succeed by just adding up totals of individual wellbeing, social sustainability, wellbeing and justice, and the politics of wellbeing.

Keywords: wellbeing, well-being, ranking, global village, human development, goals, multidimensional, happiness

This chapter begins from Barbara Grandin's original work on participatory wealth ranking (1988). It then sketches the shift towards the use of human wellbeing as a key framework for assessing development. It outlines some of the newer approaches to measuring and evaluating wellbeing. The fourth section briefly discusses some of the key issues related to wellbeing and development. Finally, a set of brief conclusions is offered.

The trajectory of the discussion goes from the village level to the global village level; from the local to the international. Comments are made on the following issues:

- The value of participatory methodologies for the generation of a wealth of data and for precision of analysis.
- The link between participatory approaches to development and democracy for development and governance outcomes.
- The clear message that it has proved necessary to go 'beyond Gross Domestic Product (GDP)' to assess wellbeing.
- The need for a three-dimensional understanding of wellbeing (with the subjective, objective and social dimensions of wellbeing all being vital; they also need to be kept in balance).

http://dx.doi.org/10.3362/9781780448459.009

- An insight into some of the techniques being used to generate international data on changes in wellbeing.

Generating an adequate understanding of wellbeing and justice, which takes account of international, sustainable and inter-generational understandings of human wellbeing, is complex. An inescapable conclusion is that better data and better analysis do not of themselves produce more justice or a better distribution of development; the political dimension of work for wellbeing and development is essential. What the article does not do is to outline a framework for international justice. This is for two reasons: it would fall foul of Amartya Sen's strictures against an argument based on 'transcendental justice' (see below); and because there is little appetite for major structural reform to the benefit of the world's poorer economies. The financial resources that are mobilized to address the ongoing crises (e.g. fuel, food, finance) of the South, pale into insignificance compared to the bail-outs suddenly available for the banking sector in the rich North.

Wealth ranking to wellbeing

It is often said that the problem of theoretical physics is how to provide a coherent account, which goes all the way from the very small to the very big. Perhaps this provides a useful analogy for international development. Wealth ranking has convincingly shown that local villagers can very quickly and accurately rank their neighbours according to what they regard as wealth, and then work out how they have done this. This helps bring out the implicit criteria that they were using. The key shift is to privilege the understanding of the people in context, rather than externally derived or imposed categories. On the basis of such accurate information, appropriate policy interventions can be designed. To place Grandin's work (1988) in historical context, the King of Bhutan had already criticized GDP by the 1970s (see below), and Robert Chambers had a well formulated approach to wellbeing, illbeing and participatory methodology by the early 1980s (Chambers, 1983). Meanwhile, Amartya Sen can draw on Indian and Greek sources extending back well over 2,000 years to illustrate the longstanding debates about justice (Sen, 2009).

Grandin's initial work was 'with pastoralists for whom wealth and livestock were close to synonymous' (Chambers, 2008: 115). Retrospectively assessing the successful application of wealth ranking, there can be little doubt that it established itself as an effective tool for providing information to assist with the framing of policy interventions. As Chambers notes: 'Early in the 1990s, wealth was more and more often replaced by well-being ... which better expressed the criteria used especially by non-pastoralist people, and grouping replaced ranking.' (Chambers, 2008: 115). In another description of the shift, he states: 'When asked to card sort households in what was originally wealth ranking (Grandin, 2008) local people have so consistently sorted not by wealth but by some composite concept close to well-being, that the process has been renamed well-being ranking.' (Chambers, 2008: 191)

However, what is valuable in a clearly defined local context proves harder to compare across contexts or to build up into a more comprehensive picture. Human societies are constituted by the interplay of the material context and the cultural context. While some needs – particularly the need for food and drink – are constant, how food and drink are found or produced varies widely. Whether camels or llamas are tamed and used to carry loads depends on the context.[2] The range of cultural variation is huge; as for example, in gender relations. This is the subject matter of anthropology as a discipline: answering the question 'how do we live together?' (Carrithers, 1992: 1) and accounting for the 'great difference between biological and cultural evolution' (Harris, 1990: 502).

A standard text book on development research methodology observes: 'Scaling up wealth ranking for use in larger communities, districts, regions, etc. has proved difficult. The strength of wealth ranking is that it is based on people's knowledge of each other' (Mikkelsen, 2005: 109). Mikkelsen's book describes and reviews wealth ranking and sets it in the wider context of contemporary 'methods for development'. In addition, social life is dynamic. Societies change, and what is considered as wellbeing changes through time. So, there is change, whether it is adjudged 'good' or not.[3] Chambers deals with this by contrasting cycles of illbeing and wellbeing. His illustration of 'the deprivation trap' (an interacting dynamic of powerlessness-vulnerability-physical weakness-poverty-isolation) can already be found three decades ago (Chambers, 1983: 112) and his analysis is complemented with a later virtuous nexus (a positive spiral of reinforcing changes; the opposite of a vicious circle) of wellbeing.

Chambers gives examples of the application of participatory methodologies as the emphasis moved from Grandin's wealth ranking to 'wellbeing grouping'. Ingenious methods were devised for making comparisons on a larger scale and across communities. In a review made in 2007, Chambers lists a study of almost 10,000 households in South Africa, a study of food security in Malawi, a study of destitution in Ethiopia, and the construction of the Participatory Poverty Index in China (Chambers 2008: 116–8). Wealth ranking thus fits within the range of participatory methods in development.

It is a long way from the chapati diagram in an Indian village to the deliberations of the UN Millennium Summit. However, effective development policy has to address universal needs, contextual challenges, and the diverse views of those affected on what constitutes wellbeing. Frameworks for discussing and assessing these needs and striving towards coherence are therefore valuable (McGregor, 2004).

Recent approaches to assessing human wellbeing

The Human Development Index

It can be dangerous to personalize debates, but it is more than convenient shorthand to call attention to the work of Nobel Prize winner Amartya Sen in this context, for his personal academic work and his institutional work with the United Nations Development Programme (UNDP) (on the *Human*

Development Report) and more recently on the Sarkozy Commission. Sen's work on positive understandings of development, centred on capabilities and functionings, has been decisive in the move beyond income poverty as the way of assessing development. Since 1990, the Human Development Index (HDI) (UNDP, no date) has ranked countries according to a formula calculated from life expectancy, educational attainment and standard of living (Gross National Income per capita). Mahbub ul Haq and Amartya Sen were the two main architects of the HDI.

There is always a danger that a tool that is valuable in capturing some information inevitably excludes other information that is significant for interpreting human behaviour. There is the attendant danger of over-interpretation, and placing too much credence in the ranking of countries according to this data. Nonetheless, in a reflective piece introducing a book of essays on human development, Sen notes three 'obvious limitations' of the HDI (2003: x–xi):

> First, the well-being and freedom that we enjoy have much internal diversity, and they are influenced by a great variety of factors – political, economic, social, legal, epidemiological, and others. These factors are distinct, but they also interrelate with each other ...
> Second, when the ingredients of a judgement are diverse, any aggregate index with *constant* weights would tend to oversimplify the evaluative exercise ...
> Third, another dichotomy involves the time dimension. We have reason to be interested in the current situation as well as future prospects. Indeed, sometimes we are particularly interested in *changes* over time.

The Basic Capabilities Index

Since 1995, Social Watch has used a different approach: the Basic Capabilities Index (BCI), which is based on under-five mortality, births attended by trained health personnel, and literacy rates and school enrolment. By taking these social indicators, 'it' or 'Social Watch' produces results that give an indication of trends in social development, not only poverty reduction measured in terms of a basic US$1, $1.25 or $2 per day measure (Social Watch, 2011: 3):

> All the indicators making up the BCI are expressed in percentages and they range from 0 to 100. Under-five mortality, which is usually expressed in number of deaths per thousand children born alive, is expressed as 100 minus that value. So that, for example, a value of 20 deaths per thousand becomes 2% and, when deducted from 100, yields a basic indicator value of 98. Thus, the theoretical maximum value in infant mortality is 100, which would mean that all children born alive survive until they are five years old. Reproductive health takes the maximum value of 100 when all women giving birth are attended by skilled health personnel. Similarly, the education indicator registers 100 when all the adults know to read and to

write, and all school age children are enrolled in education and they all attain five years of schooling. These three indicators are then averaged, so the total value of the index will vary between 0% and 100%.

The organization's self-description and main conclusions are given here (Social Watch, 2011: 2):

> Social Watch, a network of citizen organizations monitoring social policies around the world launched today a Basic Capabilities Index derived from well-being indicators which slows very slow progress in the last twenty years. This index contradicts the assessment of the World Bank, according to which extreme poverty would have halved around the world between 1980 and 2005.

The Millennium Development Goals

The Millennium Development Goals (MDGs) emerged from a series of major UN conferences on key development objectives during the 1990s. They represent a basic set of commitments by the Member States of the UN, providing a quantifiable set of objectives to be achieved within a defined time frame (see Box 9.1). These goals have been extensively discussed and debated from various perspectives. For the purposes of this article, they will be taken as an existing commitment that the world community should meet, and the point recorded that time is short to agree a next set of goals that can act in succession to the MDGs (IDS, 2010).

These goals introduce a measure of objectivity into the search for development. They are a set of minimum goals that are essential for the achievement of wellbeing.

In preparation for the UN Conference on Sustainable Development (Rio +20), the High Level Panel on Global Sustainability, in its report *Resilient People, Resilient Planet* (UN, 2012a; 2012c), has urged the agreement of a set of Sustainable Development Goals to 'mobilize global action and help monitor progress'. Given that the UN is an organization of Member States, it is not surprising that the initial call is to governments to help in this formulation. But given criticisms (however justified or unjustified) that the MDGs were a top-down initiative, developed with little direct reference to the lives of the poor, and often seen as a 'donor community agenda', the formulation of a new set of priorities for development beyond 2015 is surely an opportunity to design a more participatory process.

Wellbeing and development

The Wellbeing in Developing Countries research group at Bath University was a multiyear, interdisciplinary research programme funded by the UK Economic and Social Research Council (ESRC 2002-07). It brought together, and developed further, three perspectives: 'human needs and capabilities' (Gough and McGregor, 2007: 9–16); 'resources, livelihoods and wellbeing'

Box 9.1 About MDGs

At the Millennium Summit in September 2000 the largest gathering of world leaders in history adopted the UN Millennium Declaration, committing their nations to a new global partnership to reduce extreme poverty and setting out a series of time-bound targets, with a deadline of 2015, that have become known as the Millennium Development Goals.

The Millennium Development Goals (MDGs) are the world's time-bound and quantified targets for addressing extreme poverty in its many dimensions-income poverty, hunger, disease, lack of adequate shelter, and exclusion-while promoting gender equality, education, and environmental sustainability. They are also basic human rights-the rights of each person on the planet to health, education, shelter, and security.

Goal 1: Eradicate Extreme Hunger and Poverty
Goal 2: Achieve Universal Primary Education
Goal 3: Promote Gender Equality and Empower Women
Goal 4: Reduce Child Mortality
Goal 5: Improve Maternal Health
Goal 6: Combat HIV/AIDS, Malaria and other diseases
Goal 7: Ensure Environmental Sustainability
Goal 8: Develop a Global Partnership for Development

Source: Millennium Project, 2006

(Gough and McGregor, 2007: 17–24); and 'subjective quality of life: happiness and satisfaction with life as a whole' (Gough and McGregor, 2007: 25–33). The group came to the conclusion that it required six separate tools for detailed analysis and comparison of development challenges in Bangladesh, Ethiopia, Peru and Thailand.

The major volume emanating from this study (Gough and McGregor, 2007) and the website of the project (University of Bath, 2012) provide a significant repository of intellectual resources on wellbeing and its application in development.

How context-specific an understanding of wellbeing needs to be is illustrated by Allister McGregor:[4]

> Throughout the empirical research we had extensive discussions about what the appropriate terms in Spanish and Quechua were for wellbeing ... we mainly used "bienestar" and what it meant for people is then extensively explored and in parts with forensic psychometric detail. Of course since then the "Vivir Bien" movement has gathered pace and this leans towards the environmental sustainability narrative in Andean cosmology."[5]

The tools designed have to be broad enough for comparative purposes, yet context-specific enough to provide a real insight into particular social realities; as Allister McGregor puts it, not to 'ask about llamas in Bangladesh or about *madrassa*[6] in rural Peru' (Gough and McGregor, 2007: 340). The composite methodology is outlined in Table 9.1.

In a later elaboration, which clearly has relevance for development policy, McGregor and Andy Sumner have outlined a distinctive understanding of a three-dimensional (3-D) understanding of human wellbeing: 'Human wellbeing ... can be conceived of in terms of the interplay of three dimensions: the material, the relational and the subjective (also referred to

Table 9.1 Composite methodology

Outcomes	*Structures*	*Processes*
Resources and Needs Questionnaire (RANQ) Resources – material, human, social, cultural and naturalneeds, e.g. health, education, food and housing	Community profiling – describing demographic, social and physical characteristics of community	Process research – thematic (e.g. local collective action, livelihoods or migration) and core cases (more detailed diary work, repeated interviews)
Wellbeing and Development Quality of Life (WeDQoL) Phase 1 – bottom-up work with community identifying essential elements of QoL in their community. Phase 2 – formulation of appropriate workable definition of QoL and strategy for implementation	Structures research and welfare regimes addressing national systems and features, analysing how actors mediate between households and outside organizations and institutions including government, business and civil society	Income and expenditure research. Bangladesh and Peru – household data collected three times per year. Ethiopia and Thailand – monthly diaries (more qualitative information, smaller sample size)

Source: Author, based on Gough and McGregor, 2007: 339–44

as perceptual).' (McGregor and Sumner, 2010: 104). The authors stress that different kinds of indicator are needed for each dimension. For example (ibid.):

- 'needs satisfaction indicators' for the material level – such as the target for MDG 1 on child malnutrition;
- 'material asset indicators, multidimensional resource indicators, human agency indicators' for the relational aspect – such as the gender empowerment target of MDG 3;
- 'quality-of-life indicators' for the subjective or perceptual evaluation.

The Multidimensional Poverty Index

The Multidimensional Poverty Index (MPI) (Oxford Poverty & Human Development Initiative, 2011) works with 10 indicators. It breaks down education, health, and standard of living still further and, increasingly, also

Table 9.2 3-D wellbeing: dimensions, areas of study and indicators

Dimensions of wellbeing	*Material*	*Relational*	*Subjective*
What is to be studied?	The objectively observable outcomes that people are able to achieve	The resources that a person is able to command and the extent to which they are able to engage with others in order to achieve their particular needs and goals	The meanings that people give to the goals they achieve and the processes in which they engage
Indicators	Needs satisfaction indicators (Take, e.g. the target for MDG1 on child malnutrition)	Material asset indicators. Multidimensional resource indicators. (Take, e.g. the target for MDG 3 on gender empowerment)	Quality-of-life indicators

Source: McGregor and Sumner, 2010: 105

gives sub-regional data for over 100 developing countries.[7] Sabine Alkire, who is one of the architects of this method,[8] has taken up the challenge issued by Sen to develop the UNDP/HDI further, and has written extensively on Sen's approach.

The 10 MPI indicators are set out below:

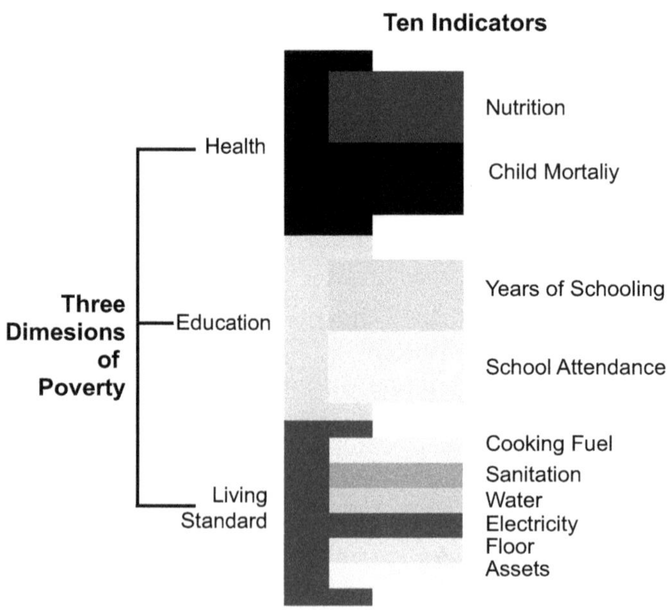

Figure 9.1 The Multidimensional Poverty Index (MPI)
Source: Oxford Poverty and Human Development Initiative (OPHI) (no date a)

Inside the MPI

The MPI has three dimensions and uses 10 indicators, which reflects some of the MDGs and thus International standards of poverty (Alkire and Santos, 2010; Alkire et al, 2011). Each dimension is equally weighted, and each indicator within each dimension is equally weighted. The MPI metholdology follows Alkire and Foster (2011)

1. Education (each indicator is weighted equally at 1/6)
Years of Schooling: deprived if no household member has completed five years of schooling
School Attendance: deprived if any school-aged child is not attending school in years 1 to 8

2. Health (each indicator is weighted equally at 1/6)
Child Mortality: deprived if any child has died in the family
Nutrition: deprived if any adult or child for whom there is nutritional information is malnourished

3. Standard of Living (each indicator is weighted equally at 1/18) **carriage return Electricity**: deprived if the household has no electricity **Drinking Water**: deprived if the household does not have access to safe drinking water or it is more than 30 minutes' walk away **sanitation :** deprived if they do not have improved sanitation or if their toilet is shared
Flooring: deprived if the household has a dirt, sand or dung floor
Cooking Fuel: deprived if the household cooks with wood, charcoal or dung
Assets: deprived if the household does not own more than one of : radio, TV, telephone, bike, motorbike, or refrigerator, and does not own a car or tractor
What makes a person MPI poor?
A person is identified as multidimensionally poor if he or she is deprived in at least one-third of the dimensions. One deprivation alone may not represent poverty.

Figure 9.2 Inside the MPI
Source: OPHI (no date b)

The Sarkozy-Sen-Fitoussi Commission

This Commission was established by the French Government of Nicholas Sarkozy. It stressed that it is necessary to shift emphasis from measuring economic production to measuring people's wellbeing (Stiglitz et al.,

2009: 12). At least in principle, these dimensions should be considered simultaneously:

- material living standards (income, consumption and wealth);
- health;
- education;
- personal activities including work;
- political voice and governance;
- social connections and relationships;
- environment (present and future conditions);
- insecurity, of an economic as well as a physical nature.

All these elements shape human wellbeing, and yet many of them are missed by conventional income measures. Stiglitz says of the Commission: 'We unanimously agreed not only that GDP was a bad, and potentially misleading, measure but that it could be improved upon. ... The Organisation for Economic Co-operation and Development (OECD), the organization of the advanced industrial countries, has undertaken a large project following up on our work.' (Stiglitz, 2012: 232).

Bhutan's Initiative at the UN

The definition of Gross National Happiness (GNH), developed over the past 40 years in Bhutan, draws both on Buddhist values and on modern social science methodology and wellbeing indicators, which are formulated in much wider categories than income or wealth.[9] The key areas are: psychological wellbeing, health, time use, education, culture, good governance, ecology, community vitality, and living standards. International attention has only begun to focus on this initiative recently, as a result of the efforts of the government of Bhutan to use the UN machinery to gain international acceptance for the approach. The route taken has been to try to get all UN Member States to focus policy around measuring happiness and wellbeing, rather than taking GDP as the measure of social progress.

> The General Assembly today called on United Nations Member States to undertake steps that give more importance to happiness and well-being in determining how to achieve and measure social and economic development.
>
> In a resolution adopted without a vote, the Assembly invited countries 'to pursue the elaboration of additional measures that better capture the importance of the pursuit of happiness and well-being in development with a view to guiding their public policies.'
>
> The resolution said "the pursuit of happiness is a fundamental human goal" and embodies the spirit of the globally agreed targets known as the Millennium Development Goals." (UN, 2011).

In order to assess GNH in Bhutan, the government has selected a wide range of indicators, some of which would probably be surprising to Western secular development specialists (see Ura et al., 2012) as they include questions about spirituality and personal attitudes (Centre for Bhutan Studies & GNH Research, 2010). The Alkire-Foster methodology, which underlies the MPI (see above), also informed the formulation of the GNH Index developed for Bhutan (Centre for Bhutan Studies & GNH Research, no date). On the occasion of the session of the UN, Secretary-General Ban Ki-Moon remarked (UN, 2012b): 'We need a new economic paradigm that recognizes the parity between the three pillars of sustainable development. Social, economic and environmental well-being are indivisible. Together they define gross global happiness.'

Three brief comments are in order at this point. The first is that Bhutan's own efforts are so context-specific and complex that it is hard to see how they can be more widely operationalized. The second is that while such a debate at the UN is an achievement for a small country, it falls far short of binding standard setting. Finally, wellbeing, as will be argued below, is more than happiness.

The World Happiness Report

The *World Happiness Report*, launched at the UN in April 2012, was co-edited by Jeffrey Sachs, John Helliwell and Richard Layard (Earth Institute, 2012; Sachs et al., 2012). The report draws heavily on existing surveys, such as the Gallup World Poll (GWP), the World Values Survey (WVS) and the European Social Survey (ESS). Having surveyed the causes of happiness and misery, it moves on to policy recommendations. The main findings are (Sachs et al., 2012: 9):

> GNP is a valuable goal, but should not be pursued to the point where economic stability is jeopardized, community cohesion is destroyed, the vulnerable are not supported, ethical standards are sacrificed, or the world's climate is put at risk. While basic living standards are essential for happiness, after the baseline has been met happiness varies more with quality of human relationships than income. Other policy goals should include high employment and high-quality work; a strong community with high levels of trust and respect, which government can influence through inclusive participatory policies; improved physical and mental health; support of family life; and a decent education for all. Four steps to improve policy-making are the measurement of happiness, explanation of happiness, putting happiness at the center of analysis, and a translation of well-being research into design and delivery of services.

The report concludes with a detailed review of the approach taken by Bhutan (Sachs et al., 2012: 108–47) and a shorter description of efforts being undertaken by the UK Government (Sachs et al., 2012: 149–51; Beaumont, 2011) and the OECD.[10] It should also be noted that many other governments are working in a similar vein, including well developed approaches in Canada and Australia.

Key issues

Wellbeing is more than happiness

It is unfortunate, for two reasons, that the coordinators of the *World Happiness Report* have chosen that title. The first is that the material does go beyond happiness (as subjective wellbeing) into social areas of wellbeing, such as the environment and governance. The second is that it is wellbeing that is the richer, more inclusive and desirable goal. However, this shortcoming is honest in one sense, in that the analysis cannot claim to provide the tools for a full evaluation of wellbeing; that would be a huge and complex task.

The shortcomings of a focus primarily on an individualistic definition of wellbeing as happiness (subjective wellbeing) are instantly apparent. Without a concentration on structural transformation and social justice, the danger is that the search for happiness can simply become an aspiration for those who already have everything. It also runs the danger of ignoring the obvious point that the fulfilment of the aspirations of the rich (as individuals and as societies) can be factors thwarting the development of the poor. The three-dimensional conception (McGregor and Sumner, 2010) of wellbeing as subjective, objective and social is an antidote to the reduction of wellbeing to individual happiness, and of development to Gross National Product (GNP).

For wellbeing to be understood adequately and operationalized fully as a framework for social welfare, it is essential to understand that it is not the same as happiness – particularly if the latter is understood in an individualistic, subjective estimate of mood. For wellbeing to be relevant in a development context, a richer and more comprehensive understanding is required.

There is a basic difference between a utilitarian understanding of happiness, and wellbeing, derived from an application of the ethical traditional following Aristotle. Bruni (2009: 206–7) explains it as the difference between 'happiness ... conceived as the effect of earning income aimed at purchasing commodities' or 'a meaningful life or well-being in the sense of actualisation of human potentials through intrinsically motivated activities in a context of interpersonal relationships'.[11] The contrast between these two approaches has been aptly described by Erich Fromm as 'to have or to be?' (Fromm, 1976).[12] Work is developing fast in this field, but much of the more comprehensive data is focused on highly developed, industrialized countries with a high level of income. The New Economics Foundation (NEF) in the UK has published a comprehensive review of evidence (Stoll et al., 2012).

Welfare economics – not just adding individual 'wellbeings'

As Partha Dasgupta says: 'Social well-being is an aggregate of individual well-beings. Economists have generally speaking aggregated individuals' well-beings by summing them.' (Dasgupta, 2007: 146)

Even though, other things being equal, the marginal dollar of income in a rich country could do more good in a poor country, development is far more complex than taking some of the surplus from the rich and giving it to the poor. Peter Singer has developed an interesting argument in his book *The Life You Can Save*, based around the following argument (Singer, 2009: 15):

> First premise: Suffering and death from lack of food, shelter and medical care are bad.
> Second premise: If it is in your power to prevent something bad from happening, without sacrificing anything nearly as important, it is wrong not to do so.
> Third premise: By donating to aid agencies, you can prevent suffering and death from lack of food, shelter, and medical care, without sacrificing anything nearly as important.
> Conclusion: Therefore, if you do not donate to aid agencies, you are doing something wrong.

Singer's argument is not designed to prove that development depends on individual acts of financial generosity, transferring money from the rich to the poor of the world through aid agencies; it is intended to challenge citizens of the rich world to ask whether wellbeing can be enhanced by use of resources in situations of extreme poverty, rather than relative wealth.

If, as an increasing number of authors are now arguing – and would seem to be the common sense conclusion – an extra dollar of purchasing power is of more significance to a poor person than a rich one, the poor person will gain more in welfare than the rich person loses; a strong moral argument for well-administered development aid (see Layard, 2005: 52; Rifkin, 2009: 51).

The calculation of overall wellbeing is made much more complex by the fact that interests are often incompatible. A significant increase in the wellbeing of one section of the community can, in certain circumstances, only be achieved by a change in behaviour in another section. At global level, we see this being played out in international climate change talks. The central dilemma between high-carbon-use developed countries, the 'emerging giants' (India and China) and low-energy-consuming (more precisely, low-level fossil fuel-consuming) countries, is that most climate scientists are convinced that human-caused global warming is largely the result of burning fossils fuels such as oil and coal. Unless the rich economies restrict their use of fossil fuels, there will be little scope for developing countries to increase their use, and the latter need to do that in order to develop. 'The developing countries, understandably, argue that their per capita energy use is a mere fraction of the per capita energy used in wealthy countries like the United States, and to deny them the opportunity to increase their economic development is to keep them locked into poverty and despair.' (Rifkin, 2009: 508).

Even if the methodology existed to show that redistribution of fossil fuel-based energy use towards poorer countries and people would increase the overall sum of human welfare, one would still need a mechanism to persuade or coerce the rich to do so; the political process is unavoidable.

Social sustainability

In discussing individual and social wellbeing, Partha Dasgupta distinguishes between the constituents of wellbeing and the determinants of wellbeing. By the constituents, he means '[v]arious kinds of civil liberty, various aspects of health, and so on'. By determinants, he means 'not only such necessities as food and shelter, but also access to knowledge and information'. He concludes: 'One may think of the constituents and determinants of wellbeing as "ends" and "means", respectively.' (Dasgupta, 2007: 143)

In his book *Economics: A Very Short Introduction* (Dasgupta, 2007), Dasgupta shows that a 'beyond GDP' measure of sustainability is conceptually convincing, yet complex to calculate. It involves calculating changes in manufactured capital, human capital and natural capital relative to the growth in population. He takes the reader through the five stages that he considers necessary to make the calculation of sustainability for a society (132):

> First, estimate the value of changes in the amounts and compositions of manufactured capital, human capital, and natural capital – which we will call *inclusive investment*. (If inclusive capital is found to be positive, we may conclude that manufactured capital, human capital, and natural capital, taken together, grew over the period.) Second, estimate the change in total factor productivity. Third, transform the two figures in a way that enables us to calculate the effects of the two sets of changes on the productive base. Fourth, combine the two resulting estimates into a single number that can be taken to reflect the change that took place in the economy's productive base. Fifth, make a correction for demographic changes to arrive at an estimate for the change that took place in the economy's productive base relative to population.

This is a complex and condensed explanation of how to assess whether economic change is moving in a positive direction (i.e. increasing – but not necessarily positive in a normative sense) and sustainable. If we take it step by step it becomes clearer. Step one is the calculation of the increase or decrease in value of manufactured capital (e.g. factories), human capital (the work force) and natural capital (e.g. fish stocks or forests). It is often thought that depletion of fish stocks or forests is like the deterioration of roads or bridges, but there are important differences. They make take a long time to recover, or may collapse suddenly – even completely (Dasgupta 2007: 129). An example is the collapse of the fish stocks off Canada (Coulthard et al., 2011: 3). 'Total factor productivity' (used in step two) is a technical term which is used to account for the surplus added to an economy by technological change. It is the residual, or what is unaccounted for, when the usual inputs (investment and labour) have been factored in; an example could be a rise in productivity as a result of computerization. Together, these elements (steps three and four) show the impact on the productive base, and finally (step five), take account of the impact of population change.

At a 'Planet under Pressure' conference in March 2012, the International Human Dimensions Programme (IHDP) of the United Nations University (UNU), Brazil and India presented a new report that sought to take into account the adverse impact of economic growth on the natural capital of rapidly developing countries, taking Brazil and India as prime examples (UNU, 2012):[13]

> Between 1990 and 2008, the wealth of these two countries as measured by GDP per capita rose 34% and 120% respectively. But a myopic focus on economic capital is flawed, scientists and economists at the conference argue. Natural capital, the sum of a country's assets, from forests to fossil fuels and minerals, declined 46% in Brazil and 31% in India, according to a new "Inclusive Wealth Indicator" designed to augment GDP as a measure of economic progress.

Only when calculations of this kind have been made can one assess whether development can be sustained through time.

It is clearly a very fertile time in terms of attempting to move from narrow measures, such as GNP or GDP, to a more realistic assessment of individual and social wellbeing. As the example cited from Dasgupta shows, however, this is no easy task. His calculation, which attempts to measure sustainability by adding depletion of natural resources into the equation, is already complex enough.

Wellbeing and justice

Nobel Prize winner Amartya Sen has made many important contributions to the study of development. His book *The Idea of Justice* (2009) provides a systematic overview or framework to much of his thinking on human welfare. The entire book requires careful study. One central thrust of his argument is that formulation of an ideal theory of the perfect society, or perfect institutions, is not the way ahead; but that there are ways of working out how to make interpersonal and social judgements around how to achieve more welfare for more people. We cannot hope for a theory to sort out all disagreements; for a perfect set of institutions to allocate welfare between competing interests; or to create perfect people to run these systems. 'We go as far as we reasonably can,' (p. 401). Going as far as we reasonably can requires action to alleviate deprivation, marginalization and vulnerability, in so far as this is possible. At its best, the study of development is a process of action and reflection.

So Sen's approach to justice does not begin from theoretical formulation of a perfect society or perfect social institutions. In fact, the entire book can be read as a critique of what he calls 'transcendental' approaches to justice.

> A transcendental approach cannot, on its own, address questions about advancing justice and compare alternative proposals for having a more just society, short of the utopian proposal of taking an imagined jump to a

> perfectly just world. Indeed, the answers that a transcendental approach to justice gives – or can give – are quite distinct and distant from the type of concerns that engage people in discussions on justice and injustice in the world (e.g. iniquities of hunger, poverty, illiteracy, torture, racism, female subjugation, arbitrary incarceration or medical exclusion as social features that need remedying) (Sen 2009: 96).

As he says: 'A theory of justice must have something to say about the choices that are actually on offer, and not just keep us engrossed in an imagined and implausible world of unbeatable magnificence.' (Sen 2009: 106) The mechanisms for expanding the choices available (his concern in *Development as Freedom*, 1999) include a plurality of concerns, and due attention to human rights, exercised through democratic debate and widespread information. In a globalized world, '[t]here are few non-neighbours left in the world today' (Sen, 2009: 173). So rather than theoretical descriptions of the perfectly just world, Sen advances a practical and pragmatic approach: 'Justice-enhancing changes or reforms demand comparative assessments, not simply an immaculate identification of "*the* just society" (or "the just institutions")' (Sen, 2009: 401). Justice will be approached therefore by focusing on 'assessments of social realizations, that is, on what actually happens' and on 'comparative issues of enhancement of justice' (Sen, 2009: 410).

The politics of wellbeing

Wealth ranking and other participatory methodologies add to that understanding of what works. This is true whether the initiative is a local exercise in wealth ranking, or a global participatory initiative such as the Voices of the Poor project of the World Bank (World Bank, no date). The volume *Crying Out for Change* explicitly framed the global synthesis of the responses from the claimed 20,000 participants around wellbeing and illbeing – the terminology of Robert Chambers (Narayan et al., 2000: 21–43). It also stressed: 'There are 2.8 billion poverty experts, the poor themselves.' (Narayan et al., 2000: 2) Whilst it is unclear to what extent the project actually changed World Bank policy or improved the lives of the poor (surely key criteria of its success), it generated a huge quantity of illuminating material on such issues as *Measuring Empowerment* (Narayan, 2005). In his final press conference as president of the World Bank (Wolfensohn, 2005), James Wolfensohn delivered his verdict: 'I think we are getting some way to that in terms of engaging people in poverty and understanding that the poor are not the object of charity, but they are part of the solution, and that you have to come up with methodologies that allow you to replicate things and make them sustainable.'

Wellbeing provides the promise of a framework in which the essential components of 'living together well' can be brought together, weighed and tested against each other. Development is good change; this needs to be seen as helping in identifying paths towards sustainable, social wellbeing. Describing it better through more comprehensive and sophisticated analyses is one thing; achieving it is another. Neither can be accomplished without the expression of what people actually want and need in order to thrive.

A more recent process aimed at drawing together views on wellbeing is the Bellagio Initiative on 'The Future of Philanthropy and Development in the Pursuit of Human Wellbeing'.[14] This is a comprehensive attempt to involve a global constituency in reflection on the challenges to human wellbeing and formulation of responses adequate to the challenges. Preparatory materials commissioned for the Initiative (see Institute of Development Studies (IDS), 2011a) moved well beyond the standard individualistic perspective on welfare economics addressing, for example, the care economy (Eyben and Fontana), a critique of consumerist values (Kasser), the need for coordination in delivery of aid (Picciotto), and the constraints in energy and resource use that require a reorientation if the benefits of development are to be widely shared (Evans and Evans). Interim conclusions from the process can be accessed online (IDS, 2011b).

During the Bellagio summit, Jay Naidoo offered a salutary perspective on wellbeing (Bellagio Initiative, 2011). He related the experience of the student generation of 1976 being crushed when they rose up against apartheid, and that it took 18 further years of opposition, action by civil society and mobilization through social movements to create the political stalemate that formed the platform for non-racial elections. Now, a further 18 years later, the distribution of wealth within the society (as measured by the Gini coefficient[15]) is still massively unequal. Establishing social justice and achieving even a relatively equal distribution of wellbeing is a huge undertaking, which will not happen by chance or through the play of market forces alone (Naidoo, 2010). There is no way round debate on social justice, nor of avoiding political struggle within societies and the world community on how to move forward toward social justice.

Conclusion

Analysis is important for achieving effective, evidence-based policy. It makes a huge difference to policy prescriptions for poverty eradication, whether one decides with Paul Collier that the most important 'core fact' is that about 50 countries, mostly conflict-affected, with a population of about a billion people, urgently need corrective action (Collier, 2007); or that it is more important to emphasize that most of the world's absolutely poor people live in Middle Income Countries with huge disparities of wealth, as Sumner has argued (Sumner, 2010). Choosing the right things to analyse and the best analysis is important.

However, one can question how many more detailed ways we need to show that most of the sub-Saharan African countries are really poor and to design policies to counter this. You can take it as a rule of thumb that whichever index you look at, whether it is recording GDP per capita, multidimensional poverty, food security, or happiness, that rich (OECD) and oil-rich countries will be at the top and much of sub-Saharan Africa will be at the bottom. How much further confirmation do we need that sub-Saharan African countries are in crisis before urgent action is taken?

It has been necessary to cover a wide terrain in the journey from Grandin's method of wealth ranking of Kenyan pastoralists, to global discussions of 3-D wellbeing (taking subjective, objective and interpersonal/social wellbeing as a framework). Along the way we have considered new initiatives to assess progress in wellbeing; and sustainable development and the necessity of not depleting the basis of life for future generations. Even though the picture is confusing, it is a sign of great intellectual vitality and a readiness to ensure development work is more rigorously grounded. There are some common threads: participatory methodology; understanding the views and priorities of those affected by policies; and the need for evidence-based policy.

The adoption of the MDGs has galvanized debate and action at global level about a set of targets. It has also generated critiques of where these targets came from and why these goals should be prioritized. Global crises relating to fuel, food and finance – as well as crises in multilateral institutions trying to get to grips with issues such as trade (the 'development round') and climate change – make it clear that prospects for wellbeing at local and national levels are bound up with complex and far-reaching sets of relationships. The formulation of a new set of internationally agreed targets will not be enough to secure 'development' for the world's poorest and most vulnerable people. Readers will draw their own conclusions, but the experience of these 30 or more years of work and reflection on human rights, peace and development issues suggest to me that the creation of more just societies is related to struggle, solidarity, subsidiarity and sustainability. Struggle, because no society has ever been transformed without organization and political initiative by those excluded from benefits of that society. If people do not 'do it for themselves' no good change will happen or stick. Solidarity, because committed and sensitive support from external allies can help tip the power balance and dismantle some of the connections that hold existing injustice in place. Subsidiarity, because while decisions need to be made as close to the people as possible, they must also be made at the right level. Decisions addressing global public goods and problems which do not need visas to cross boundaries cannot be made effectively at local level. Sustainability, because patterns of production and consumption that undermine the basis of future social existence are detrimental to intergenerational wellbeing.

This is a complex conclusion – unavoidably so. Politics, process and pragmatism are involved. Politics – as Sen has shown – because arguments about how to move to better social arrangements, institutions and governance are best conducted democratically. Process, because the participatory methodologies generate answers that are different from, and richer than, those of external 'experts'; and pragmatism, because better solutions, which approximate to a good society, are preferable to 'perfect' societies, which are never implemented (or implementable). The 3-D framework that includes material, relational and subjective aspects enables the vital dimensions of human wellbeing to be spelled out in valuable ways. Living together well depends on the basic prerequisites for life, the subjective dimension of satisfaction, and the right relationships. A strength of the MDGs is that they are clear and quantifiable. Considerable progress has been made on development indices that go well beyond GDP, and much ingenuity has been applied in finding intelligent proxies for desirable qualities (public goods), such as using air quality as an indicator for environment. Finding reliable and agreed quantitative indicators for good governance, sound institutions and social justice is far harder – though impressive arguments have been made to show the adverse impacts that extreme inequality has both within societies (Wilkinson and Pickett, 2009) and internationally (UNDP, 2011). As was noted at the outset, at present there is little basis for optimism that a major international realignment is likely; one that would allow significant progress to be made on trade, agricultural subsidies, climate change, technology transfer, lack of infrastructure, or any of the other multilateral issues that have such an adverse effect on the development of poorer countries.

One of the key messages of the Bellagio Initiative (2011) was the lack of trust in the development 'system'. Much has been promised, much has been tried, but the results for the most vulnerable and poorest people are woefully inadequate. Development reality is notoriously more complex than binary divisions (planners versus searchers – (Easterly, W. 2006); top-down or bottom-up; aid or trade; international versus locally owned). Even a major systematic attempt to embrace participatory methodology, such as the World Bank's Voices of the Poor project, was criticized as being 'window dressing' (Patel, 2008), which did not really change the fundamental policies or approach of the organization. It is important that those who use participatory methodologies are also aware of the danger of 'ventriloquising the poor' (Cornwall and Fujita, 2012) by selecting quotations from poor people to illustrate, embellish, and provide plausibility to an analysis developed away from the context.

There is a need for expertise. Development priorities are not only a matter for 'what the community thinks'. To give one illustration: the best choices in terms of tree planting for the next 30 years or more are a matter of immediacy in many communities, since trees have a long life and their growth could be affected by climate change in years to come. To ensure wise decisions, it would be necessary both to have detailed information on climate change for the region and also scientific understanding of the impact of change. It is not just a question of hearing as many voices as possible. It is also a matter of communities having access to information in a comprehensible form, which helps them to determine what is in their best interests.

In the context of the post-2015 debate on successor targets to the MDGs, the 'what' and 'how' of development take on a particular urgency. As Laderchi et al. pointed out in the context of the MDG discussion (2006), how you define and measure poverty matters. They distinguish between monetary approaches, capability approaches, social exclusion approaches, and participatory approaches. In the same volume, Sumner looks at the multidimensionality of wellbeing and comments that there still tends to be a predominance of economic indicators of wellbeing, because of the assumption that these are more readily quantifiable and objective (2006: 69). This bears out Nobel Prize winner Daniel Kahneman's (2012) contention that 'economists have a mystique among social scientists because they know mathematics'.

This chapter can be challenged on the grounds that it does not engage in a sufficiently robust critique of the various attempts to move beyond GDP to wellbeing, but its main message is something different. It is rather to show the complexity of doing so and of getting international agreement – particularly at a time when so many specialists are working on different conceptualizations.

As an element of the international process for deciding successor targets to the MDGs, also informing the work of the High Level Panel, the Participate initiative (co-convened by the IDS at the University of Sussex and the Beyond 2015 network; see IDS, no date) has been developed, which augments the process with, for example, plans for Ground Level Panels. This has involved reviewing 84 participatory studies, which comment on a total of 107 countries (Leavy and Howard, 2013). Four key themes have emerged (Leavy and Howard 2013: 6–7):

- Development frequently doesn't reach the very poorest and most marginalized.
- Development that is sustainable requires meaningful participation that leads to local ownership.
- Poverty is increasingly characterized by uncertainty, crisis, conflict, insecurity and volatility.
- Poor governance reinforces poverty for the poorest and most marginalized.

It remains to be seen whether the international community is capable of doing development differently – so that poor and vulnerable people have a genuine say in strategies which may help to eradicate the obstacles that stand in the way of their objective impoverishment, and their subjective lack of wellbeing.

Notes

1. The author is grateful to Allister McGregor and John Rowley for comments.
2. Professor Allister McGregor provided valuable methodological advice, conceptual and chronological restructuring of the paper. This is one of the points for which I am indebted.
3. 'Development means good change' according to a definition by Chambers (from 1995) (Chambers, 2005: 184). He spells out his personal commitment in his reflections on 'Responsible Well-being' (Chambers, 2005: 184–220).

4. Allister McGregor: Director of the ESRC Research Group at Bath; now Professor at the Institute of Development Studies, University of Sussex.
5. Personal communication. As with Grandin's methodology, the key terms for determining key factors in the social setting are defined by those who live there. Participatory methodologies have a much deeper history than this, of course. An earlier example is Paulo Freire's *Pedagogy of the Oppressed*, an approach to literacy work, which simultaneously assisted ordinary Latin Americans in developing the capacity to 'read' their social situation with radicalizing impact. (Freire, 1972a and 1972b; for a very clear introduction to the method, see Hebblethwaite 1993: 169–78).
6. Islamic school for religion-based study (footnote in original).
7. For a note on the Alkire Foster method used in the calculation of the MPI, see OPHI (no date b).
8. It is worth noting that Alkire had already contributed a chapter on 'Measuring freedoms alongside wellbeing' in the WeD volume (Alkire, 2007).
9. 'Gross National Happiness is a term coined by His Majesty the Fourth King of Bhutan, Jigme Singye Wangchuck in the 1970s. The concept implies that sustainable development should take a holistic approach towards notions of progress and give equal importance to non-economic aspects of wellbeing. The concept of GNH has often been explained by its four pillars: good governance, sustainable socio-economic development, cultural preservation, and environmental conservation. Lately the four pillars have been further classified into nine domains in order to create widespread understanding of GNH and to reflect the holistic range of GNH values. The nine domains are: psychological wellbeing, health, education, time use, cultural diversity and resilience, good governance, community vitality, ecological diversity and resilience, and living standards. The domains represents each of the components of wellbeing of the Bhutanese people, and the term "wellbeing" here refers to fulfilling conditions of a "good life" as per the values and principles laid down by the concept of Gross National Happiness.' (Centre for Bhutan Studies and GNH Research, no date).
10. Within the OECD, there is the attempt to measure wellbeing – as recorded in their Report "How's Life" and the on-line resource, the Better Life Index (which is compiled from data on housing, income, jobs, community, education, environment, governance, health, life satisfaction, safety and work-life balance in each of the OECD countries (OECD, no date)). Obviously, the OECD countries have a huge head start in terms of the statistical data available to them. But it is clear that, were such information available for all UN member countries, this would provide a huge asset in efforts to assess the relative wellbeing of countries. There would still be issues surrounding what elements are valued most highly in different contexts, whether the measures chosen are the right ones, and so on.
11. The full quotation, despite its complexity, if worth considering: 'Relative consumption and treadmill explanations are based on a hedonic/utilitarian understanding of happiness: happiness is conceived as the effect of earning income aimed at purchasing commodities. From an Aristotelian eudaimonian perspective this conception is too restrictive and – because of

this restriction – even biased. Earning money and purchasing commodities in the context of a market economy is at best only an aspect of what eudaimonia stands for – a meaningful life or well-being in the sense of actualisation of human potentials through intrinsically motivated activities in a context of interpersonal relationships.' Bruni (2009: 206–7).

12. Fromm further specifies the 'having mode' as related to 'The Acquisitive Society', taking up the title of the classic by R.H. Tawney (Tawney, 1943).
13. For a note describing the methodology used, see International Human Dimensions Programme on Global Environmental Change (no date).
14. The Bellagio Initiative is a series of global consultations to produce a new framework for philanthropic and international development collaboration in pursuit of human wellbeing in the 21st century. The project is led by the Institute of Development Studies (IDS), the Resource Alliance and the Rockefeller Foundation. The preparatory materials and information generated through the Summit are available on the Initiative's website (Institute of Development Studies, 2011a).
15. The Gini coefficient is a mathematical calculation of inequality within society. For a technical description see: <http://data.worldbank.org/indicator/SI.POV.GINI> [accessed 14 May 2014].

References

Alkire, S. (2007) 'Measuring freedoms alongside wellbeing', in Gough, I. and McGregor, J.A. (eds) *Wellbeing in developing countries: from theory to research,* Cambridge: Cambridge University Press.

Beaumont, J. (2011) *Measuring National Well-being: A Discussion Paper on Domains and Measures,* Newport: Office for National Statistics. <http://www.ons.gov.uk/ons/dcp171766_240726.pdf> [accessed 30 April 2014]

Bellagio Initiative (2011) 'Protecting and promoting human wellbeing in the 21st century' [online video recording of panel discussion]. <http://www.bellagioinitiative.org/resource-section/multimedia/> [accessed 30 April 2014]

Bruni, L. (2009) 'Happiness', in Peil, J. and van Staveren, I. (eds) *Handbook of economics and ethics,* pp.202–9. Cheltenham & Northampton, Mass.: Edward Elgar.

Carrithers, M (1992), *Why Humans Have Cultures, Explaining Anthropology and Social Diversity,* Oxford and New York: Oxford University Press

Centre for Bhutan Studies & GNH Research (no date) 'Gross National Happiness Index' [website] <www.grossnationalhappiness.com> [accessed 30 April 2014]

Centre for Bhutan Studies & GNH Research (2010) 'GNH Survey Findings 2010' <http://www.grossnationalhappiness.com/docs/2010_Results/PDF/National.pdf> [accessed 3 May 2014]

Chambers, R. (1983) *Rural Development: Putting the Last First,* London, Lagos, New York: Longman.

Chambers, R. (2005) *Ideas for Development,* London: Earthscan.

Chambers, R. (2008) *Revolutions in Development Inquiry,* London: Earthscan.

Collier, P. (2007) *The Bottom Billion: Why the Poorest Countries are Failing and What Can Be Done About It,* Oxford: Oxford University Press.

Cornwall, A. and Fujita, M. (2012) 'Ventriloquising "the Poor"? Of voice, choices, and the politics of "participatory" knowledge production', *Third World Quarterly* 33:9 1751–65.

Coulthard, S., Johnson, D. and McGregor, J.A. (2011) 'Poverty, sustainability and human wellbeing: A social wellbeing approach to the global fisheries crisis', *Global Environmental Change* 21 (2): 453–63.

Dasgupta, P. (2007) *Economics: A Very Short Introduction*, Oxford and New York: Oxford University Press.

Earth Institute (2012) 'First World Happiness Report launched at the United Nations' [website] <http://www.earth.columbia.edu/articles/view/2960> (posted 02 April 2012) [accessed 30 April 2014]

Easterly, W. 2006. Planners versus Searchers in Foreign Aid, Asian Development Review, Vol.23, No. 2. pp 1-35.

Freire, P. (1972a) *Pedagogy of the Oppressed*, London: Penguin (First English edition 1970 – Continuum).

Freire, P. (1972b) *Cultural Action for Freedom*, London: Penguin (First US edition Harvard Education al Review 1970).

Fromm, E. (1976) *To Have or To Be?* London: Penguin.

Grandin, B. E. (1988) *Wealth Ranking in Smallholder Communities: A Field Manual*, Rugby: Practical Action Publishing.

Gough, I and McGregor, J.A. (2007) *Wellbeing in Developing Countries: From Theory to Research*, Cambridge: Cambridge University Press.

Harris, M. (1990) *Our Kind; Who we are; where we came from; where we are going*, New York: Harper & Row.

Hebblethwaite, M. (1993) *Base Communities: An Introduction*, London: Geoffrey Chapman.

International Human Dimensions Programme on Global Environmental Change (IHDP) (no date) *Inclusive Wealth Report* [online resource] <www.ihdp.unu.edu/file/get/8751> [accessed 30 April 2014]

Institute of Development Studies (IDS) (2011a) 'The Bellagio Initiative: the future of philanthropy and development in the pursuit of human wellbeing' [website] <www.bellagioinitiative.org/> [accessed 30 April 2014]

IDS (2011b) 'Documenting the Bellagio Initiative Summit' [aide-memoire available online] (posted December 2011) <www.bellagioinitiative.org/wp-content/uploads/2011/12/Bellagio_Aide-m%C3%A9moire_final.pdf> [accessed 30 April 2014]

IDS (no date) 'Participate: Knowledge from the margins for post-2015' [website] <http://www.ids.ac.uk/participate> [accessed 1 May 2014]

Kahneman, D. (2012) 'This much I know: Daniel Kahneman' [online interview] <www.theguardian.com/science/2012/jul/08/this-much-i-know-daniel-kahneman> (posted 8 July 2012) [accessed 1 May 2014]

Laderchi, C. R., Saith, R. and Stewart, F. (2006) 'Does it matter that we do not agree on the definition of poverty? A comparison of four approaches' in McGillivray, M. and Clarke, M. (eds) *Understanding Human Well-being*, Tokyo, New York and Paris: United Nations University Press, pp.19–53.

Layard, R. (2005) *Happiness: Lessons From a New Science*, New York: Penguin.

Leavy, J. and Howard, J. (2013) *What Matters Most? Evidence from 84 Participatory Studies with Those Living with Extreme Poverty and Marginalisation*,

Participate, Brighton: IDS. <www.ids.ac.uk/files/dmfile/ParticipateSynthesis-WhatMattersMost.pdf> [accessed 3 May 2014]

McGregor, J.A. (2004), 'Researching well-being: Communicating between the needs of policy-makers and the needs of the people', *Global Social Policy* 4 (3): 337–358.

McGregor, J.A. and Sumner, A. (2010) 'Beyond business as usual: What might 3-D wellbeing contribute to MDG momentum?' *IDS Bulletin* 41 (1): 104–12.

McGillivray, M. and Clarke, M. (eds) (2006) *Understanding Human Well-being,* Tokyo, New York and Paris: United Nations University Press.

Millennium Project (2006) [historical website] <http://www.unmillenniumproject.org/goals/index.htm> [accessed 3 May 2014]

Naidoo, J. (2010), *Fighting for Justice: A Lifetime of Political and Social Activism,* Johannesburg: Picador.

Narayan, D., Chambers, R., Shah, M.K. and Petesch, P. (2000) *Voices of the Poor: Crying Out for Change,* New York, N.Y.: Published for the World Bank, Oxford University Press. <http://go.worldbank.org/XMWSK7EMS0> [accessed 30 April 2014]

Narayan, D. (ed.) (2005) *Measuring Empowerment: Cross-disciplinary Perspectives,* Washington D.C.: World Bank.

Organisation for Economic Co-operation and Development (OECD) (no date), 'Better Life Index' [website] <www.oecdbetterlifeindex.org/> [accessed 3 May 2014]

Oxford Poverty & Human Development Initiative (OPHI) (2011) 'Multidimensional Poverty Index 2011' [website] <http://www.ophi.org.uk/wp-content/uploads/OPHI-MPI-Brief-2011.pdf?cda6c1> [accessed 3 May 2014]

OPHI (no date a) 'Global Multidimensional Poverty Index' [website] <www.ophi.org.uk/multidimensional-poverty-index/> [accessed 14 May 2014]

OPHI (no date b) 'Global Multidimensional Poverty Index' [website] www.ophi.org.uk/wp-content/uploads/MPI-One-Page-final.pdf [accessed 14 May 2014]

OPHI (no date c) 'Alkire Foster Method' [website] <http://www.ophi.org.uk/research/multidimensional-poverty/alkire-foster-method/> [accessed 3 May 2014]

Patel, R. (2008) 'Interview with Raj Patel' [online], Washington, D.C.: National Family Farm Coalition. <http://nffc.net/Pressroom/2008RajPatelInterview.htm> [accessed 1 May 2014]

Peil, J. & van Staveren, I. (eds) (2009) *Handbook of Economics and Ethics.* Cheltenham & Northampton, Mass.: Edward Elgar.

Rifkin, J. (2009) *The Empathic Civilization: The Race to Global Consciousness in a World in Crisis*, Cambridge: Polity.

Sachs, J.D., Helliwell, J.F. and Layard, R. (2012) *World Happiness Report,* Columbia University: Earth Institute.

Sen, A. (1999) *Development as Freedom*, New York: Knopf.

Sen, A. (2003) 'Foreword' in Fukuda-Parr, S. and Shiva Kumar, A.K. (eds) *Readings in Human Development*, pp. vii–xiii, Oxford University Press and New York: UNDP.

Sen, A. (2009) *The Idea of Justice*. London: Penguin.

Singer, P. (2009) *The Life You Can Save: Acting Now to End World Poverty*. New York: Random House; London, Basingstoke and Oxford: Picador.
Social Watch (2011) 'Social Watch launches 2011 Basic Capabilities Index' [press release] <www.socialwatch.org/sites/default/files/press-SW-BCI2011-1.pdf> [accessed 3 May 2014]
Stiglitz, J.E. (2012) *The Price of Inequality*. London and New York: Penguin.
Stiglitz, J.E., Fitoussi, J.P. and Sen, A. (2010) *Report by the Commission on the Measurement of Economic Performance and Social Progress*, Paris: Commission on the Measurement of Economic Performance and Social Progress. <http://www.stiglitz-sen-fitoussi.fr/documents/rapport_anglais.pdf> [accessed 3 May 2014]
Stoll, L., Michaelson, J. and Seaford, C. (2012) *Well-being Evidence for Policy: A Review*, London: New Economics Foundation. <www.neweconomics.org/publications/entry/well-being-evidence-for-policy-a-review> [accessed 3 May 2014]
Sumner, A. (2006) 'Economic well-being and non-economic well-being' in McGillivray, M. and Clarke, M. (eds) *Understanding Human Well-being*, pp. 54–73, Tokyo, New York and Paris: United Nations University Press.
Sumner, A. (2010) 'Global poverty and the new bottom billion', *IDS Working Paper* 349: 01-43.
Sumner, A. and Melamed, C. (2010) 'Introduction – the MDGs and beyond: pro-poor policy in a changing world', *IDS Bulletin* 41 (1): 1–6.
Tawney, R. H. (1943; 1st edn 1921), *The Acquistive Society*, London: G. Bell & Sons.
UN (2011) 'Happiness should have a greater role in development policy – UN Member States', UN news story [website], <www.un.org/apps/news/story.asp?NewsID=39084> (posted 19 July 2011) [accessed 30 April 2014]
UN (2012a) 'Global Sustainability Panel says a "Future Worth Choosing" must be based on true costs to people and the environment' [press release] (posted 30 January 2012) <http://www.un.org/gsp/sites/default/files/event_attachments/Addis%20Launch-Press%20Release.pdf> [accessed 3 May 2014]
UN (2012b) 'Happiness and well-being: defining a new economic paradigm', Remarks made by UN Secretary-General at High Level Meeting [website] (posted 2 April 2012) <www.un.org/apps/news/infocus/sgspeeches/statments_full.asp?statID=1493> [accessed 30.04.2014]
UN (2012c), *Resilient People, Resilient Planet: A future worth choosing*, Report by UN Secretary General's High-Level Panel on Global Sustainability, New York, N.Y.: UN <www.un.org/gsp/sites/default/files/attachments/GSP_Report_web_final.pdf> [accessed 14 04 2012]
UNDP (2011) *Human Development Report 2011: Sustainability and Equity: A Better Future For All*, New York: UNDP.
UNDP (no date) 'Human Development Index' [website] <http://hdr.undp.org/en/statistics/hdi/> [accessed 3 May 2014]
United Nations University (2012) 'Barriers to change' [online press release] Press Release from Planet Under Pressure conference. <www.vie.unu.edu/file/get/9757.pdf> (posted March 2012) [accessed 30 April 2014]
University of Bath (2012) 'Wellbeing research in developing countries' [website] <www.welldev.org.uk/> [accessed 3 May 2014]

Ura, K., Alkire, S., Zangmo, T. and Wangdi, K. (2012) *A Short Guide to Gross National Happiness Index*, Bhutan: Centre for Bhutan Studies. <http://www.grossnationalhappiness.com/wp-content/uploads/2012/04/Short-GNH-Index-edited.pdf> [accessed 3 May 2014]

Wilkinson, R. and Pickett, K. (2010) *The Spirit Level: Equality is Better for Everyone*, London: Penguin.

Wolfensohn, J. (2005) 'A decade of dedication to poverty eradication'. Final assessment by James Wolfensohn, president of the World Bank, prior to leaving office [website] <http://go.worldbank.org/JSOOEIWEM0> [accessed 30 April 2014]

World Bank (no date) 'Voices of the poor' [website] <http://go.worldbank.org/H1N8746X10> [accessed 30 April 2014]

About the author

Roger Williamson is currently a Visiting Fellow at the Institute of Development Studies (IDS), Sussex University, and a member of the Development Board of the Oxford Mindfulness Centre, Oxford University. His previous career spans over 20 years working on peace, human rights and development issues for NGOs, and more than a decade organizing over 70 sustainable development and international affairs conferences for Wilton Park, the academically – and financially – independent centre attached to the UK Foreign and Commonwealth Office. Since joining IDS, he has worked as a core member of the team that conducted the Bellagio Initiative on philanthropy, wellbeing and international development; on urban poverty; and on preparations for the 50th anniversary of IDS in 2016.

CHAPTER 10

Conclusions about wellbeing assessments and ideas for the future

John Rowley

This chapter looks at the main messages from the different chapters in this book and links them to trends in assessing poverty and wellbeing. The increased interest in wellbeing could translate into international development agencies adopting more complex understanding of poverty in the design and evaluation of initiatives. However, this seems unlikely in the short term, as the pressure for narrow measures of results may continue to force aid agencies into seeking simplistic estimates of impact. The level of interest in wellbeing is rather patchy, and some important aid agencies are apparently not exploring multi-dimensional definitions of poverty. This may be because wellbeing has many different definitions or because there is no agreement on a simple method that can be applied to assess it. Wellbeing is not a declared objective of development work, although assessments of wellbeing could be helpful in designing, monitoring and evaluating development interventions.

Keywords: wellbeing, well-being, ranking, health, agency, multi-dimensional assessment

If you ask people about their wellbeing, for example, in asking them to carry out a wellbeing ranking, you are likely to receive a lot of ideas on a wide range of issues relating to wellbeing and illbeing or poverty. Material wealth will be mentioned as one of the factors and is likely to be central to the discussions of wellbeing that follow. However, economic wealth will not be the exclusive concern, and will be surrounded by diverse other aspects of human life, including social, spiritual, attitudinal and other issues. This was well known to those who tried the simple tools of wellbeing ranking, or the 'heap-of-beans' exercise (Schaeffer, 1992) in the early 1990s. Even when they focused on wealth during the ranking exercises, they were shown a mixture of interrelated criteria drawn from many different aspects of life.

This finding was reinforced by the Voices of the Poor project (Narayan et al., 2000), in which large numbers of people in 23 countries were asked about a range of elements in their livelihoods and took part in wellbeing ranking exercises. Thousands of people were asked about their situation and offered the tools to help them talk about it. They described poverty in a broad range of ways and brought in many interconnected dimensions. In many cases, material wealth was not the highest priority. Often, intangible social factors,

http://dx.doi.org/10.3362/9781780448459.010

or feelings of security or of being valued, for example, were rated as more important than material wealth.

Voices of the Poor did not emerge from a vacuum. The World Bank had produced a report monitoring poverty since 1978, and continues to do so every year. The *World Development Report* (World Bank, 2013) is strongly focused on economic income and provides comparable statistics from countries where data are available. The year 1999 saw, perhaps partly in response to the focus on material poverty, the launch of the Voices of the Poor project, aiming to include a wide range of factors and allowing the poor themselves to say what they found important in their assessments of wellbeing.

The findings from Voices of the Poor are echoed in industrialized countries. In 2011, the UK Office for National Statistics (cited in OECD, 2013), found that only 30% of nearly 7,000 respondents considered economic measures to be a good measure of national wellbeing. By contrast, 80% endorsed health data, 79% 'life satisfaction', and 62% 'income distributions' as better indicators. The top-ranked indicator of wellbeing by visitors to the OECD Better Life Index is 'life satisfaction'. This is followed by health, education, the environment, and work-life balance, all apparently more important to respondents than explicit descriptions of material wealth.

The OECD (2011) *How's Life?* framework for measuring wellbeing is based on three aspects: material living conditions, quality of life, and sustainability. The framework depends to a great extent on the Fitoussi-Sarkosy-Sen ideas explored by Roger Williamson in Chapter 9 of this book ('Wealth ranking to wellbeing: where next for development?', Williamson, 2014). In the OECD model, material living conditions include: income and wealth; jobs and earnings; and housing. Sustainability of wellbeing is based on preserving four forms of capital: natural, economic, human, and social. Quality of life covers many of the same issues as are raised in wellbeing ranking exercises, including health, education, social connections, civic engagement, governance, personal security, and 'subjective wellbeing'.

The meaning of subjective wellbeing is taken up in the recent OECD *Guidelines for Measuring Subjective Well-being* (2013), which offers a comprehensive guide to carrying out assessments on the basis of three areas of enquiry. There is a great deal of advice on how to shape questionnaires and how to phrase questions, with some fascinating findings on how people respond differently to different phrases – phrases which appear at first glance to be very similar. The components of the assessment include levels of satisfaction with work, health, and income, and how people react to their situation and make sense of it. The language used is rather off-putting and the vocabulary is, unfortunately, likely to exclude the ordinary interested reader.

The details of the analytical framework may not be as important as the fact that the OECD has a wellbeing unit, and is taking very seriously the possibility of measuring subjective wellbeing. In the preface, the suggestions that it is too difficult to measure, or that we don't know enough to carry out assessments, are dismissed as excuses. What seems surprising is that the effort to determine how to assess wellbeing does *not* include participatory wellbeing assessment exercises, which could be used to explore key issues and could be developed with the people who would provide their own understanding. This may be evidence of the decline of participatory methods, as the very idea of designing the framework and testing the assessments with local people does not appear.

The World Bank Group is also working on multidimensional understanding of poverty. The paper *A Common Vision for the World Bank Group* (World Bank Group, 2013) includes the statement (para 13):

> Ending poverty and sharing prosperity are unequivocally about progress in non-monetary dimensions of welfare, including, but not limited to, education, health, nutrition, and access to essential infrastructure, as well as about empowerment and enhancing voice and participation in economic, social, and political spheres, especially for women and other vulnerable groups.

This follows a sequence of initiatives in which the multi-dimensional nature of poverty was made explicit by the International Finance Corporation (IFC) as reported in the Road Map (Financial Years 13–15) (IFC, 2012) and work was subsequently done on reaching a definition of a poverty focus. The current Road Map (Financial Years 14–16) continues this direction and makes reference to the Voices of the Poor project (IFC, 2013: para 3.20). The reference is only with respect to levels of employment, but it is a significant acknowledgement of that remarkable initiative. The World Bank Group is making important efforts to come up with better definitions of poverty and, of course, better ways of measuring changes in poverty. Although it is acknowledged that poverty assessment should be based at household level (IFC 2012: 96, para 94), the cost of working at this level, it is suggested, may be prohibitive. This is different from the position of the OECD, which dismissed cost as an excuse. However, one wonders whether the authors have considered a potential role for wellbeing ranking, or for wellbeing assessment methods like those described in Chapter 8, 'Wellbeing assessment in practice: lessons from Wellbeing and Poverty Pathways', by Sarah White and her colleagues (Marshall et al., 2014).

Voices of the Poor was also mentioned by Duncan Green in a blog published in May 2013. Green was expressing the view that a sequence of shocks (the financial crisis, spikes in food prices, and the Arab Spring) have made us think differently about the nature of poverty and comments that, 'As the World Bank's path-breaking and unsurpassed "Voices of the Poor" study in the 1990s showed, to be poor is as much about anxiety, vulnerability and shame as about income levels.' Green wonders if an awareness of the complex nature of poverty and a focus on power and agency in development will help aid agencies to reach a more human understanding of the nature of poverty and power.

These cases of interest in wellbeing by large development agencies are only recent examples of the trends explored in Chapter 9 by Roger Williamson (2014). He shows how the concept of wellbeing grew and was tested by a range of leading thinkers over time. If the interest in wellbeing leads to a desire to find ways of allowing poor people to explain how they perceive the nature of poverty and how interventions have changed levels of wellbeing, then wellbeing ranking would be a good candidate tool. Clearly this is not a recommendation for a single tool to be used on its own, but rather in combination with other methods in a sequence of exercises.

Assessments of wellbeing actually work, despite the uncertainties and possibilities of error, and as Polly Hill (1972) says, there is no point in pretending that the categories produced by ranking do not represent real differences in levels of wellbeing. The usefulness of the assessments for higher-level influence and policy making was pointed out in a review of Polly Hill's publication shortly after it was published. The reviewer suggests that the information and insight into how farmers of different capacities, with different levels of wealth, produce food, should be used in the design of state agricultural policies and in externally funded development projects (Ortiz, 1974). Although it is clear that such information would be useful in policy formulation, no mechanism is obvious. My own work in agricultural development in Africa in the late 1970s and early 1980s did not include ideas of assessing the wellbeing of the proposed beneficiaries, or of designing interventions that might be appropriate to producers of different levels of wellbeing. In fact, the opposite seems to be true: development initiatives tended to be uniform, and likely to be of help only to the most well-off producers who had the capacity to invest and the ability to take risks.

Anton Simanowitz has shown in Chapter 6 ('Using participatory wealth ranking in a South African microfinance organization: the value of scale', Simanowitz, 2014) that wellbeing ranking can be applied across a range of situations and can provide robust and locally meaningful assessments of poverty. He makes it clear that the quality of facilitation is crucial to success but that, despite those difficulties, the method, which had been perceived to be only narrowly applicable to very local situations, can in fact be extended across substantial areas. The method still takes account of a range of material, social and personal factors in its assessments.

It is not obvious that managers in development agencies would have the confidence to evaluate the effectiveness of their work by using wellbeing assessment methods. One obstacle might be a concern over the quality of facilitation and interview work. Claire Heffernan and Federica Misturelli show in Chapter 7 ('Wellbeing ranking, semi-structured interviews and practitioner bias: personality traits and participatory narratives', Heffernan and Misturelli, 2014) that the quality of facilitation really matters, and in ways that might not be expected. There are no clear, shared quality standards, and bias is always likely. Clearly, it is necessary to be alert and self-critical in order to notice and manage bias or other distorting effects in interviews. The quality of engagement seems to matter a great deal in interviews, and this probably applies to all interviews regardless of the methods used or the overall aim. Participatory methods may require good personal qualities as well as good facilitation skills. A good process, in which findings are checked and used to design the next steps in cycles of learning, can resolve issues that might result from any particular interview.

The OECD manual referred to above (2011) contains ample guidance on the design and implementation of questionnaire surveys. It seems that people can be very perverse in answering questionnaires; for example, they sometimes arbitrarily select the first of a range of options, but also select the last of the range. This is only one example, and people who design and administer questionnaires must be alert to these and other issues and apply skill and fine judgement to their work. The quality of the tools and their administration seem to be important to any information collection method.

Sarah White and colleagues show in Chapter 8 (Marshall et al., 2014) that the use of multi-dimensional assessment of wellbeing can work, and could be used across a wide range of circumstances. There is a clear need for testing, and scrupulous attention to detail both during the testing and perhaps especially when interpreting the initial results. The difficulties associated with adopting wellbeing assessments do not seem to be linked to the methods themselves.

It may be that widespread adoption of wellbeing assessment methods is hampered by a perceived problem with participatory approaches. Participatory methods work well in a good process, where interview methods are honed through repeated cycles of learning and, as mentioned in Chapter 5, the facilitator does not give up too soon (Pretty et al., 1992). It is also important that the methods are used with a positive attitude towards learning, which is sometimes expressed as believing that local people are experts in their own lives. Following this approach leads to the development of wellbeing assessments that are based on the views of local people, and give rise to detailed, rich and context-specific observations of wellbeing. This could make it more difficult to aggregate results over a wide area, and might make the whole approach less attractive to those people managing systems that require simple, single observations of impact. At the same time, familiarity with participatory methods is dwindling among the staff of international development agencies, and the image of participatory methods is gathering a negative reputation. This may be partly because of a presumption that methods are almost always participatory, and that the approach has been mainstreamed, thereby making it inappropriate to call it into question. It may be partly because participation is seen as 'old', amid the faddishness of the development aid business where energy and enthusiasm normally attach to things that are new.

Voices of the Poor seemed to offer the possibility of working with locally relevant understanding, and an interpretation of poverty that incorporated many nuanced interconnected factors. However, almost immediately the aid agencies focused on the Millennium Development Goals (MDGs), which are the opposite of this approach. The MDGs are a set of simple statements that are applied globally and require no interpretation or local input at all. They were probably helpful in mobilizing donor funds and focusing attention on some issues of extreme poverty. Certainly no one could argue against them in terms of not desiring better health, better education, etc., and the definitions are simple, which ought to allow easy measurement of progress. However, the MDGs are not useful at local level and risk treating entire nations as a single entity; a bad case of 'Homogeneous Blob Syndrome' a phrase coined by Alice Welbourn to describe a failure to recognize differences at community level (1991).

The MDGs are examples of the 'Simple, quantitative, unambiguous targets [that] are important political rallying points and valuable markers of progress', cited by Rick Davies (1997) in *Beyond Wealth Ranking*. Yet, simple rallying cries, such as those slogans promoted by many agencies to encourage staff and supporters to 'Make Poverty History' or 'End Poverty', also deny the 'complexity of the concept of "poverty", the importance of issues like participation and social inclusion, and the imperative of privileging local perceptions' (Davies, 1997, citing Aidan Cox).

The successors to the MDGs will almost certainly aim to, among other things, 'end poverty' and improve 'shared prosperity', and are likely to require the same simple, single measures made up of scaled-up averages and aggregation of data; phrases that will be easy to say and provide an illusion of impact and control. They may be more open to local perceptions of poverty, but they will probably be used alongside the powerful and ever-growing demand for evidence of impact. Participation as an approach is not likely to be an overt aspect of the post-2015 aid agenda.

Tina Wallace et al. (2007) say that the relationships between the actors in international development are perverse, and tend to prevent the flow of learning from poor people to those funding initiatives that are meant to help the poor. The power in the relationships between funders, intermediary agencies, local partners and, eventually, beneficiaries, tends to discourage honest dealing with the demands for evidence of impact. The increase in pressure to produce simple statements of impact has aggravated these problems. This is not a simplistic demonization of donors as the source of all problems; overall, though, the ability of local partners to develop locally appropriate means of assessing changes in wellbeing is diminished by the reporting requirements according to which they operate.

The drive for evidence of impact may have improved some areas of reporting, but it has also had some perverse consequences. The demand for results has not been easy to accommodate in many areas where results are hard to observe and take a long time to come about. Perversely, the drive for evidence of impact may be producing the opposite effect, as implementing agencies increasingly separate monitoring and information collection into different functions: one to support their own learning; and the other to report to donors.

The *Big Push Forward* (2013) provides an analysis of this situation, including views on the pressures that donor agencies are under and the nature of the relationships involved. It is interesting to consider whether wellbeing assessments have a role to play in this. Could they provide some of the observations that would satisfy the need for evidence? Could they be used as a starting point for other work that would deliver better evidence?

Do development programme staff need to know about wellbeing if their business is simply reducing income poverty? Is it possible to argue that the business of an externally funded development project is merely to help some of the poorer in a community become less poor? This argument might observe that many aspects of wellbeing are related and correlate well with material wealth. Therefore, the argument would continue, it is only necessary to know that some who were among the poorer have become better off. In any case, the social, personal, and other intangible aspects of poverty and wellbeing are beyond the influence of the external agent, who cannot take responsibility for improving these intangible aspects of wellbeing. However, that is not what the use of wellbeing approaches and the Voices of the Poor tell us. Their main message seems to be that being poor is made up of a wide range of things, not just material wellbeing; and that becoming less poor involves changes in many of those aspects of life. This would make it right to try to monitor such changes, using methods that are sensitive to the diverse elements perceived to make up wellbeing.

Wellbeing is not a slogan in high-level development goals and not a declared aim of most development work. Development aid initiatives do not focus on wellbeing as an objective; they focus on education, health, access to water, increased income, and similar aims. It is true that such programmes have impacts on wellbeing aside from their declared targets. For example: an income-generating project may increase wellbeing through increased social links and solidarity among the participants and increased prestige in their families and community. Although wellbeing offers the potential to assess and describe a situation and monitor changes in meaningful and locally appropriate ways, in international development aid it is unlikely to become a focus for action. In other contexts such as health care in the UK, on the other hand, the phrase wellbeing may have meaning as a desirable objective and be a focus for action and understanding (NHS, 2013).

The situation in international aid at this moment seems to contain some competing trends. First, there is an upwelling of interest in wellbeing and definitions of poverty as complex and multifaceted. This includes suggestions for methods of assessing poverty according to the understanding and aspirations of local people. It also includes a number of models of wellbeing that have been tested and shown to provide the kind of insight and understanding that is required. This book adds to the evidence around this trend and contributes this observation: that the simple tools of wellbeing ranking can also provide insight into, and understanding of, the complex and nuanced nature of poverty.

Second, there is a strong and growing need among donors and agencies in international development for evidence of impact, where impact means numbers of people experiencing lower levels of poverty. The 'What We Do' page of the DFID website (2013) includes statements that, by 2015, DFID will: help 9 million children in primary school; help 2 million children in lower secondary school; train more than 190,000 teachers; and many more targets in the same style, involving vague ideas of improvement and massive numbers. Of course, staff within DFID have complex and subtle ideas about improving the wellbeing of poor people, but the agency demands data to support simplistic statements like the examples above.

Third, the concepts and language of participation seems to be considered weak or faulty. This makes it more difficult to present, even-handedly, the evidence of the effectiveness of methods that emerged from the time when participation was more easily accepted and seen as an important approach. Although all development agencies still speak of their work as participatory, one of the core strands in the participatory approach, addressing power issues in development aid processes, has gone missing. Part of the decline in attention to participatory processes may relate to internal divisions between social and economic interests within development agencies; these may map onto differences in the use of qualitative and quantitative measures and assessments. When economists and quantitative methods have greater influence, then participatory methods may have less importance.

Fourth, there is the ongoing design of the successors to the MDGs, which seem likely to be built around very simple statements about ending poverty. Perhaps there will be room within statements about sharing prosperity to recognize the usefulness of wellbeing assessments of local differences. The evidence from this book seems to suggest that wellbeing works as a way of understanding the complex nature of poverty, and as a way of assessing changes, both in terms of reducing poverty and sharing in prosperity. Wellbeing also works as a way of being more realistic and more intelligent in managing development efforts. Perhaps there are ways in which the local nuanced understanding and the global slogans can be made to work together. It may be that wellbeing assessments can take on a greater importance in those spaces within international development where demands for simplistic evidence of impact carry less influence. This may require some decentralization, so that the work of projects and programmes is respected at the level at which they operate.

References

Big Push Forward (2013) [website] <http://bigpushforward.net/> [accessed 3 May 2014]

Department for International Development (DFID) (2013) 'What WDo' [website] <www.gov.uk/government/organisations/department-for-international-development/about> [accessed 3 May 2014]

Green, D. (2013) 'How have a series of global shocks changed the way we think about development?' [blog] <www.oxfamblogs.org/fp2p/?p=14558> (posted 9 May 2013) [accessed 3 May 2014]

International Finance Corporation (IFC) (2012) *IFC Road Map FY13–15: Creating Innovative Solutions in Challenging Times* [online resource] <www.ifc.org/wps/wcm/connect/87c9800046b649beaa04abb254bfb7d4/Road+Map+FY13-15.pdf?MOD=AJPERES> [accessed 3 May 2014]

IFC (2013) *IFC Road Map FY14–16: Leveraging the Private Sector to Eradicate Extreme Poverty and Pursue Shared Prosperity* [online resource] <www.ifc.org/wps/wcm/connect/1d30b9004028f151b28fff23ff966f85/Road+Map+FY14-16+redacted.pdf?MOD=AJPERES> [accessed 3 May 2014]

Heffernan, C. and Misturelli, F. (2014) 'Wellbeing ranking: Semi-structured interviews and practitioner bias: Personality traits and participatory narratives', in Rowley, J. (ed.) *Wellbeing Ranking: Developments in Applied Community-level Poverty Research*, pp. 89–110, Rugby: Practical Action Publishing, <http://dx.doi.org/10.3362/9781780448459.007>

Hill, P. (1972) *Rural Hausa – A Village and a Setting*, Cambridge: Cambridge University Press.

Marshall, N., White, S.C., Gaines, Jr., S.O. and Jha, S. (2014), 'Wellbeing assessment in practice: Lessons from wellbeing and poverty pathways', in Rowley, J. (ed.) *Wellbeing Ranking: Developments in Applied Community-level Poverty Research*, pp. 111–126, Rugby: Practical Action Publishing, <http://dx.doi.org/10.3362/9781780448459.008>

National Health Service (NHS) (2013). See for example 'Tools: wellbeing self-assessment' [website] <http://www.nhs.uk/Tools/Pages/Wellbeing-self-assessment.aspx> [accessed 3 May 2014]

Narayan, D., Chambers, R., Shah, M.K. and Petesch, P. (2000) *Voices of the Poor: Crying Out for Change*, New York, N.Y: Published for the World Bank, Oxford: Oxford University Press.

Organisation for Economic Co-operation and Development (OECD) (2011) *How's Life?: Measuring well-being*, Paris: OECD. *<http://dx.doi.org/10.1787/9789264121164-en>* [accessed 3 May 2014]

OECD (2013) *OECD Guidelines on Measuring Subjective Well-being*, Paris: OECD. *<http://dx.doi.org/10.1787/9789264191655-en>* [accessed 3 May 2014]

Ortiz, S. (1974) 'Obstacle to Agricultural Growth in Hausaland Viewed through a Village Study', *Development and Cultural Change* 23 (1) 163–68.

Pretty, J., Subramanian S., Kempu Chetty, N., Ananthakrishnan, D., Jayanthi, C., Muralikrishnasamy, S. and Renganayaki, K. (1992) 'Finding the poorest in a Tamil Nadu village: a sequence of mapping and wealth ranking', *RRA Notes* 15: 39–42, London: International Institute for Environment and Development (IIED).

Schaefer, S.S. (1992) 'The "beans-game" – experiences with a variation of wealth ranking in the Kivu Region, Eastern Zaire' *RRA Notes* 15: 27–28, London: IIED.

Wallace T., with Bornstein, L. and Chapman, J. (2007) *The Aid Chain: Coercion and Commitment in Development NGOs*, Rugby: Practical Action Publishing.

Welbourn, A. (1991) 'RRA and the analysis of difference', *RRA Notes* 14: 14–23, London: IIED.

Williamson, R. (2014) 'Wealth ranking to wellbeing: Where next for development?', in Rowley, J. (ed.) *Wellbeing Ranking: Developments in Applied Community-level Poverty Research*, pp. 127–152, Rugby: Practical Action Publishing, <http://dx.doi.org/10.3362/9781780448459.009>

World Bank (2013) 'World Development Reports' [website] <http://econ.worldbank.org/external/default/main?contentMDK=23044836&theSitePK=8258025&piPK=8258412&pagePK=8258258> [accessed 3 May 2014]

World Bank Group (2013) 'A common vision for the World Bank Group' Development Committee Paper, Spring 2013, Section 2: Defining goals for the World Bank Group [online] <http://siteresources.worldbank.org/DEVCOMMINT/Documentation/23394965/DC2013-0002%28E%29CommonVision.pdf>

About the author

John Rowley is an international development professional with over 30 years' experience working for national and international NGOs, government agencies, bilateral and multilateral donors and commercial companies in the UK, Africa and elsewhere.

ANNEXES

Annex 1: How to do wellbeing ranking

Purpose

- To understand insiders' ideas of wellbeing.
- To identify local indicators and criteria of wellbeing.
- To establish the relative position of different households in a community; this could serve to monitor changes.

How to:

List all the households

Make a list of all the households in the community. You need to decide what the best social unit is for your work. It may be family or household or individual adults.

This can be done in a number of ways. It may be necessary to ask an insider to recall the names of all the households that they can remember. It may be necessary to develop different lists for men and women, especially if the informants consider that people of different wellbeing live together (e.g. rich men with poor wives).

Be prepared to split a community into sections (e.g. dividing a village into different quarters) if that is how the informant understands the situation, or if they say that they know one section but not another.

Prepare papers or cards

Put the name of each household on a separate card or piece of paper. It will be useful to give each card a unique number.

Choose the participants

Participants should know the people in the community very well and will probably have lived in the community for a long time. You will probably need to do the ranking with men and with women separately. It is almost always best for men to rank men, and for women to rank women.

Individual or group interviews?

In a classic wellbeing ranking, it is necessary to interview informants individually and to do separate rankings with three or more informants. It is, however, possible to do the exercise with a group. In the first case, you carry out the cross-checking yourself on the separate results. In the second case, the cross-checking occurs during the interview as the participants check each other's ideas.

Start ranking the households

- Decide on the word or phrase that you will use for 'wellbeing'. Try to find a word that implies social, spiritual, and/or human wellbeing as well as material well-being. Make sure you do not give any suggestions or examples. If you are asked, 'what do you mean by "wellbeing"?', do not give an answer, but say that the exercise depends on what they mean by wellbeing. In English, the term wellbeing is very vague and can allow participants to choose what they think is important.
- Ask the key informant to sort the cards into groups according to the wellbeing of the household. They can have as many groups as they like. Designate one end of the space where the cards are being placed for high wellbeing, and the other end for low wellbeing.
- Begin by offering a card and reading the name. The second card can be placed above or below the first according to the judgement of the informant.
- Pass the cards to the informant and ask them to place each one in the right category of wellbeing. Encourage them to create new groups if they don't find it easy to fit a household into the groups that they have created so far. It often helps to ask if the next household goes above or below the previous one.
- Allow the informant to discard some households if they say they don't know them. Informants need *not* classify their own household.
- Continue until all the cards have been placed in one or other of the groups.

Check the groupings

Take each group in turn and read out the names of the households in the group. Ask the informant if they are happy that the households should be put together. Move some cards to other groups, if necessary. Allow large groups to be split into smaller groups if the informant finds that the households are not sufficiently similar to each other.

Identify the criteria being used

Ask what the households in each category have in common: why they are in the same group. The reasons given will be the criteria for judgement of well-being. Repeat for each group. Probe for further criteria of wellbeing by asking how a household could change from one group to another, e.g. How could someone in this group move into a higher group? How could they fall into a lower group?

Write the ranks on each card

Mark the back of each card with the category that they have been put into. If the informant has created five categories of wellbeing, the cards in the highest category should be marked 1/5; those in the next group 2/5; and those in the lowest 5/5. If the next informant were to create six groups, then the marks would be 1/6, 2/6, etc., down to 6/6.

Calculate the wellbeing categories

Add the scores of the different informants to get a single score for each household.

Arrange the households in order of their combined scores. The lowest scores represent those thought to have the best wellbeing; the largest scores represent the worst-off in the community. This is most easily done using a spreadsheet programme on a computer.

You can divide the community list into different categories, from highest level of wellbeing to the lowest level of wellbeing, if you find this helpful. You can have as many groups as you like, but you should not have more groups than the number chosen by the informants.

Cross-checking

Look out for anomalies where a family is ranked as high by one informant and low by another. Discuss anomalies with participants, if possible. There is almost always a simple explanation. Where the households are ranked in a consistent way by all the informants, you can be confident that the ranking reflects local views of wellbeing.

Further sources

Pretty, J.N., Guijt, I., Thompson, J. and Scoones, I. (1995) *Participatory Learning and Action, A Trainer's Guide*, London: International Institute for Environment and Development (IIED), pp. 253–60.

Grandin, B.E. (1988) *Wealth ranking in Smallholder Communities: A Field Manual*, Rugby: Practical Action Publishing.

Guijt, I. (1992) 'A user's note on wealth ranking by cards', *RRA Notes* 15:65–69, London: IIED.

Annex 2: How to do wellbeing groups – heap-of-beans exercise

Purpose

- To understand insiders' ideas of wellbeing.
- To identify local indicators and criteria of wellbeing.
- To identify/understand differences and inequalities within a community.

This tool is particularly valuable in assessing the different impacts of projects on people with different levels of wellbeing.

Preparation

Decide on the word or phrase that you will use for 'wellbeing'. If you are interested in sharing ideas on a broad understanding of wellbeing, then you need to find a word or phrase that implies social, spiritual and/or human wellbeing as well as material wellbeing.

If your primary interest is, in fact, material wellbeing, then you can let the participants take the exercise in that way. Material wellbeing is often the first direction chosen in interviews.

Have a small amount of beans or maize grains or similar with you, just in case it is difficult to find something convenient at the site where the interviews take place.

Process

- Explain that you would like to learn more about wellbeing in the community.
- Present the participants with the heap of beans. Say, 'These beans represent all the men [or women, or heads of households, or the members of whatever group you are interested in] in the community.' Say, 'Can you divide them according to their different levels of wellbeing? You can have as many groups as you like.'
- Demonstrate cutting the pile into larger and smaller groups.
- Refuse to give examples of attributes of wellbeing or a definition of wellbeing. If asked, say that you are interested in the participants' ideas of wellbeing.
- Encourage someone in the group to start. Usually the exercise is very quick once someone makes a start.
- If there is one very large pile you can ask if it really represents a single group. Ask, 'Are there some people in this large group who have a higher level of wellbeing and some who have a lower level?' The participants may agree to split the group into smaller groups.
- When the participants are satisfied with their groupings be sure that you understand which piles represent higher wellbeing and which represent lower wellbeing. Point to one group and ask: 'How do the people in this

group resemble each other? What do they have in common?' Make a note of their characteristics.

- Repeat for each group and note the characteristics of *people in each group*.
- Ask: 'How can someone from this group move up to this group?' The answers may give you more information, or they may confirm the characteristics of each group. You could also ask how someone could fall from a higher group into a lower group.
- If you have a special interest, e.g. evaluating a project, you can ask:
  'In which groups would I find people who took part in the project?'
  'In which groups would I find people who have adopted the new practice?'
- If you are interested in specific elements of wellbeing you can ask:
  'In which groups would I find people with a mobile phone?', '...who own a radio?', etc.

Always repeat the exercise with two or three other informants. This usually produces different ideas on wellbeing.

Index

www.ingramcontent.com/pod-product-compliance
Ingram Content Group UK Ltd.
Pitfield, Milton Keynes, MK11 3LW, UK
UKHW021010120926
8556IPUK00029B/445

9 781853 398452